Second Edit...

6840404916 1 899

Rewarding Learning

WITHDRAWN FROM STOCK

ICT
for GCSE

Student's Book

- Siobhan Matthewson
- Gerry Lynch
- Margaret Debbadi

D1421817

HODDER
EDUCATION
AN HACHETTE UK COMPANY

Endorsed by CCEA on 31st March 2011. If in any doubt about the continuing currency of CCEA endorsement, please contact Michael McAuley in CCEA at mmcauley@ccea.org.uk.

Whilst the publisher has taken all reasonable care in the preparation of this book CCEA makes no representation, express or implied, with regard to the accuracy of the information contained in this book. CCEA does not accept any legal responsibility or liability for any errors or omissions from the book or the consequences thereof.

The Publishers would like to thank the following for permission to reproduce copyright material:

Photo credits

p.160 *T* © ZTS/Fotolia; *B* © Radius Images/Corbis; **p.161** *T* © Jorgen Udvang/Istockphoto; *M* © Ewa Walicka/Fotolia; *B* © Sergey Peterman/Fotolia; **p.162** © Protouch Manufacturing Limited; **p.163** *T* © Krzysiek z Poczty/Fotolia; *B* © Ermin Gutenberger/Istockphoto; **p.164** *T* © justin maresch/Fotolia; *B* © Vidady/Fotolia; **p.165** *L* © liquidImage/Fotolia; *C* © Ashley Whitworth/Fotolia; *R* © Fatman73/Fotolia; **p.166** *T* © Doctor Stock/Science Faction/Corbis; *B* © David J. Green/Alamy; **p.167** *T* © Konstantin Shevtsov/Fotolia; *B* © ussatlantis/Fotolia; **p.168** © Ragnarock /Shutterstock; **p.170** *T* © Ilja Mašík/Fotolia; *MT* GreenGate Publishing Services; *MB* © Yong Hian Lim/Fotolia; *B* © Rafa Irusta/Fotolia; **p.170** *TL to TR* © Mardis Coers/Fotolia; © Dan Marsh/Fotolia; © vetkit/Fotolia; © Daniel James Armishaw/Fotolia; *BL to BR* © maron/Fotolia; © Artostock/Alamy; © Daniel Hughes/Fotolia; **p.172** © Andrew Barker/Fotolia; **p.179** © Art Directors & TRIP/Alamy; **p.180** © Feng Yu/Fotolia; **p.187** *T* © Kurt De Bruyn/Fotolia; **p.192** © Jenson/Fotolia; **p.196** *L* © amana images inc./Alamy; *C* © John Crowe/Alamy; *R* © cphoto/Fotolia; **p.197** *T* © titelio/Fotolia; *M* © Georgios Alexandris/Alamy; *B* © yordan marinov/Fotolia; **p.206** © Hugh Threlfall/Alamy; **p.217** *T* © effe45/Shutterstock; **p.221** © quayside/Fotolia; **p.222** © Ace Stock Ltd/Alamy; **p.225** © The UK Cards Association; **p.226** *T* © Monkey Business/Fotolia; **p.236** *T* © Leah-Anne Thompson/Fotolia; *B* © Thomas Pullicino/Shutterstock; **p.237** © Peter Menzel/Science Photo Library; **p.238** © Bernhard Classen/Alamy; **p.243** *TL* © Brian Jackson/Fotolia; **p.244** *B* © Goygel-Sokol Dmitry/Shutterstock; **p.245** *T* © Dean Mitchell/Shutterstock; **p.251** *BL* © Vladislav Gajic/Fotolia; **p.255** © Ilona Baha/Fotolia; **p.265** *TL* © Marcus Clackson/Istock; *TC* © L. Shat/Fotolia; *TR* © GoodMood Photo/Fotolia; *BL* © Brian Jackson/Fotolia; *BR* © liquidImage/Fotolia.

Acknowledgements

Google for the screenshots on **pp. 3, 4** and **6**; IAC Search & Media Europe Ltd for the screenshot on **p.3**; Pixlr.com for the screenshots on **pp. 101–103**; Flybe.com for the screenshot on **p.135**; Ticketmaster for the screenshot on **p.135**; Protouch Manufacturing Limited for the photo on **p.162**; EasyJet for the screenshot on **p.181**; WinZip for the screenshot on **p.193**; AVG Technologies for the screenshot on **p.202**; British Telecommunications plc for the advertisement on **p.211** © British Telecommunications plc 2010. Copyright in this article is reproduced with the permission of British Telecommunications plc; BroadbandMax.co.uk for the screenshot on **p.216**; The UK Cards Association for the photo on **p.225**; My Space Inc., Twitter, YouTube and Last.fm Ltd. for the logos on **p.251**; Tesco PLC for the screenshot on **p.256**; FAST (The Federation against Software Theft) for the screenshot on **p.263**.

Adobe product screenshots reprinted with permission from Adobe Systems Incorporated.

Microsoft product screenshots reprinted with permission from Microsoft Corporation.

Although every effort has been made to ensure that website addresses are correct at time of going to press, Hodder Education cannot be held responsible for the content of any website mentioned in this book. It is sometimes possible to find a relocated web page by typing in the address of the home page for a website in the URL window of your browser.

Hachette UK's policy is to use papers that are natural, renewable and recyclable products and made from wood grown in sustainable forests. The logging and manufacturing processes are expected to conform to the environmental regulations of the country of origin.

Orders: please contact Bookpoint Ltd, 130 Milton Park, Abingdon, Oxon OX14 4SB. Telephone: (44) 01235 827720. Fax: (44) 01235 400454. Lines are open 9.00–5.00, Monday to Saturday, with a 24-hour message answering service. Visit our website at www.hoddereducation.co.uk

© Siobhan Matthewson, Margaret Debbadi and Gerry Lynch
First published in 2011 by
Hodder Education,
An Hachette UK Company
338 Euston Road
London NW1 3BH

Impression number   5 4 3
Year   2015 2014 2013 2012

All rights reserved. Apart from any use permitted under UK copyright law, no part of this publication may be reproduced or transmitted in any form or by any means, electronic or mechanical, including photocopying and recording, or held within any information storage and retrieval system, without permission in writing from the publisher or under licence from the Copyright Licensing Agency Limited. Further details of such licences (for reprographic reproduction) may be obtained from the Copyright Licensing Agency Limited, Saffron House, 6–10 Kirby Street, London EC1N 8TS.

Cover photo © Ingram Publishing Limited
Illustrations by GreenGate Publishing Services and Alex Machin
Typeset in Minion 12pt by GreenGate Publishing Services, Tonbridge, Kent
Printed in Italy

A catalogue record for this title is available from the British Library
ISBN: 978 1444 109603

LEICESTER
LIBRARIES

Askews & Holts	31-Jul-2013
	£19.99

Contents

Foreword

This book is the Second Edition of ICT for GCSE. The book's title reflects its purpose and content. It has been written primarily to support the CCEA GCSE ICT Full and Short courses (Revised specification).

■ Full course GCSE ICT

The Full course GCSE ICT has three Units.

- Unit 1 Tools and applications – 30%
- Unit 2 Using multimedia and games technology – 30%
- Unit 3 Understanding ICT systems in everyday life and its implications for individuals, organisations, society and the wider world – 40%

Units 1 and 2 are assessed through Controlled Assessment. Unit 3 is assessed through a terminal examination. The terminal examination will also assess elements of Units 1 and 2.

■ Short course GCSE ICT

The Short course GCSE ICT has two units.

- Unit 1 Tools and applications – 60%
- Unit 2 Understanding ICT systems in everyday life and its implications for individuals, organisations, society and the wider world – 40%

Unit 1 is assessed through Controlled Assessment and Unit 2 is assessed through a terminal examination. The terminal examination will also assess elements of Unit 1.

■ Overview

The book mirrors the specification in structure and sequence and takes students through the Controlled Assessment Units by using detailed scenario based tutorials. Students are encouraged to evaluate their products using simple criteria.

The book has been updated to include new sections on games technology and emerging wireless technologies. The text acknowledges the changing ways in which technology affects how we live and examines the legal and environmental implications of using ICT.

The aim of the book is to prepare students for assessment in the relative units and ultimately to enable them to achieve an optimum grade.

1 Communication software

What you will learn in this section

In this section you will learn about using a search engine, an email package and a VLE (Virtual Learning Environment). Through the worked example you will gain skills which will assist you in:

- understanding how a web address is constructed
- using the features of a web browser
- using a search engine for simple and complex searching techniques
- creating an address book for your email account
- attaching a file to an email
- using Cc (carbon copy) and Bcc (blind carbon copy) to send an email to a group of contacts
- using message options and creating personal folders
- understanding the features of a VLE.

This is assessed through the following components:

Unit 3 Terminal Examination
Unit 1 Controlled Assessment.

■ Searching the internet

The World Wide Web (WWW) consists of a vast number of pages provided by individuals, organisations and businesses. When the pages are grouped together they form a website and the first page on a website is known as the home page. Most websites contain pages in multimedia format as they consist of a mixture words, sounds, videos, images and animations. Pages on a website are linked together using hypertext links. Hypertext refers to keywords highlighted in a different colour or graphics, that when clicked on, move from page to page or website to website. The cursor normally changes from a pointer to a hand when it recognises a hypertext link. Each website has its own unique address.

Website addresses

A website will have its own unique identification or address. The website address is formally called a Uniform Resource Locator (URL). Consider the URL: http://www.ccea.org.uk

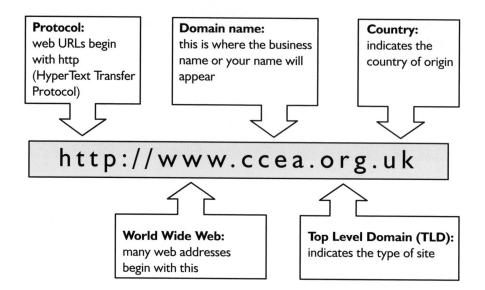

You may see different references to top level domain names. Although there are many domain names used, the table below shows some of the common ones in use.

Top level domain	Meaning
.co	Indicates a company
.com	A commercial organisation
.org	Reference to a charity or non-profit organisation
.ac	Reference to a university or college
.sch	Reference to a school
.gov	Indicates a government agency
.net	Reference to a network

Web browser

Many ICT users refer to the term 'surfing the net'. A web browser is a software package that allows the user access to the internet. Most computers use Microsoft Internet Explorer as their web browser, but Netscape Navigator and Firefox are also examples of web browsers. Opposite is a diagram that shows you the features of a typical browser.

These browsers also use internet search engines which allow the user to enter keywords/phrases to find information quickly. Each search engine maintains a large database of websites. There are many search engines available such as:

- Google
- Ask Jeeves
- Excite
- Lycos
- AltaVista
- Yahoo!
- Metacrawler
- Bing

Back Button and Forward button to go to previous and next page

Menus available in a search engine

Address bar to enter web address

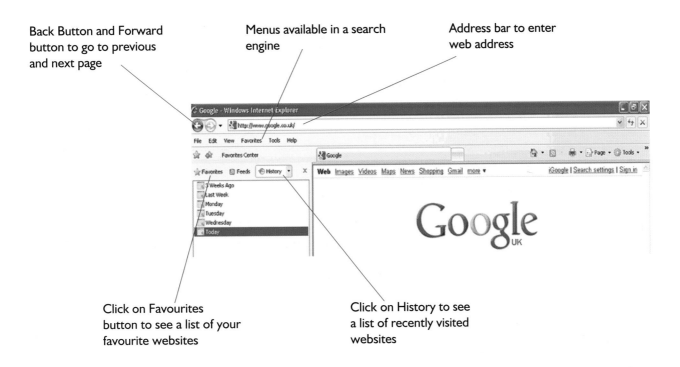

Click on Favourites button to see a list of your favourite websites

Click on History to see a list of recently visited websites

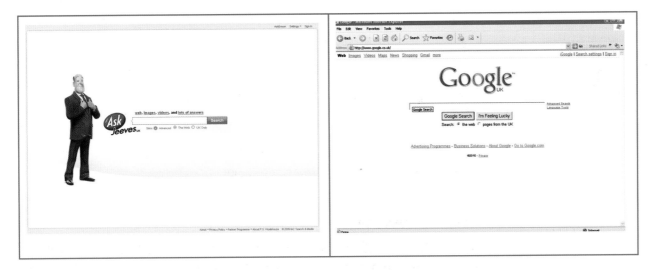

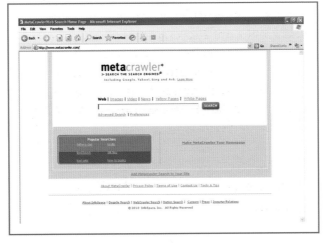

Most search engines such as Google and Yahoo! also include an advanced search facility for more experienced users.

■ Searching techniques

It is important to employ a number of techniques when using a search engine. Inexperienced users tend to type a keyword or a phrase into the text box provided by the search engine. This will usually return a vast number of websites which can often be unhelpful. To refine your search you should consider some of the following searching techniques.

Using capital/small letters

When you enter keywords and phrases in small letters, the search engine will return websites that consist of both lower and upper case versions of websites. Whereas keying in capital letters will usually return only an exact match of the keyword or phrase. For example entering madrid will retrieve websites that contain both MADRID and madrid.

Using wildcards

The asterisk (*) can help searching. It acts as an additional character in a keyword. For example, entering Schoo* returns websites containing school or schools or schooling. By entering Colo*r returns color and colour. Therefore it is best used for singular or plural words and also when a word may have different spelling such as an English spelling and an American spelling.

Quotation marks

Using quotation marks ('') around keywords or phrases will assist in more exact searches including words side by side in the same order. For example, 'apartments to rent in spain' will only return websites matching this phrase exactly.

Keywords first!

Using good grammar techniques is important when writing in English. When you decide on a suitable phrase, it is important to type a phrase using appropriate grammar. If you list the words in the phrase in order of importance, it will lead to a better search. For example, if you want to search for websites that allow you to choose a dog breed that would be suitable as a family pet, you may enter the search as dog breed family pet choose. This means the search will initially focus on the type of pet.

Plus (+) and minus (–)

Using the plus and minus signs in front of keywords allows the user to force inclusion or exclusion from phrases. For example, the phrase spain+cities-madrid will return websites referencing all Spanish cities except Madrid. Therefore entering the phrase revision+GCSE-history will return websites that refer to GCSE revision in subjects except history.

Complex logic

This involves using AND, OR and NOT.

school AND pupil
(returns websites that contain both 'school' and 'pupil')

school OR pupil
(returns websites that contain either 'school' or 'pupil')

school NOT pupil
(returns websites that contain 'school' but not 'pupil').

Example of using a variety of searching techniques

Consider a situation where you invite your friends around to your house for dinner. You are told that most of them are vegetarians and one of them is celebrating their birthday. You then decide to use the internet to search for: vegetarian recipes for special occasions. You plan the following searches:

Search	Comments on search
vegetarian	one keyword will return millions of websites, making the search ineffective
vegetarian AND recipe	websites must include both keywords, therefore it narrows the search
vegetarian AND recipe*	returns websites where recipe and recipes (singular OR plural) occur, therefore widens the search
(vegetarian OR vegan) AND (recipe*)	putting brackets around keywords will assist the search. (vegetarian OR vegan) will only search for either of these two words excluding other keywords initially and then will continue the search looking for either of these words *and* occurrences of recipe
(vegetarian OR veggie OR vegan) AND (recipe* OR cook*) AND ('special occasion*')	narrows website hits as the phrase 'special occasion' or 'special occasions' must be in each website

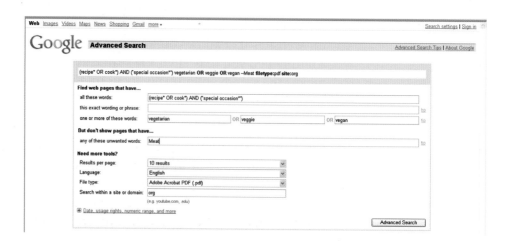

When setting up a search on the internet you should follow some simple guidelines including:

- Always do a plan.
- Build a simple initial search, usually one or two keywords, and test it.
- Add one refinement at a time to a copy of the previous working search and perform the search.

Email systems

When you open your email account, the **Inbox** displays all emails that have been sent to you.

To create a new email, contact or distribution list, click on the **New** button and select an option from the menu.

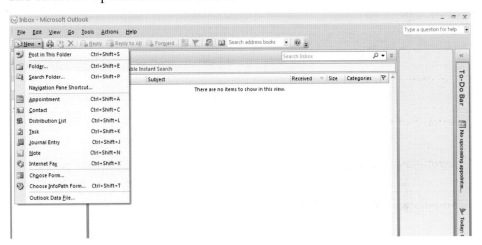

If the email address you are sending to is stored in your address book, then click on the **Address Book** icon.

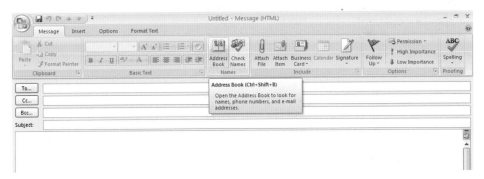

Then select the name from the stored list in your contacts. If you want to send the same email to another contact, their details can be entered in Cc (carbon copy) box. Alternatively, if you want to send an email to a contact but you do not want the other contacts to know this, their details can be entered in Bcc (blind carbon copy) box.

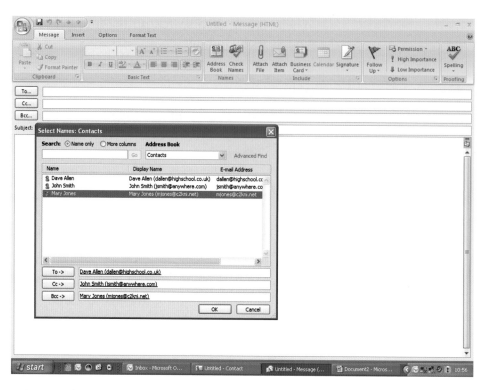

When the contact details have been entered you can then add an email title in the **Subject** box and the details of the email message in the main body.

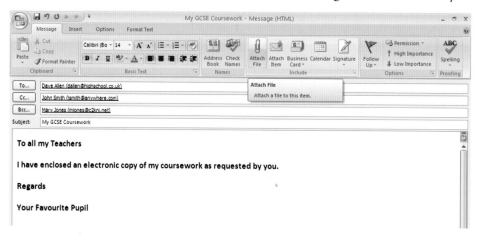

To send an email attachment, click on the **Attach File** icon and this will open **My Documents** folder, you can then insert a file or a number of files including a graphic or a video clip which is displayed below your Subject box.

Before sending the email the user can add **Message Options** such as clicking on the **High Importance** icon and selecting '**request a read receipt for the message**'. This will mean the email will appear at the top of the recipient's Inbox and when they open the email an automatic confirmation of reading the email will be sent back to the sender.

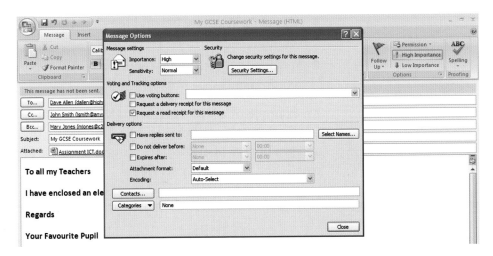

To help the user organise their emails they can create a number of Personal Folders and each folder can then store emails received from a named recipient.

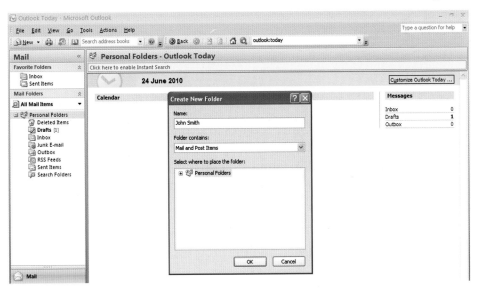

■ Virtual learning environment (VLE)

A virtual learning environment (VLE) is a software tool which is used in many schools to assist in the delivery of courses. Collaboration between students and teachers from a school or even a number of schools becomes possible. The main advantages of VLEs are:

● Organised central storage method for a number of digital resources.

● Staff and pupils can share resources for teaching and learning.

● Incorporates multimedia into lessons, which appeals to different learning styles.

- Allows for learning beyond the classroom with 24/7 individual access to the VLE.
- Personalised learning with lessons tailored to individual pupil requirements.

An example of a VLE is LearningNI. This will allow a student to access the course they are currently enrolled on, create their own personal web page, access a library of electronic resources, receive announcements, access their emails and many other services.

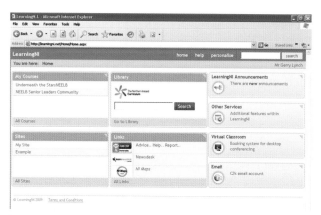
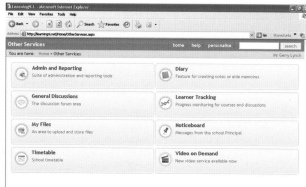

Other services available for learners include uploading files, accessing their timetable and participating in discussions. For teachers there are tools available for administration and reporting on pupil progress, accessing a notice board to receive messages from the school principal and dedicated tracking tools for pupils who are currently taking part and being assessed in courses.

To illustrate tracking of courses the teacher and pupil can see the courses taken and the progress being made.

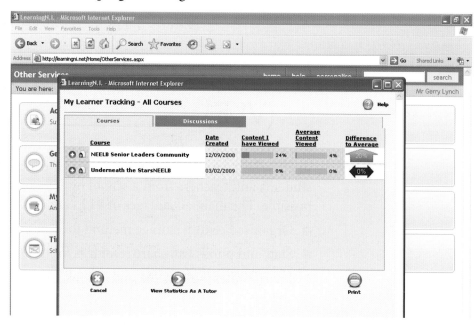

To use the library of resources the user can select a Key Stage, an area of learning and keywords can be entered into the dedicated search engine.

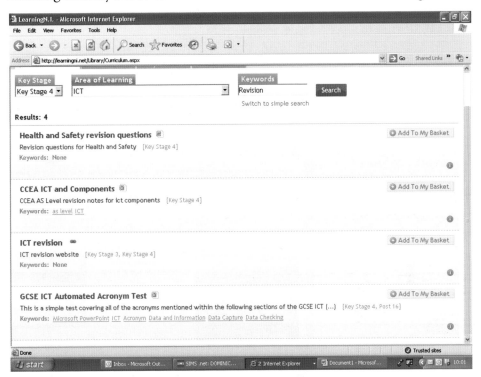

There are also dedicated hyperlinks built into the VLE such as the Newsdesk to allow the user to view up-to-date daily news.

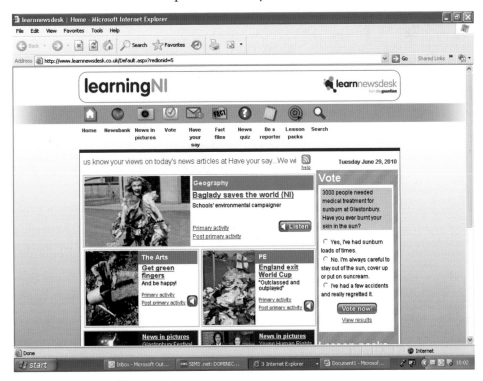

An integral part of a VLE for pupils and teachers is a 'virtual' Advice and Help centre which will cover areas such as cyberbullying, hacking, and so on.

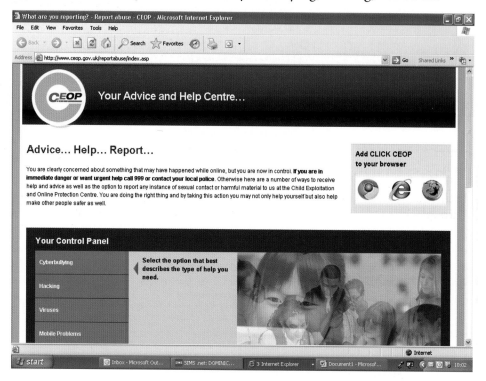

2 Presentation package

What you will learn in this section

In this section you will learn how to use a presentation package to present information effectively. Through the worked example you will gain skills which will assist in:

- understanding the features provided in a presentation package
- developing a presentation that is fit for purpose and meets the needs of a target audience
- explaining the main features of presentation software
- creating a presentation using presentation software
- sequencing and structuring the presentation to meet user requirements
- evaluating a presentation.

This is assessed through the following components:

Unit 3 Terminal Examination
Unit 1 Controlled Assessment Task 3 (7.7 hours).

This section is supported by the following digital media which may be accessed through www.hodderplus.co.uk/cceaictgcse:

Earhart Data.xlsx
Anna.jpg
song.mp3
piano.mp3
drums.mp3
logo.jpg
Evaluating Presentation.docx

■ The features of a presentation package

A presentation package provides users with the features to create presentations which combine text, graphics, sound and video. Users can select backgrounds for their presentation and can add buttons to allow other users to navigate through it.

Users can create slide masters. A slide master is a slide which is used to include features which will appear on every slide. This slide is created only once and can be applied to all of the slides in the presentation.

Timings can also be added so that the presentation will play automatically or loop continuously without intervention. Animation can be added to objects on the slides, this will affect the way they behave and move onto and off the slide. Transitions can also be added. A slide transition affects the way each slide appears and disappears.

■ Consider the following scenario

Ruth Earhart of the Earhart School of Music is going to apply to the local community drama fund for funding to help her school travel to Vienna.

As part of her application she must make a presentation to the funding co-ordinators. She must include:

- general information about where her school is located
- information on the number of pupils and classes
- information about the income from her classes
- an approximate costing showing the amount of funding she will require
- some examples of students' work.

Ruth will plan her presentation and undertake the following:

- Produce a storyboard for presentation.
- Include a newly designed school logo.
- Plan the content of the slides in her presentation.
- Design the layout of each slide.
- Design a slide master for the presentation.
- Collect the digital assets required for the presentation.

Ruth decides that there will be seven slides in the presentation. She then draws out the plan for navigating through her presentation.

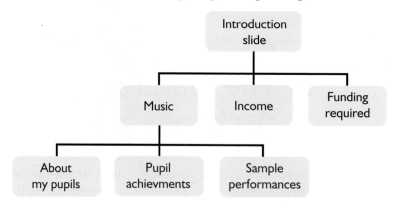

Selecting an application to create the presentation

Ruth has considered the different tools available for creating multimedia presentations. She has decided to use Microsoft PowerPoint. You may wish to research the different applications available for creating a presentation.

■ How to create and edit a multimedia presentation

1   Open PowerPoint. You will see a blank slide.

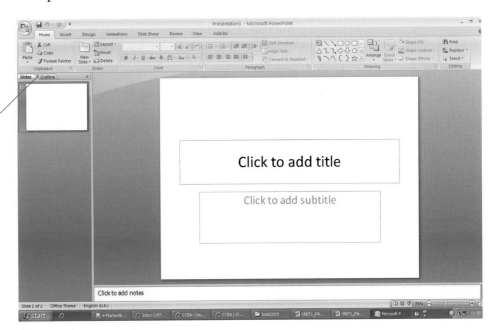

The Slides/Outline tabs which show slides as thumbnails and allows the reorganisation of the slideshow

2   Select the **Design** tab.

3   Select the 'flow design' theme from the selection shown.

In PowerPoint when a user selects a template or theme it usually includes a background, a colour scheme and settings for the size of bullet points and the font type used. This can be applied to the entire presentation. In this case the 'Flow Design' theme will be used so that all slides look similar

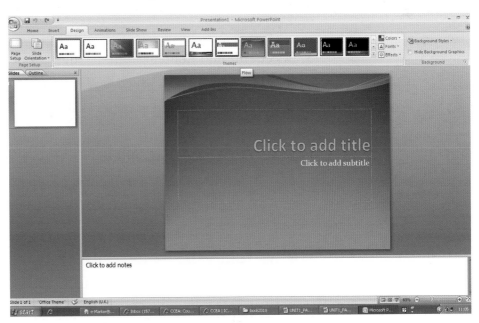

4   Click and add the title '*The Earhart School of Music*'.

5   Add a subtitle '*Music tuition and enjoyment for all*'.

6   Save the presentation as '*Earhart*'.

Adding new slides

The Music, Income and Funding Slides will contain a title, text and a graphic.

1   Click the **Home** tab.

2   Select the **New Slide** icon.

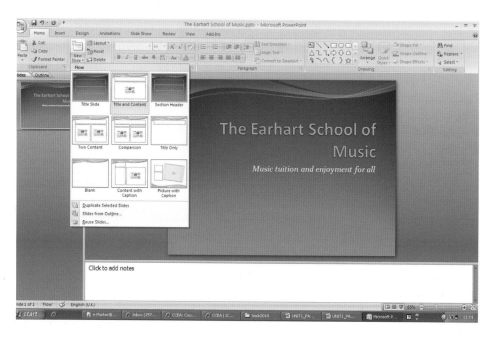

3   Select **Title and Content** from the slide layout menu as shown.

4   Insert three new slides which have **Title and Content** layout.

5   Insert the title, text and graphics as shown below.

Prepare the Music slide

1   Add the heading text '*Music at Earhart*' and format it appropriately.

2   Add the text below and format it appropriately.

- We are located in the North West and have over 70 pupils.
- Age range 4–22.
- We teach 10 different instruments.
- We provide accompanists for local drama groups.

- We perform free of charge at old people's homes and local schools every month.
- We participate in festivals and competitions.

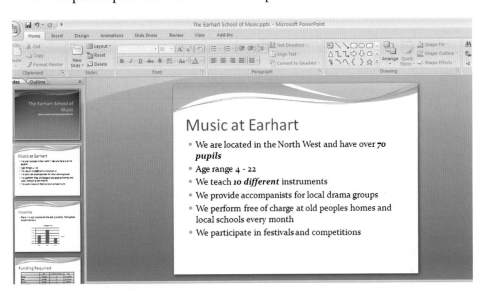

Prepare the Income slide

1. Add the heading text '*Income*' and format it appropriately.

2. Add the text '*Below is our income for the last 3 months, from grade examinations*' and format it appropriately.

   You will need to include a chart from the worksheet *Income Data* in the spreadsheet *Earhart Data.xlsx*.

3. Copy the chart from the worksheet and paste it into the slide.

4. Click on the chart you have pasted and the **Design** tab will allow you to select a style for the chart. You can also use the different group options, for example **Chart Layouts**, to format the chart.

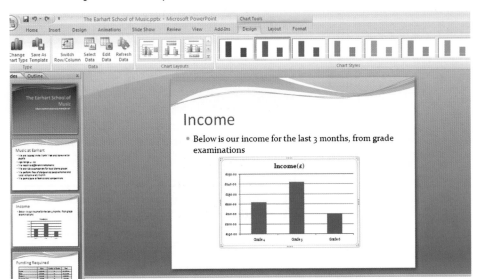

Note: When you copy and paste a chart into your presentation, the data in the chart is **linked** to the Excel worksheet. If you want to change the data in the chart, you must make changes to the original worksheet within Excel. The Excel file is separate and is not saved with the PowerPoint file.

If you want to **embed a chart** you must use the **Insert** tab, **Illustration Group**, **Chart** icon. A sample spreadsheet will appear. You can replace the data by clicking on any cell. This chart would then be embedded in the presentation. You could edit the data directly by double clicking on it and you would not need the associated spreadsheet file.

Prepare the Funding Required slide

1 Add the heading text '*Funding Required*' and format it appropriately.

You will need to include data from the worksheet *Funding Data* in the spreadsheet *Earhart Data.xlsx*.

2 Copy a selection of data from the spreadsheet and paste it into the slide.

3 Click on the table you have pasted and the **Design** tab will allow you to select a style for the table. You can also use the different group options, for example **Draw Borders**, to format your table.

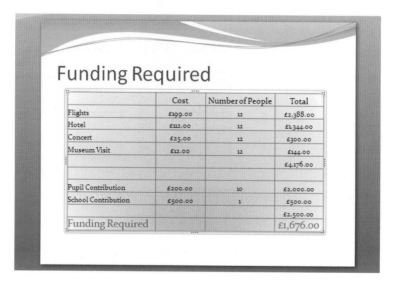

Prepare the Pupil Achievements slide

Ruth wants to use a table in this slide.

1 Add a new slide which will contain a **Title only**.

2 Add the heading text '*Pupil Achievements*' and format it appropriately.

3 Click on the **Insert** tab then click the **Table** icon and insert a 3×3 table as shown.

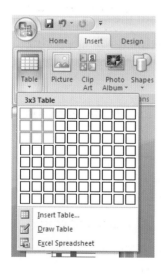

4 Insert the following data into the table.

Examination results	Competition successes	National successes
All pupils who entered grade examinations this year gained at least a Merit Grade.	11 first prize winners at the local festival.	Top scoring pupil in Grade 5 Piano, Grade 6 Flute examinations.
85% of pupils gained Distinction.	Top rock band prize at Battle of the Bands competition.	Two pupils presented with High Achievers Awards for violin.

Formatting text in a multimedia presentation

1 Highlight the text in row 1.

2 The text in row 1 should be:

Style: Bold
Font: Constantia
Font size: 22
Aligned: Centre

Prepare the About My Pupils slide

For this slide Ruth has decided to include one of her pupils and give a brief profile about how she has benefited from the school of music.

1 Add a new slide which will contain a picture with caption.

2 Add the following text to the **Title** box:

About My Pupils
Anna – Singer

3 Add the following text to the text box:

I have been with the Earhart School of Music for 6 years. I study Piano and Classical Singing. I have also learned to play the Guitar and got into a rock band with Cormac, Eoin and Ian. We have a brilliant time and have just landed a couple of gigs in a few local night spots. Happy Days. Thank goodness for Earhart!

4 Click and add the picture of Anna, *Anna.jpg*.

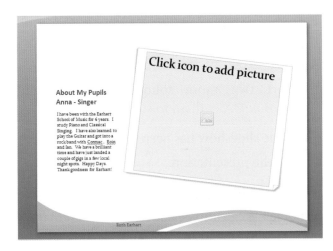

Prepare the Sample Performances slide

1 Add a new slide which has a title and content.

2 Add the heading text '*Sample Performances*' and format it appropriately.

3 From the **Insert** tab select **Text Box**.

4 Click on the slide and add the following text to the slide '*Anna sings solo*'.

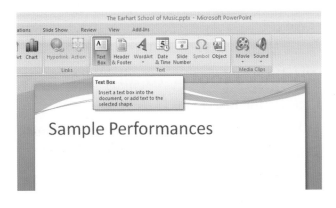

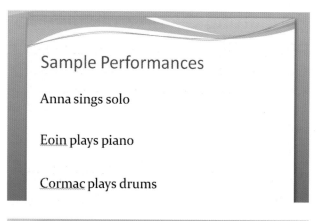

These mp3 files are linked to the presentation. This means that you will have to copy both the **linked files** and the presentation file if you want to give the presentation to your audience. You should copy all three mp3 files to the same folder as your presentation.

However, .wav files which are smaller than 100kB can be **embedded** in the presentation. This means they become part of the presentation once it is saved and do not need to be copied with it.

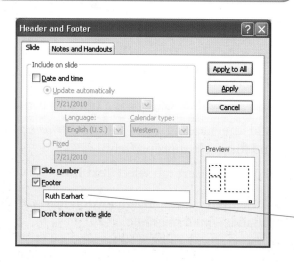

5   Add two more text boxes with the following text:

Eoin plays piano
Cormac plays drums

6   Format the text:

Font: Constantia
Size: 36

Linking sound files

1   From the **Insert** tab, select the **Sound** icon and browse to find the file *song.mp3*.

2   Set the sound so that it will start **When Clicked**.

3   Insert two more sounds *piano.mp3* and *drums.mp3*. Set them to start when clicked.

The basic slideshow has been created.

4   Save the presentation.

5   View the presentation.

A movie file can also be added to the presentation by selecting the **Insert** tab and clicking on the **Movie** icon from the **Media clips** group.

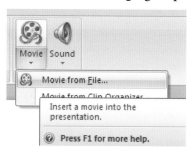

Adding a footer to all slides

1   Select the **Insert** tab.

2   From the **Text** group select **Header and Footer**.

3   The following dialogue box will appear.

Enter Ruth's name as shown.

4   Click **Apply to All**.

Creating a slide master

Ruth wishes to add her name to every slide. She also wants to add a button to each slide which will take the user back to slide 1. This could be done by adding the details to each slide individually. Another way of doing this is to create a **Slide Master**. A Slide Master contains details which will appear on every slide in the presentation.

Adding a hyperlinked action button to a Slide Master

1 From the **View** tab, in the **Presentation Views** group, click **Slide Master**.

2 Select the first Slide Master layout.

3 From the **Insert** tab, in the **Illustrations** group, click **Shapes**.

4 From the **Action Buttons** select **Action Button: Home**.

5 Drag the Action Button on to the slide master.

6 Ensure the Action Button is **Hyperlinked** to the **First Slide** as shown.

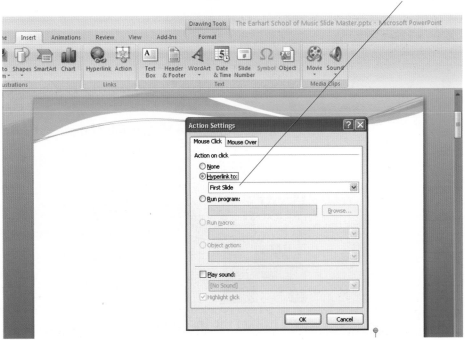

Editing different Slide Master layouts

You may find that the Action Button does not appear on the Picture with Caption Layout slide.

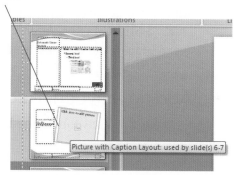

1 Stay in Slide Master view.

2 Copy and paste the Action Button onto this layout.

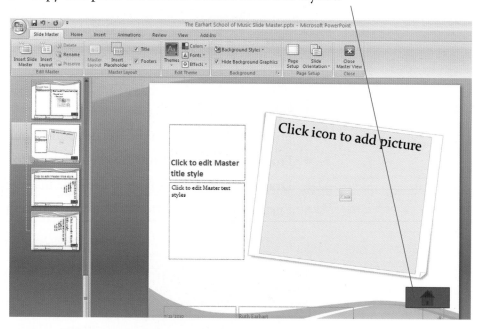

3 Click on the **Slide Master** tab and select **Close Master View**.

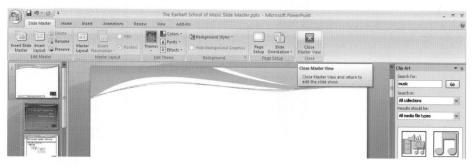

4 Click on the **Insert** tab.

5   From the **Shapes** menu, add an **Action button** to the Music at Earhart slide.

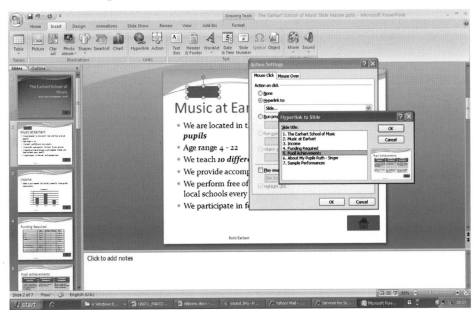

6   Use the **Hyperlink** function to link the button to the **Pupil achievements slide**.

7   From the **Format** tab, select **Text Box**.

8   Enter the text '*Pupil achievements*'.

9   Select the **Home** tab and format the text on the button appropriately.

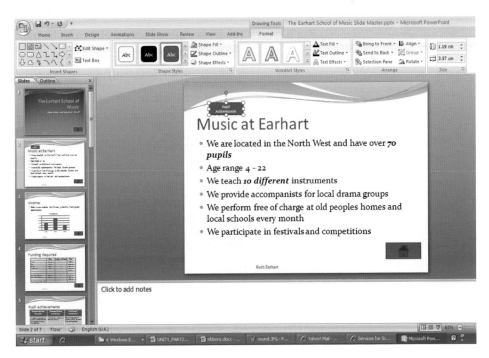

10 Add two further buttons to the Music slide which will link to the **About My Pupils** and **Sample Performances** slides.

11 Format and position the buttons appropriately.

12 Save the presentation.

Adding the company logo

Ruth has developed a new logo and wants to include it in the first slide. She wants to animate the logo as it enters the screen.

Insert the file *logo.jpg* onto slide 1.

Drawing a custom animation path

1 Click on the **Animations** tab.

2 Select **Custom Animation**.

3 Click the **Add Effect** button.

4 Select **Motion Paths**.

5 Select **Draw Custom Path**.

6 Select **Curve**.

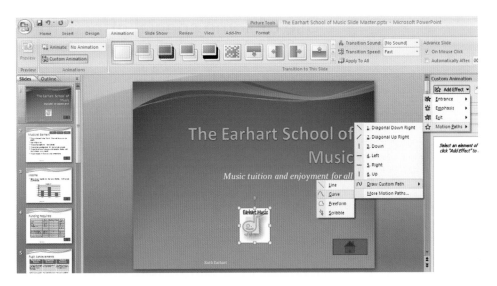

7 Draw an animation path for the logo to follow.

8 Set the animation to start **With Previous**.

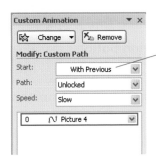

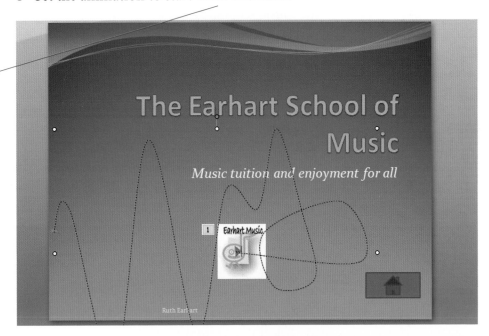

Adding a sound effect

1 Double click on the animation path.

2 The following dialogue box will appear.

3 Add an **Applause** sound effect.

4 Save the presentation.

Use of some special effects for display

1 Select the **Animations** tab.

2 Click on the thumbnail of slide 2 in the **Slide Sorter**.

3 From **Transition to This Slide** group select a transition which you will apply to the slide.

4 Set the speed of the transition.

5 Apply a transition to each slide.

6 View the slide show.

7 Save the presentation.

Extension activity: Using timings to control the display sequence

Ruth has decided to make a new copy of the slide show to run in the hall of the music school.

1 Save your presentation as *The Earhart School of Music Timing.ppt*.

2 Go to the **Slide Master** and remove the Home Action Button.

3 Close the Slide Master view.

4 Click on the thumbnail of slide 2 and remove all of the buttons from the slide.

5 Select the **Animations** tab.

6 In the **Advance Slide** section uncheck the button which says **On Mouse Click**.

7 Tick the box which says **Automatically After**.

8 Set the seconds to 3.

9 Apply a transition to the slide.

10 Click on the **Apply To All** button.

11 Save your presentation.

12 View the presentation.

Printing slides

1 Select the **Office** button.

2 Select **Print**.

3 Select **Handouts (3 slides per page)**.

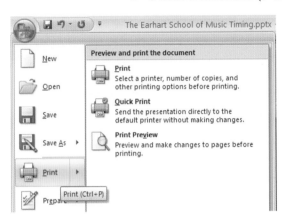
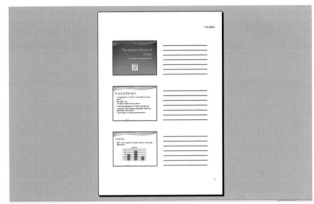

Evaluating a presentation

When you have completed your presentation create a table as shown below. Consider how well it achieves its objectives. This is called evaluation. Here are some points you could think about when evaluating the presentation. Open the file called *Evaluating Presentation.docx* and complete it or copy and complete the following grid.

My presentation is:	1 – Strongly disagree 5 – Strongly agree					Evidence to support my statements	Areas for improvement
	1	2	3	4	5		
Accurate						I have checked all slides and 6 out of the 7 slides have accurate information. There are no spelling mistakes.	Ruth has added two new classes and she has pupils at secondary school. The information on the Music slide is not accurate – it should be changed.
Complete							
Fully tested							
Working correctly							
Suitable for the intended audience							
Communicates the message well							
Makes appropriate use of multimedia assets							

3

Information handling package

What you will learn in this section

In this section you will learn about information handling. Through the worked example you will gain skills which will assist you in:

- understanding the basic data structures and features of a database
- developing a database that is fit for purpose and which meets the needs of a target audience
- explaining the main features of database software
- creating a database solution
- producing information to meet user requirements
- selecting, searching and sorting a database
- creating and formatting reports
- mail merging to select and sequence recipients for a mail shot
- testing and evaluating a database.

This is assessed through the following components:

    Unit 3 Terminal Examination
    Unit 1 Controlled Assessment Task 1.

This section is supported by the following digital media which may be accessed through www.hodderplus.co.uk/cceaictgcse:

    Music.mdb – a Microsoft Access database file
    Accompanist.xls – a Microsoft Excel file
    Mainletter.doc – a Microsoft Word file
    Mergedletter.doc – a Microsoft Word file
    Evaluation.doc – a Microsoft Word file

■ A word about flat files

Data stored on an ICT system is stored and organised in **files**. When the data is organised in rows and columns with data values being repeated, it is called a flat file. A flat file looks like a spreadsheet, it is two dimensional and has no related files (or tables).

Files are made up of **records** and each record is made up of a set of **fields**.

Data fields

A field is the smallest single piece of data in a file. Fields can hold different types of data, such as:

- numeric
- text
- boolean
- date
- currency.

See section on validation for definitions.

Records

A record is a unit of data which is made up of a number of fields.

Look at this spreadsheet. The structure of the spreadsheet could be described as a flat file.

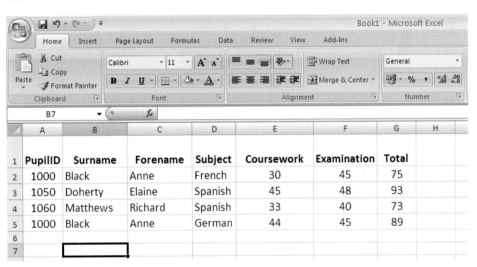

Can you identify records and fields in this file?

There are **four records** and each record is made up of **seven fields**. The fields names are Pupil ID, Surname, Forename, Subject, Coursework, Examination, Total.

The data types for each field are:

Field Name	Data Type
Pupil ID	Numeric
Surname	Text
Forename	Text
Subject	Text
Coursework	Numeric
Examination	Numeric
Total	Numeric

Redundancy

This file has a very simple rows and columns structure. The main weakness of this type of file is that data has to be repeated. Look at the entry for 'Anne Black', her name is recorded twice because she studies two languages. In a relational database system, this would not happen. The Surname and Forename of each person would be stored only once and a related table would be created to hold the rest of the data. The two tables would then be linked. When data is repeated unnecessarily it is said to be 'redundant'. If another entry is made for Anne Black the file would now look like this:

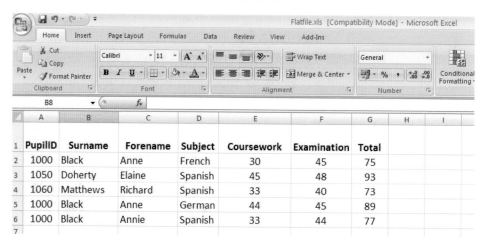

The new entry contains data which is not correct. Anne Black's Forename has been recorded as 'Annie'.

Integrity

The more often data has to be recorded the higher the possibility of the data having an error or inconsistency. The user of the data must be able to rely on the correctness and accuracy of the data. The correctness, reliability and accuracy of the data is called data integrity.

■ Relational databases

A relational database holds information in files or tables which are linked together using relationships between fields in the tables.

Data is less likely to be repeated so there is *less* data redundancy. The number of times that data has to be re-typed is kept to a minimum so data is more likely to be free from typing errors. This means that the *integrity* of the data is likely to be better.

Key field

Each table in a relational database has a field which is called a **key field**. The key field is a value which will uniquely identify each record in the table. In the case of the Pupil, the unique key field would be the Pupil ID.

Relationships

Relationships are links that have been made between two tables. The links are made using fields that are contained within both tables.

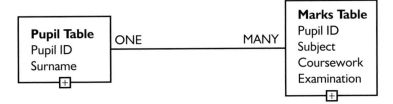

One Pupil has *many* Marks. This means that there is a one-to-many relationship between the two tables.

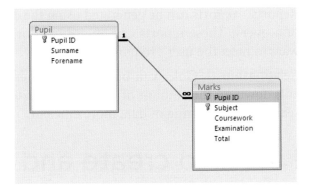

A one-to-many relationship created between two tables in Microsoft Access.

When the tables are created and the data is entered, each pupil's name is entered only once regardless of the number of results that have been recorded for that pupil.

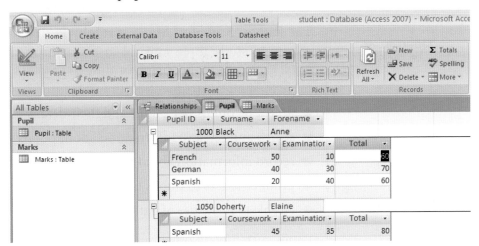

■ Data security

Data must be kept secure so that there is no unauthorised access to it. It is easier to keep the data secure in a relational database because only one copy of the data is held.

■ The features of a database package

A database package is designed to allow users to collect and structure data usually in the form of fields and records.

The database package will provide:

● Query facilities – the user can search for information which fulfils given criteria.

● Forms – the user can create forms to capture data onscreen.

● Methods of validating data, for example range checks and presence checks, can be done when data is being entered to ensure it is correct.

● Reports – reports can be generated using the data in tables or the results of a query. These reports can be grouped or organised in a variety of ways to meet the user's requirements.

● Relationships – tables can be linked together using relationships. This cuts down on the amount of data which has to be stored and makes the searching and sorting of data more efficient.

■ How to create and edit a database

As part of your controlled assessment, you are required to use database software effectively to produce information.

Consider the following scenario

Earhart School of Music

Name:

Address:

Town:

Postcode:

Do you need an accompanist for your exam?   Y/N

Parent's signature:

Date:

The Earhart School of Music is run by Ruth Earhart. She offers pupils the chance to study three musical instruments at three different grades. Any pupil can study violin, piano or flute to grades 3, 4 or 5. Some pupils study more than one instrument. Ruth wants to:

● keep a record of her pupils and their details

● search and retrieve information about pupils

● record information about when they pay to take the music examinations

● produce letters to pupils using the Mail Merge facility

● be able to make use of data from other software packages in the database.

Pupils currently fill out a manual form like the one shown on the left.

Having studied database software at a night class she has decided to set up a database with the following structure. Here is a typical record from the database.

PupilNumber	Surname	Forename	Street	Town	Postcode	AccompanistRequired	DateJoined
1000	Black	Ellen	23 Long Road	Coleraine	BT99 0JJ	Yes	12-Dec-03

■ Creating a database

There are many different types of database software. Microsoft Access is a database software tool. In order to create a database:

1 Open **Microsoft Access**.

2 Click on **Blank database**.

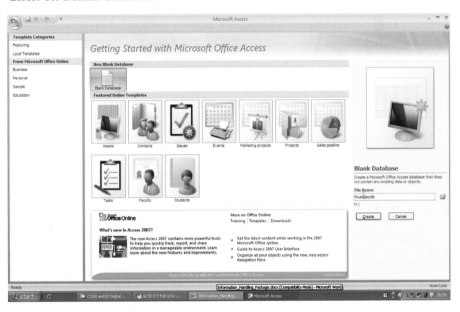

3 Give the file the name *Music*.

4 Click **Create**.

5 Click on the **Create** tab.

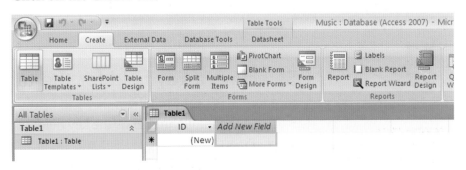

The **Table design** window will appear.

■ How to structure a database

Data in a database is organised into fields.

1 Enter the following field names into the **Table design** window.

Field name	Data type
PupilNumber	Number
Surname	Text
Forename	Text
Street	Text
Town	Text
Postcode	Text
AccompanistRequired	Yes/No
DateJoined	Date/Time

2 **Save** the Table as *Pupil*.

3 View the Pupil table in **Design View** by clicking on the **View** icon, then select **Design View** as shown on the left.

4 The **Table design** window will look like the one below when all of the fields have been entered and the table has been saved.

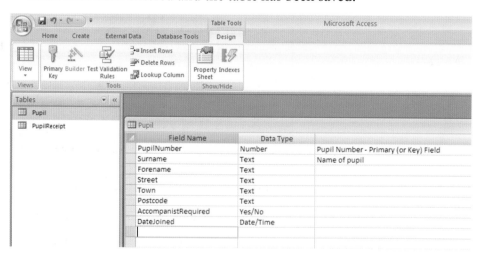

Selecting a key field for the table

In this case the field PupilNumber will be the key field.
To set the PupilNumber as the key field:

1 Highlight the row which contains the field PupilNumber.

2 Click on the **Primary Key** icon.

Primary
Key

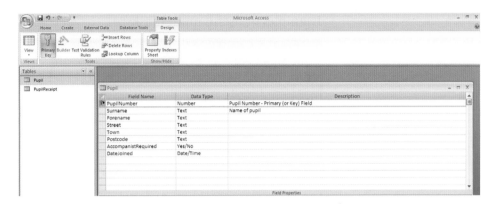

A key symbol will appear beside the PupilNumber field showing that it is now the Primary Key or key field in the Pupil table.

Validation and input masks

Once the table structure has been set up data can be entered into the table. In Chapter 10 – Data and information, you can look at the ways in which data can be validated when it is being input to a computer system.

When data is being collected it should be validated to ensure that it is in the correct range or is of the correct type. Access has some special facilities that allow for validation and format checking.

Input masks

An input mask controls how data is entered into the database. The input mask defines the format of the data being entered. Here are some examples:

0	Accepts a digit 0 to 9. Plus and minus signs not allowed. Entry required.
9	Accepts a digit (0 to 9) or SPACE. Plus and minus signs not allowed. Entry NOT required.
#	Accepts a digit or space. Plus and minus signs allowed. Entry NOT required.
L	Accepts a letter A to Z. Entry required.
?	Accepts a letter A to Z. Entry NOT required.
A	Accepts a letter or digit. Entry required.
a	Accepts a letter or digit. Entry NOT required.
&	Any character or a space. Entry required.
C	Any character or a space. Entry NOT required.
<	Will convert all characters that follow to lowercase.
>	Will convert all characters that follow to uppercase.

Examples of useful input masks:

Sample input mask	Acceptable values
(000) 00-00000	(028) 71-77775
(0000) AAA-AAAAA	(9445) 555-PUPIL
#999	–20 or 123
>L????L?000L0	BLACKGR678H4 YYY R 765Y8
>L<?????????????	Annabel
>LL00000-0000	AC45654-3209

There are some ready-made input masks available in Microsoft Access. One of these is for a postcode. This can be applied to the Postcode field by following the steps outlined.

1   Select the Postcode field.

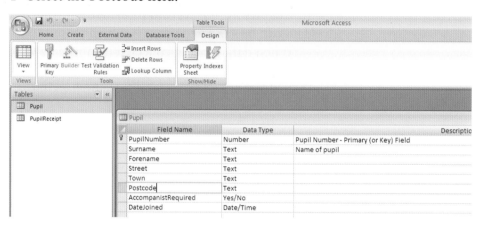

2   Click on the **Input Mask** row in the Field Properties table.

3   Click on the ellipsis icon. ⊡

4   Select the Postcode input mask from the **Input Mask Wizard**. Follow through the wizard leaving the placeholder as the '_' character.

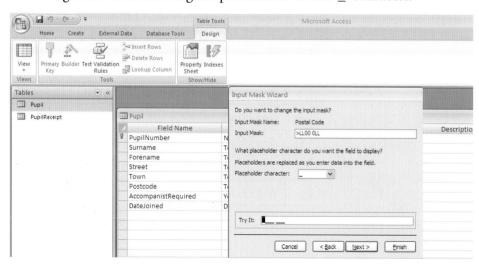

5 In order to ensure that the space in the Postcode appears we select the **With the symbols in the mask** option button. Click **Finish**.

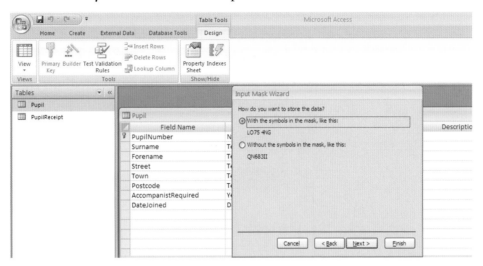

6 The input mask for the Postcode now appears in the input mask row.

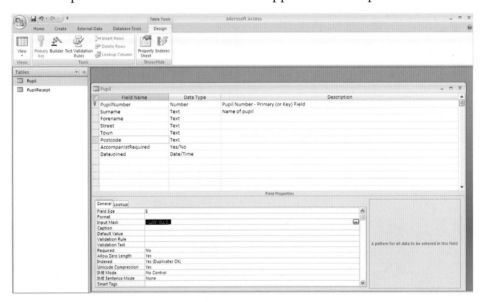

Design input masks for each of the following:

● Ensure that the PupilNumber field accepts four digits between 0 and 9. Entry is required.

● Ensure that the Surname and Forename fields format data with capital letters at the beginning of each field.

Formatting the DateJoined field

Another way of controlling the way in which data is to be held in a database is to use some of the data formatting tools.

Ruth wants the DateJoined to be held in the following format: 24-Apr-04.

The field can be formatted so that regardless of how the data is entered into the database, it will be shown in the required format. This is done by using the Format utility.

1 Select the DateJoined field.

2 Select the **Format** row for this field.

3 Click on the list box and select **Medium Date**. This will ensure that the DateJoined is captured in the correct format.

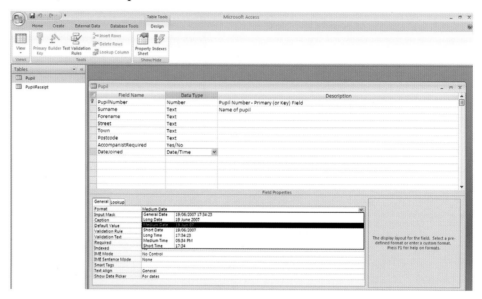

■ Validation in Microsoft Access

Validation ensures that data is present, in the correct range and format. You can read more about this in Chapter 10 – Data and information.

Ruth has decided that she will start the PupilNumber at 1000. There are 25 pupils in her school at present, she has decided that the school will never have more than 100 pupils.

The PupilNumber will have values 1000–1100.

She wishes to add validation to ensure that the PupilNumber is in the correct range.

Access allows data to be validated using the **Validation Rule** and **Validation Text** rows.

The **Validation Rule** row is the place where the range check or rule for data entry is placed.

The **Validation Text** is the text which will appear in a message box if the data entered does not satisfy the Validation Rule.

● In the **Validation Rule** row enter: *>=1000 and <=1100*.

● In the **Validation Text** row enter: '*You must enter a value between 1000 and 1100*'.

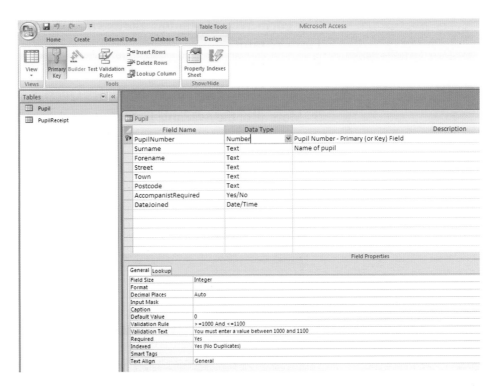

Ruth wishes to make sure that the DateJoined is validated. The school was opened in September 2007.

● Create a **Validation Rule** for the DateJoined field.

● **Save** and **Close** the Pupil table.

You will test the validation in the table later.

■ Creating a data entry form

Chapter 10 – Data and information examines the role of data capture forms in data entry.

Database software usually provides some method of designing forms for data capture. Access allows users to create such forms. It makes data entry more user friendly.

1 Select the **Create** tab.

2 Click on the **Forms** icon as shown. A pupil form will appear by default.

The **Form Wizard** window allows you to structure your form. To use the Form Wizard:

3 Select **More Forms** then **Form Wizard** as shown on the left.

4 Select **Table: Pupil** from the **Tables/Queries** drop-down list.

5 Move all of the **Available Fields** into the **Selected Fields** box by clicking: >>

6 Click **Next**.

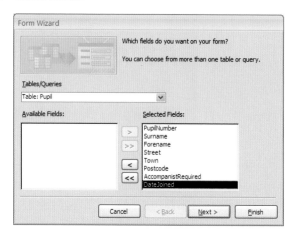

7 Select **Columnar** layout.

8 Click **Next**.

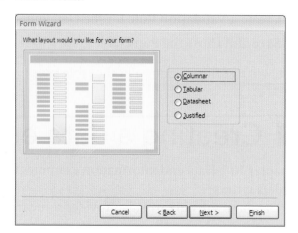

9 Select **Origin** style for the form layout.

10 Click **Next**.

11 Save the form as *Pupil*.

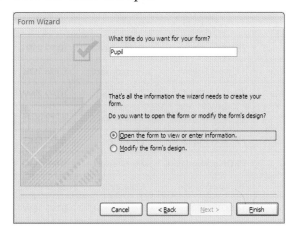

The finished form is shown below:

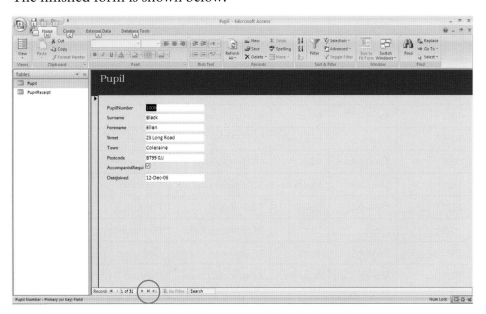

The form can be used to view data or to enter new data.

To enter new data click on the new record icon.

Using the newly designed form, enter the following data into the database.

							Pupil	
PupilNumber	Surname	Forename	Street	Town	Postcode	AccompanistRequired	DateJoined
1000	Black	Ellen	23 Long Road	Coleraine	BT99 0JJ	Yes	12-Dec-09
1001	Green	Hugh	27 High Street	Portstewart	BT96 1UJ	Yes	21-Oct-07
1002	Matson	Mary	1 Shipquay Street	Coleraine	BT99 9YY	No	19-Sep-07
1003	Ross	Richard	23 Main Street	Coleraine	BT99 2WW	Yes	12-Jun-08
1004	Barkley	Susan	12 Culmore Ave	Portrush	BT95 5TT	Yes	21-Oct-07
1005	Mackle	Edward	120 West Road	Portstewart	BT96 1IK	No	12-Jun-08
1006	Smith	Rochelle	5 The Strand	Coleraine	BT99 2WG	Yes	21-Sep-07
1007	Kane	Philip	98 Richmond Park	Portrush	BT95 5XD	Yes	21-Oct-07
1008	Rawdon	Kim	12 Clarendon Park	Portstewart	BT96 1UJ	Yes	18-Aug-09
1009	Parke	Anne	78 William Street	Coleraine	BT99 2SR	Yes	21-Oct-07
1010	Rodgers	Caroline	1 Orchid Square	Portstewart	BT96 1OH	Yes	14-Aug-09
1011	Garner	Heather	4 Atlantic Road	Coleraine	BT99 2WW	Yes	21-Oct-07
1012	Caldwell	Rose	90 Portlock Ave	Coleraine	BT99 3GH	Yes	12-Jun-10
1013	Buckley	Brenda	73 Papworth Drive	Portrush	BT95 5HG	Yes	21-Oct-07
1014	Anderson	Claire	99 Drummond Park	Portstewart	BT96 1QQ	No	19-Sep-09
1015	Thompson	June	19 Bishop Street	Coleraine	BT99 7YH	Yes	01-Sep-08
1016	Kelly	Charles	14 Main Street	Portstewart	BT96 1EW	No	12-Jun-10
1017	Lambe	Laura	51 Lower Pier	Portrush	BT95 6YH	Yes	07-Sep-10
1018	Huey	Earl	77 Woodbrook West	Coleraine	BT99 9UH	No	21-Oct-07
1019	Walsh	John	19 Epworth Park	Coleraine	BT99 3JK	Yes	21-Oct-07
1020	Evans	Orla	23 Wesley Street	Portrush	BT95 6TF	Yes	21-Oct-07
1021	Smyth	Naomi	88 Lisdillon Road	Portstewart	BT96 1VS	Yes	12-Jun-08
1022	Walker	Michael	91 Hillview Park	Coleraine	BT99 1QS	No	14-Sep-09
1023	Paynter	Mirella	85 Foyle Road	Coleraine	BT99 5DC	No	12-Jun-08
1024	Swann	Margaret	13 Petri Way	Portrush	BT95 6UK	Yes	21-Oct-09
1025	Cunningham	John	107 Baronscourt	Portstewart	BT96 1NB	Yes	27-Oct-10
1026	Sheridan	Moorlene	100 Garden City	Coleraine	BT99 4BN	Yes	08-Nov-09
1027	McNicholl	David	1 Talbot Ave	Portrush	BT95 5TR	Yes	12-Jun-08
1028	Lynch	Ivor	14 Hamstead Park	Portstewart	BT96 1AF	No	12-May-08
1029	Doherty	Jack	16 Greenpark Close	Coleraine	BT99 7HH	Yes	05-May-10
1030	Moore	Amanda	8 Kensington Drive	Portrush	BT95 5TD	Yes	12-Jun-10

Test the validation

1 Open the Pupil table in table view.

2 Go to the second record in the Pupil table.

3 Change the PupilNumber to 12001. You will see that validation text appears, click OK.

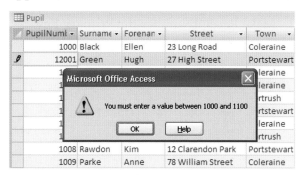

4 Return the PupilNumber to 1001.

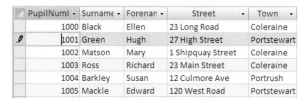

5 Now test your validation for DateJoined.

Ruth has now decided to record information about when pupils pay for their examinations.

She needs to know:

● which pupil has paid

● what the pupil has paid for

● what date the payment was made

● the amount of the payment that has been made.

One pupil studies many instruments. She proposes a table with the following structure.

Field name	Data type
ReceiptNumber	AutoNumber
PupilNumber	Number
GradeTaken	Text
Instrument	Text
DateOfPayment	Date/Time
Amount	Currency

Create this table. Click on the **Create** tab then select **Table Design** as shown.

1 Make ReceiptNumber the Primary Key.

2 Save the table as *PupilReceipt*.

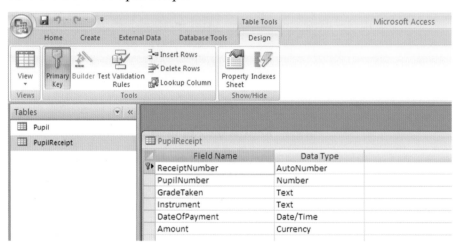

3 Add suitable validation to the database to take account of the following:

- The GradeTaken can only be 'Grade 4', 'Grade 5' or 'Grade 6'.

- The Instruments taken at the school are 'Violin', 'Piano' or 'Flute'.

- The Amount for each grade taken is between £20 and £60.

Relationships

The Access database now has two tables. It is possible to relate these two tables so that data can be accessed from both of them at once.

1 Select **Database Tools** then **Relationships** as shown.

2 To set up a relationship between the two tables click on the **Relationships** icon.

The **Relationships** window will open.

3 Add each table to the **Relationships** window.

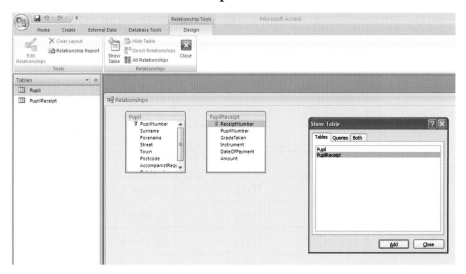

The PupilNumber occurs in both tables therefore we will set up a relationship between the two tables on the field PupilNumber.

We do this by dragging the PupilNumber from the Pupil table and dropping it on top of the PupilNumber in the PupilReceipt table.

The **Edit Relationships** window will appear.

4 Tick the **Enforce Referential Integrity** box. This means that only a PupilNumber which is in the Pupil table will be accepted in the PupilReceipt table.

Since one pupil studies many instruments the **Relationship Type** is **One-To-Many**.

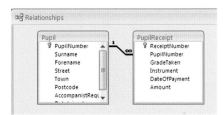

5 Close the **Relationships** window.

6 Save the changes to the relationships.

Add data to the PupilReceipt table

1 Create a form for entering the new data into the PupilReceipt table.

2 Enter the following data into the PupilReceipt table.

PupilReceipt					
ReceiptNumber	PupilNumber	GradeTaken	Instrument	DateOfPayment	Amount
1	1000	Grade 5	Violin	12-Sep-10	£40.00
2	1020	Grade 4	Piano	28-Oct-10	£24.00
3	1021	Grade 4	Piano	05-Oct-10	£24.00
4	1005	Grade 6	Flute	12-Sep-10	£50.00
5	1000	Grade 5	Piano	15-Sep-10	£30.00
6	1005	Grade 6	Violin	15-Sep-10	£47.00
7	1005	Grade 4	Piano	05-Oct-10	£24.00
8	1006	Grade 5	Flute	30-Sep-10	£35.00
9	1010	Grade 4	Violin	05-Oct-10	£28.00
10	1019	Grade 6	Piano	14-Nov-10	£55.00
11	1020	Grade 5	Flute	12-Sep-10	£35.00
12	1028	Grade 5	Violin	21-Sep-10	£40.00
13	1028	Grade 4	Flute	14-Sep-10	£22.00
14	1023	Grade 6	Flute	12-Oct-10	£45.00
15	1009	Grade 4	Piano	05-Nov-10	£24.00
16	1000	Grade 4	Piano	14-Sep-10	£24.00
17	1011	Grade 5	Piano	19-Nov-10	£30.00
18	1014	Grade 4	Violin	05-Oct-10	£28.00
19	1013	Grade 6	Flute	19-Nov-10	£45.00
20	1023	Grade 4	Piano	14-Sep-10	£24.00

3 Save the PupilReceipt table.

4 View the PupilReceipt table, it should appear as follows:

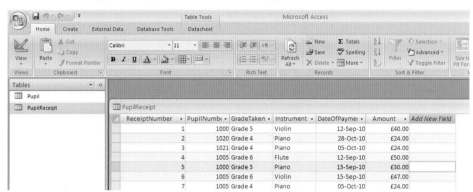

A relationship has been set up between these two tables so the related records in the PupilReceipt table are visible.

Ellen Black has paid for three examinations.

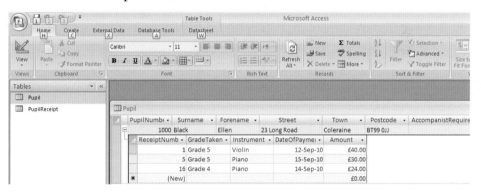

Creating a form with a sub form

Since Ruth has set up a relationship between the two tables, she can create a single form which will allow her to enter data into the two tables at once. She decides to create a form to do this.

1 Using the **Form Design Wizard** again, select the following fields from each table.

Table	Fieldname
Pupil	PupilNumber
	Surname
	Forename
	Street
	Town
	Postcode
	AccompanistRequired
	DateJoined

Table	Fieldname
PupilReceipt	ReceiptNumber
	GradeTaken
	Instrument

The finished form will look like this in **Design View**:

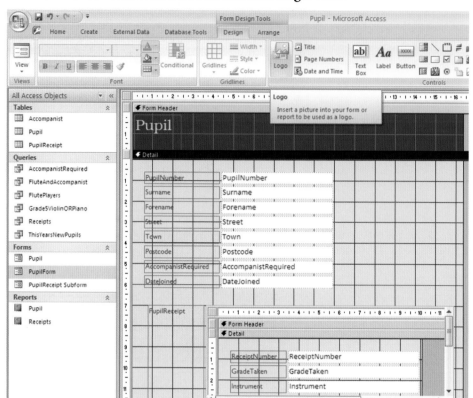

To add a logo to the form:

2   Click on the **Logo** icon as shown above.

3   Browse and add a suitable picture to the form.

Here is a view of the form with a suitable logo.

■ Querying a database

In a computerised database many records can be searched and information can be retrieved very quickly. Microsoft Access provides a Query facility. This allows users to ask the database to find records which fit certain criteria.

To create a query, click on the **Create** tab.

1 Select **Query Design** as shown.

Ruth wishes to make a list of all the pupils who require an accompanist. All of this information can be found from the Pupil table.

The **Show Table** window will appear.

2 Add the Pupil table and close the **Show Table** window.

3 Add the following fields to the **Query Design** window by double-clicking on them:

Surname
Forename
Street
Town
Postcode
AccompanistRequired

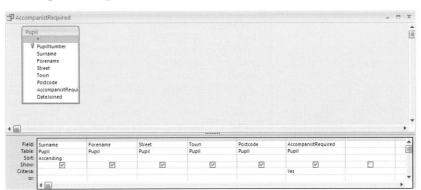

4   Type '*Yes*' into the **Criteria** row of the AccompanistRequired column. The pupils who require an accompanist will have the value 'Yes' in the AccompanistRequired field.

5   Uncheck the **Show** box in the AccompanistRequired column. This means that this field will not be shown in the results of the query.

Click on the **Run** icon to see the results of the query

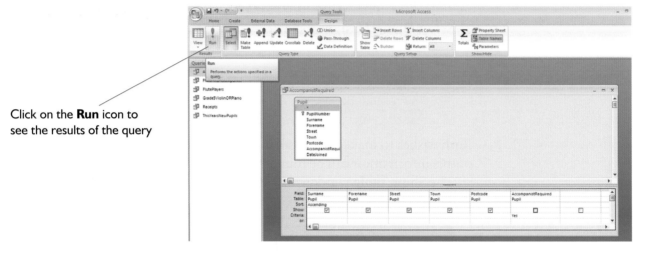

The results are shown in table format.

Surname	Forename	Street	Town	Postcode
Barkley	Susan	12 Culmore Ave	Portrush	BT95 5TT
Black	Ellen	23 Long Road	Coleraine	BT99 0JJ
Buckley	Brenda	73 Papworth Drive	Portrush	BT95 5HG
Caldwell	Rose	90 Portlock Ave	Coleraine	BT99 3GH
Cunningham	John	107 Baronscourt	Portstewart	BT96 1NB
Doherty	Jack	16 Greenpark Close	Coleraine	BT99 7HH
Evans	Orla	23 Wesley Street	Portrush	BT95 6TF
Garner	Heather	4 Atlantic Road	Coleraine	BT99 2WW
Green	Hugh	27 High Street	Portstewart	BT96 1UJ
Kane	Philip	98 Richmond Park	Portrush	BT95 5XD
Lambe	Laura	51 Lower Pier	Portrush	BT95 6YH
McNicholl	David	1 Talbot Ave	Portrush	BT95 5TR
Moore	Amanda	8 Kensington Drive	Portrush	BT95 5TD
Parke	Anne	78 William Street	Coleraine	BT99 2SR

Out of 31 pupils, 23 require an accompanist to play while they are taking their exam.

6   Save the query as *AccompanistRequired*.

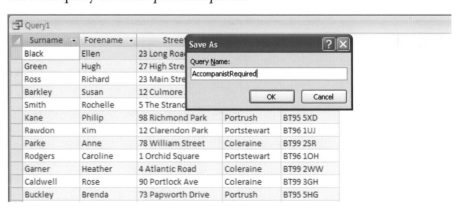

Creating queries which require more than one table

One of the main advantages of linking or relating two tables is that data from both tables can be used at the same time.

Ruth has a question. She wants to produce a list of names of all those pupils who have paid for flute exams. In order to do this data from both tables is required.

1 Create a new query in **Design View**.

2 Add both tables to the **Query Design** window.

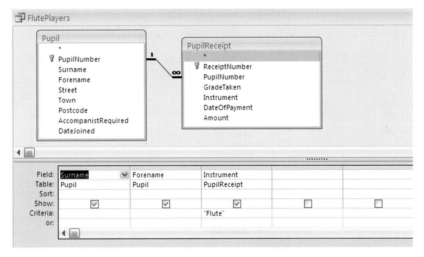

3 Add Surname and Forename from the Pupil table.

4 Add Instrument from the PupilReceipt table.

5 To search for all flute players type '*Flute*' into the **Criteria** row of the Instrument column.

6 Run the query.

7 View the results.

8 Save the query as *FlutePlayers*.

Six people have paid for flute examinations.

Creating queries using logical operators and more than one criteria

Logical operators are words like AND and OR which allow us to combine conditions.

Ruth needs answers to the following questions. The questions are outlined and the way in which the queries are designed is shown. Using the **Query Design** details create the three queries and show the output you have generated from each.

Query 1

Who are the pupils who play the flute AND need an accompanist?

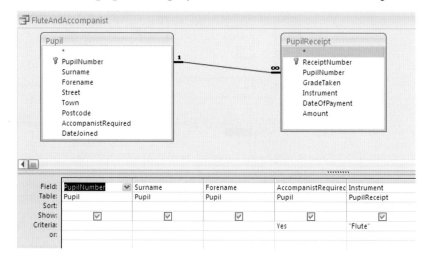

Query 2

Who are the pupils who have joined between 1 September 2007 and today?

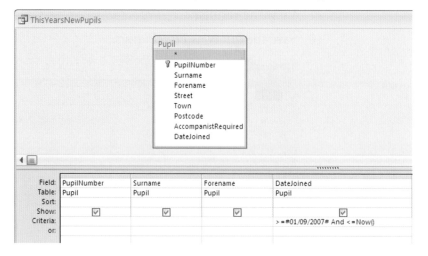

Query 3

Who are the pupils who have paid to take Grade 5 in the violin or piano?

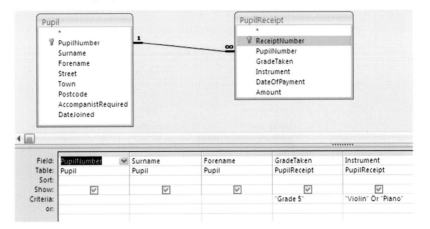

■ Reports

Ruth wants to produce a list showing what each of her students have paid for.

To do this she will need to design a report. Like queries, reports can make use of one or two tables.

To create a report, click on the **Create** tab.

1 Select **Report Wizard** as shown. The **Report Wizard** window will open.

2 Select the Pupil table.

3 Add the PupilNumber, Surname and Forename fields to the Selected Fields list.

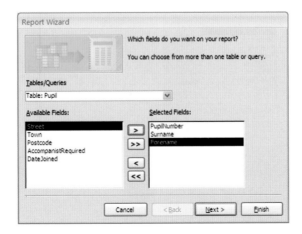

4 Select the PupilReceipt table.

5 Add the ReceiptNumber, GradeTaken, Instrument, DateOfPayment and Amount fields to the **Selected Fields** list.

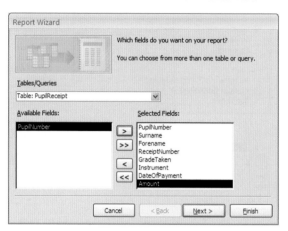

6 Ruth wishes to view the data in order of PupilNumber.

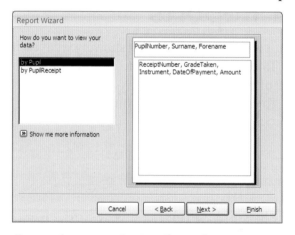

7 Group the report by PupilNumber.

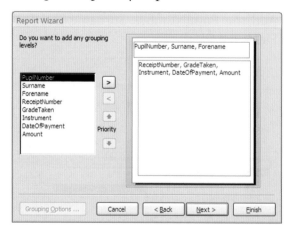

8 Sort the details for each pupil by ReceiptNumber.

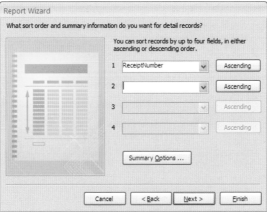

9 Since there will be so many fields on the report, it is best to select Landscape orientation for it.

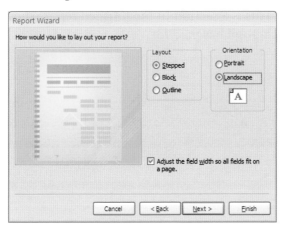

10 You can also select a style and colour scheme for the report.

This is the last stage in producing the report using the wizard.

11 Save the report as *Receipts*.

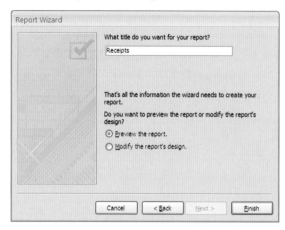

If the **Preview the report** option button is selected, Access will display the report when **Finish** is clicked.

This is a section of the finished report showing the examinations which each pupil has paid for.

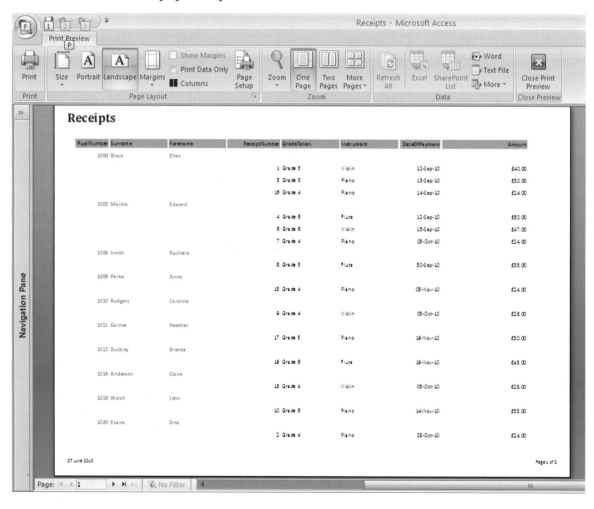

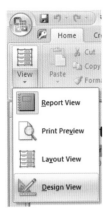

Extension activity

Some improvements could be made to the report by viewing it in design layout.

To view the report in design layout click on the **View** icon and select **Design View** as shown.

1 Change the report heading to '*Pupil Bill Details*'.

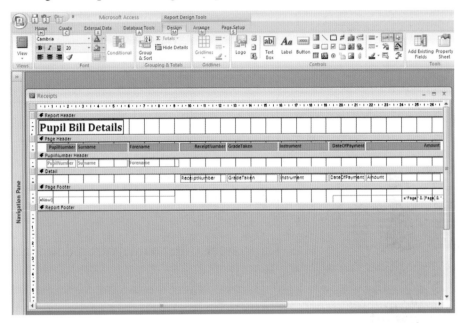

2 Save the report.

Ruth has decided that she would like to place the total amount paid by each pupil after their details on the report.

Open the Receipts report in **Design View** again.

3 Click on the **Design** tab.

4 Select the **Group & Sort** icon as shown below:

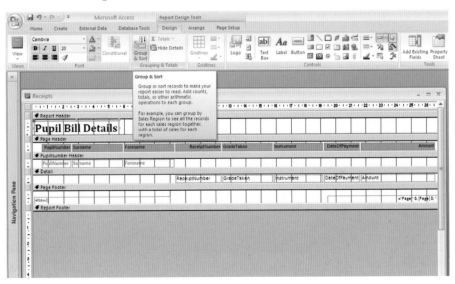

5   Select **More Options** in the **Group, Sort and Total** window below the report.

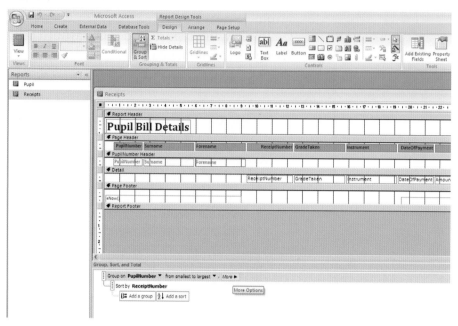

6   Click on the **with no totals** drop-down menu.

Set each of the values in the **Totals** window as shown.

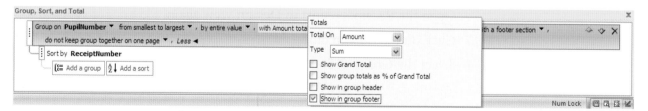

This will show on the report the amount paid by each person.

To format this value as currency:

7   Click on the newly added field.

8   Click on the **Property Sheet** icon.

9 Click on the **Format** tab.

10 Select **Currency** from the drop down list.

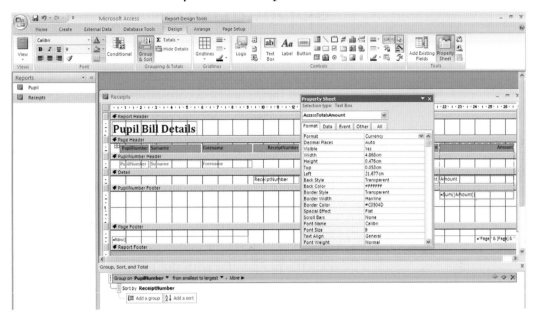

11 Save the report.

12 View the report before printing.

This is a section of the report showing a subtotal for each pupil.

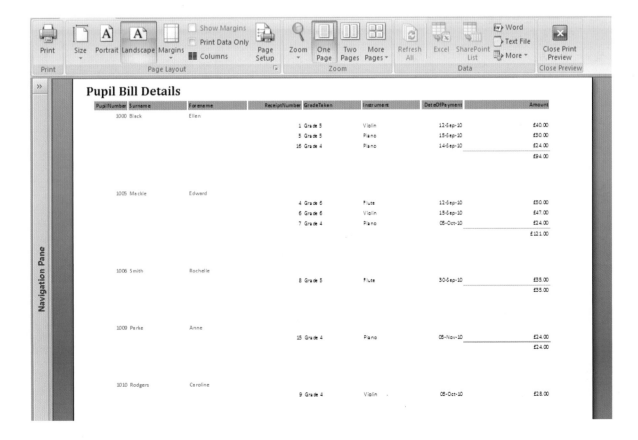

■ Sharing data between applications

Using Mail Merge

Any music pupil who requires an accompanist must come to a meeting and practise with their chosen accompanist on Friday 29 January. Ruth wants to send all of her pupils, who require an accompanist for their grade exam, a letter containing this information.

This is an opportunity to use two pieces of software to help Ruth carry out the task.

It is possible to use the AccompanistRequired query created earlier and create a letter in a word processor. The Mail Merge facility in the word processor can merge the query contents with the letter. This creates an individual letter for each pupil.

1   Create the main letter with the information, using Microsoft Word.

2   From the **Mailings** tab select **Start Mail Merge** then **Letters** as shown below.

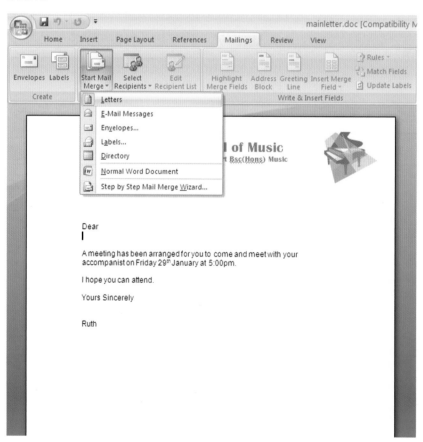

3   Click on the **Select Recipients** icon.

4 Select **Use Existing List** as shown.

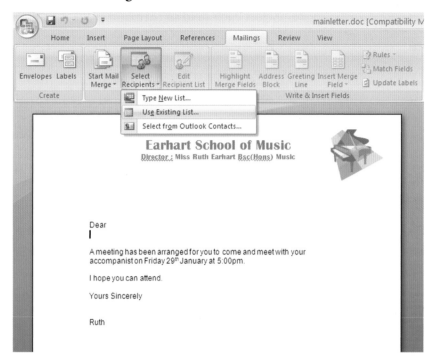

5 The **Select Data Source** window will appear. Browse and select your database *Music.mdb*.

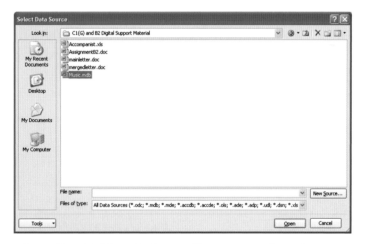

6 The **Select Table** window will appear, select the AccompanistRequired query.

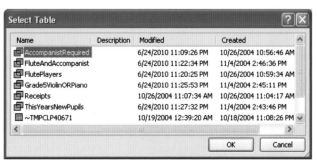

7 Add merge fields to the letter. Click the **Insert Merge Field** icon.

8 Select each field in turn and place it in the correct position on the letter.

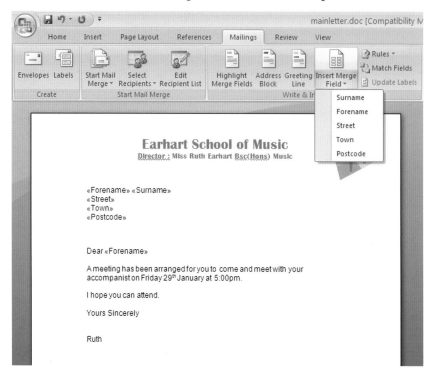

Note that merge fields are shown inside brackets << and >>. It is easy to identify where the data will appear on the letters.

If you want to select particular records for your mail merge you can do this by clicking the **Edit Recipient List** icon.

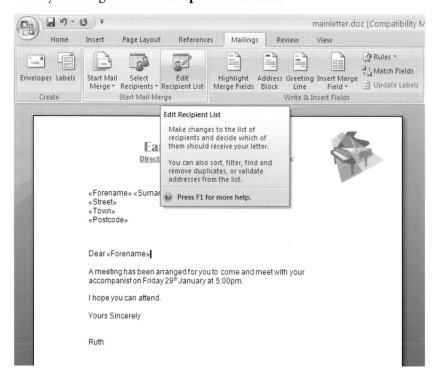

The **Mail Merge Recipients** window will appear.
You can add criteria to select recipients if required.

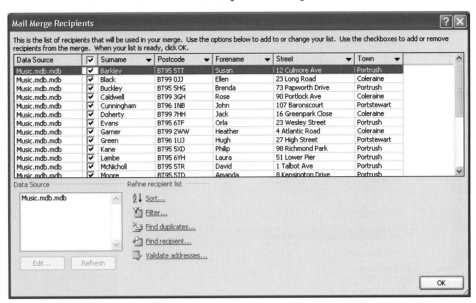

For example, selecting Portrush would merge all those people who live in Portrush.

Ruth wants to send her letter to everybody therefore select (**All**) from the drop-down menu.

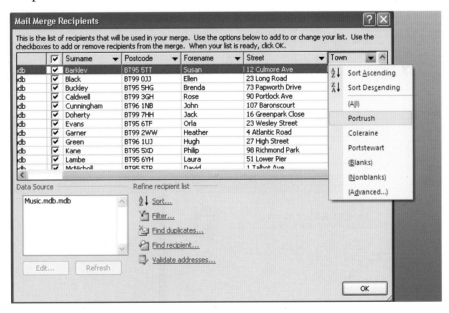

1   Merge the letter with the query, click the **Finish & Merge** icon.

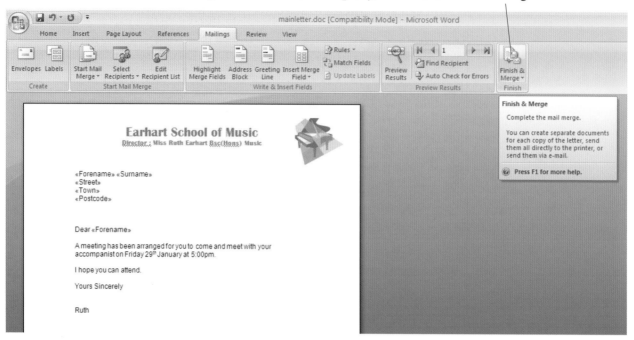

2   **Merge All** records as shown:

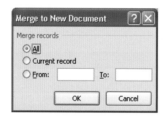

3   Preview your letters.

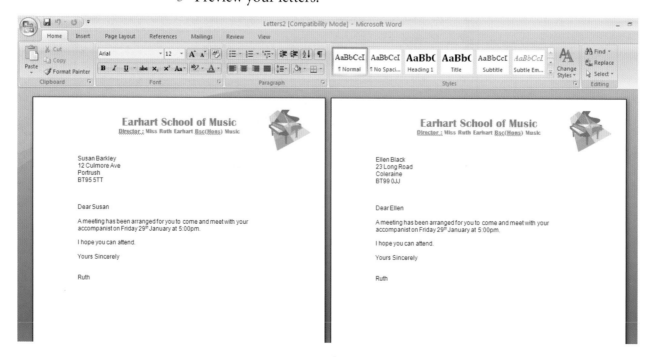

Importing files from another source

Ruth has created a list of possible accompanists and the instruments that they play. She has done this in a spreadsheet. She wishes to import the details in the spreadsheet into the database for use in queries.

1 Create a spreadsheet and enter the following data:

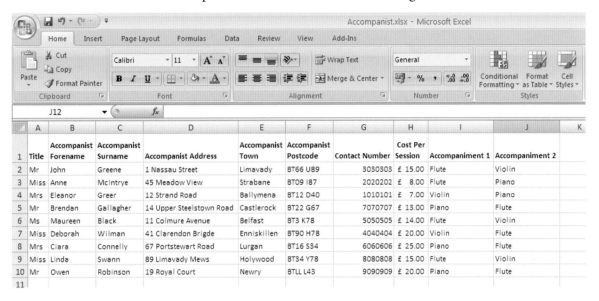

	A	B	C	D	E	F	G	H	I	J	K
1	Title	Accompanist Forename	Accompanist Surname	Accompanist Address	Accompanist Town	Accompanist Postcode	Contact Number	Cost Per Session	Accompaniment 1	Accompaniment 2	
2	Mr	John	Greene	1 Nassau Street	Limavady	BT66 U89	3030303	£ 15.00	Flute	Violin	
3	Miss	Anne	McIntrye	45 Meadow View	Strabane	BTO9 I87	2020202	£ 8.00	Flute	Piano	
4	Mrs	Eleanor	Greer	12 Strand Road	Ballymena	BT12 D40	1010101	£ 7.00	Violin	Piano	
5	Mr	Brendan	Gallagher	14 Upper Steelstown Road	Castlerock	BT22 G67	7070707	£ 13.00	Piano	Flute	
6	Ms	Maureen	Black	11 Colmure Avenue	Belfast	BT3 K78	5050505	£ 14.00	Flute	Violin	
7	Miss	Deborah	Wilman	41 Clarendon Brigde	Enniskillen	BT90 H78	4040404	£ 20.00	Violin	Flute	
8	Mrs	Ciara	Connelly	67 Portstewart Road	Lurgan	BT16 S34	6060606	£ 25.00	Piano	Flute	
9	Miss	Linda	Swann	89 Limavady Mews	Holywood	BT34 Y78	8080808	£ 15.00	Flute	Violin	
10	Mr	Owen	Robinson	19 Royal Court	Newry	BTLL L43	9090909	£ 20.00	Piano	Flute	
11											

Alternatively the digital version of the file *Accompanist.xls* can be used to complete this exercise.

To import the data into a table, open the Access database *Music.mdb*.

2 Select the **External Data** tab and click on the **Excel** icon.

The **Get External Data** window will open.

3 Use the **Browse** button to find the *Accompanist* file you created.

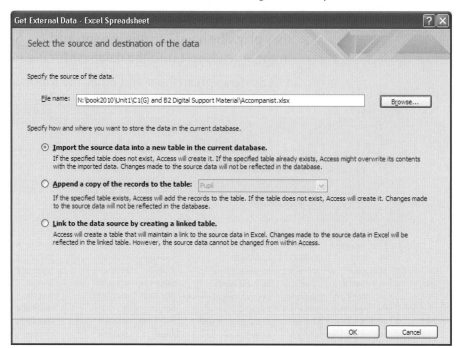

4 Click the **OK** button.

The Import Spreadsheet Wizard appears:

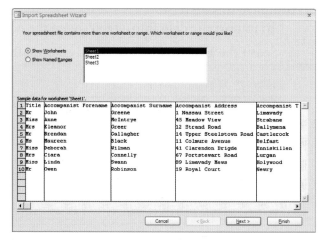

Note: It is possible to change the Data type or name of fields that are being imported or to skip them if they are not required in the database. This can be done using the dialogue box shown. You are not required to do this.

6 Click **Next**.

7 On the next screen, check the box **First Row Contains Column Headings**.

8   Click **Next**.

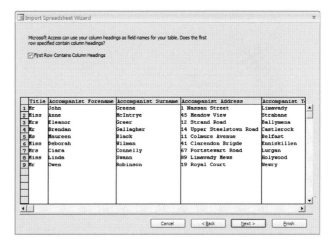

9   Click **Next**.

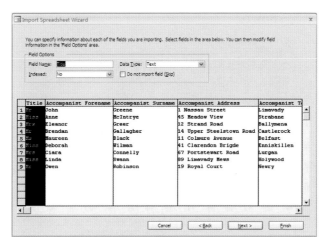

10   Select the **Let Access add primary key** option.

11   Click **Next**.

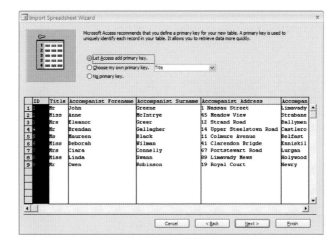

12 Call the table *Accompanist*. Click **Finish**.

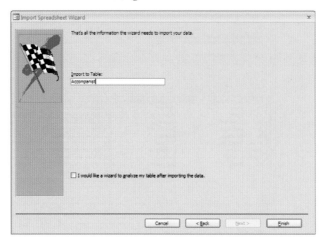

A new table will now exist in the list of tables. The structure of the new table is shown.

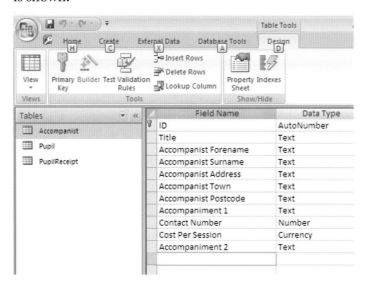

This table can now be used in queries and reports.

■ Creating a menu/switchboard for the system

All of the items created can be integrated into a menu system using a **Switchboard**. This would allow Ruth to access information at the click of a button.

1 From the **Database Tools** tab, select **Switchboard Manager**.

2 Click **Yes** if the message below appears.

The **Switchboard Manager** window will appear.

3 Click the **Edit** button.

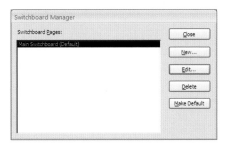

The **Edit Switchboard Item** dialogue box will appear.

4 Click **New** (this will add a button to the switchboard).

5 Complete the dialogue box as shown below:

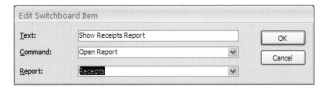

6 Add a further switchboard item as shown below:

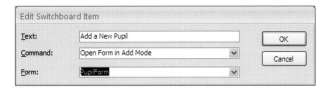

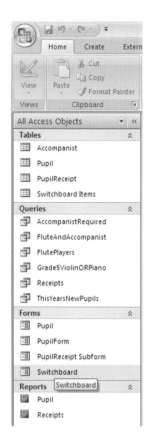

7 Add a button to close the switchboard:

8 Close the Switchboard Manager.

9 View the switchboard from the **Forms** section of Access.

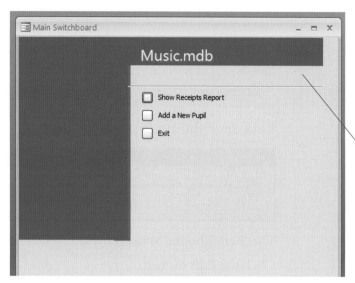

This is a very simple form which you can customise in Design View. How can this switchboard be improved?

■ Testing and evaluating

Testing and evaluating any system is important to ensure that it meets the user's requirements. At the outset, Ruth had some requirements. Copy and complete the table below to help you to reflect on how each of her requirements have been met. (Alternatively you can download the file called *Evaluation.doc* and complete it electronically.)

Requirement	Met (Yes/No)	Evidence (Describe which parts of the database show that you have met this requirement.)	Evaluation (How well do you think each part of the database you have described meets the requirements? Give a reason to support your answer.)
Keep a record of her pupils and their details	Yes	I have created a form called Pupilform. This contains a subform which allows Ruth to enter the data about a pupil and also to enter receipt/payment details. This form works fully and all data is written to the database.	Pupilform is user friendly and clearly explains what is required in each box. I have included a title, but could improve it by adding Ruth's logo.
Search and retrieve information about pupils			
Record information about when they pay to take the music examinations			
Produce letters to pupils using the mail merge facility			
Be able to make use of data from other software packages in the database			

4 Spreadsheet package

What you will learn in this section

In this section you will learn about using a spreadsheet. Through the worked example you will gain skills which will assist you in:

- understanding the basic data structures and features of a spreadsheet
- entering data and formatting different cell types
- using conditional formatting and data validation techniques
- building a formula and using inbuilt functions to carry out calculations
- replicating a cell value, formula or function by row or by column
- using more complex aspects of data modelling including IF statements and Lookup statements including absolute cell references
- creating, labelling and formatting a chart.

This is assessed through the following components:

Unit 3 Terminal Examination
Unit 1 Controlled Assessment Task 2.

This section is supported by the following digital media which may be accessed through www.hodderplus.co.uk/cceaictgcse:

Courseworkmarks.xls – a Microsoft Excel file

■ The basics

Spreadsheet packages have a number of common features as outlined in the table below.

Feature	Detail of feature
Cell	Cells can store data in the form of text, number, date, formula or reference to another cell.
Cell format	Cells can be formatted by changing font size and style. Also cells can be given borders or shading to emphasise appearance. You can also format data in cells, for example the date can be formatted to DDMMYY.
Columns and rows	The user can vary the width of columns and alter the height of cells.
Locking cells	Cells can be protected (read only), which means the user cannot change the data. Cells can also be hidden to assist in security.

Fill	A formula or value can be entered into a cell and can be automatically replicated down or across.
Mathematical functions	The user can select from a choice of in-built mathematical functions. Some of the common functions include: SUM, AVERAGE, MIN and MAX.
Graphs and charts	Data entered onto the spreadsheet can be displayed on a graph or chart. The user can choose a 2D or 3D image and can also select from a variety of chart types. Once the user has selected the data to be entered into the chart the computer will automatically draw the chart.
Conditions	This is an advanced feature which allows the user to create a condition and control possible actions by using an expression such as: IF (condition) THEN (action) ELSE (action).
Lookup tables	Another advanced feature is a Lookup table. These tables contain data that can continuously be referenced using a Lookup function. The function can use a VLookup (vertical lookup) or a HLookup (horizontal lookup).
Macros	Some experienced users can write small programs referred to as macros. This involves the user creating a series of commands that can be performed by the spreadsheet automatically.

Spreadsheets are mainly designed to perform calculations and recalculations automatically. A spreadsheet consists of a table divided into rows and columns to produce cells. Cells have a column reference (letter) and a row reference (number).

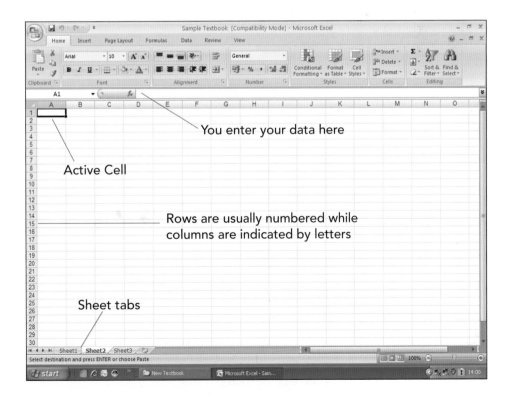

The contents of the active cell are displayed in the formula bar. The column and row reference are also indicated, such as B4. Remember the column reference (always a letter) is always first when referring to a cell. It works the same way as co-ordinates in Mathematics: horizontal reference and then vertical reference.

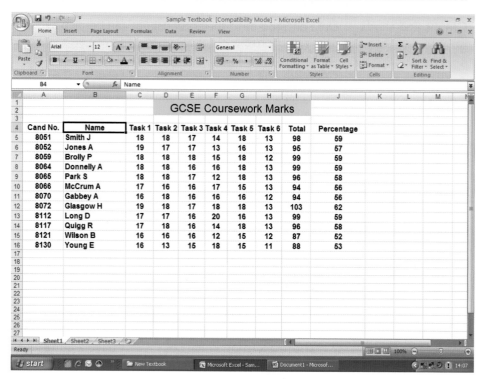

To select a row or column, click on the row number or column letter, such as C.

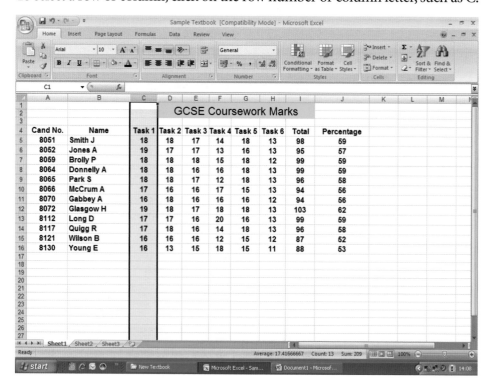

Moving the cursor to the point where column I ends and column J begins allows the user to alter the width of the column. This allows the user to insert and view a larger number of characters. The same process can be applied to rows.

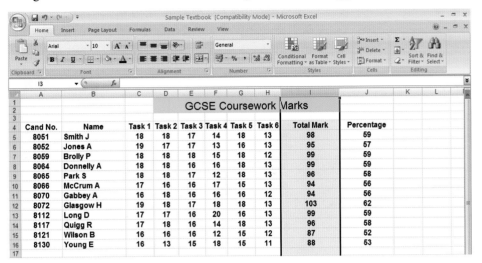

When entering data into a spreadsheet you can format the data into a specified category, such as:

- General
- Number
- Currency
- Date
- Time
- Percentage.

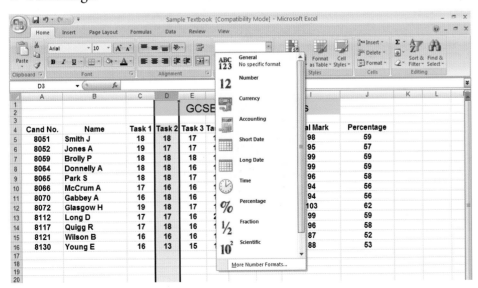

Selecting the **Format Cells** button allows the selected cell(s) to be formatted. Formatting cells allows the user to control the contents of a cell, such as cell type and font colour.

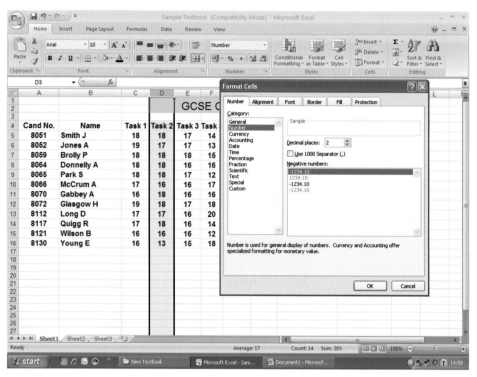

The **Format Cells** button and the **Border** tab will allow you to select borders and patterns using a variety of colours.

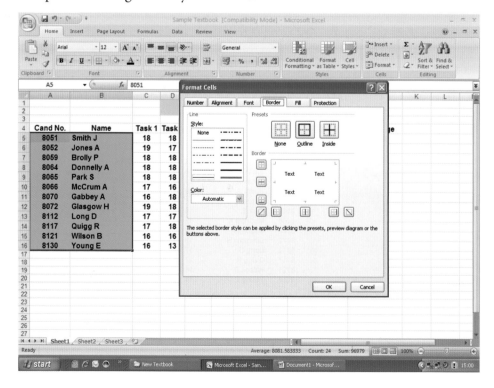

By selecting the **Format** menu you can also use a number of other formatting features such as **AutoFit Column Width**.

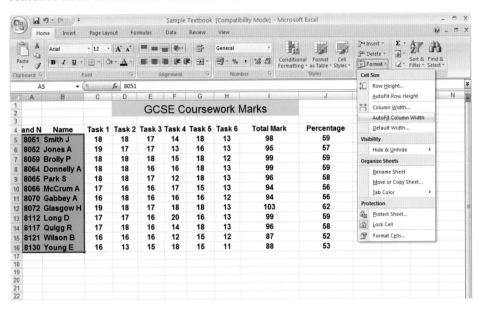

◼ Conditional formatting

Conditional formatting allows the user to include aspects such as cell shading or font colour to cells if a specified condition is true. In this example we want to display any total score between 91 and 99 in a different font colour.

1 Select the cells that display Total Marks, then click on the buttons **Conditional Formatting**, **Highlight Cells Rules** and **Between**.

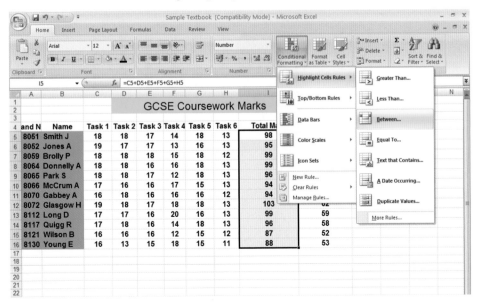

2 Enter the values *91* and *99* in the **Between** dialogue box and select **Red Text**.

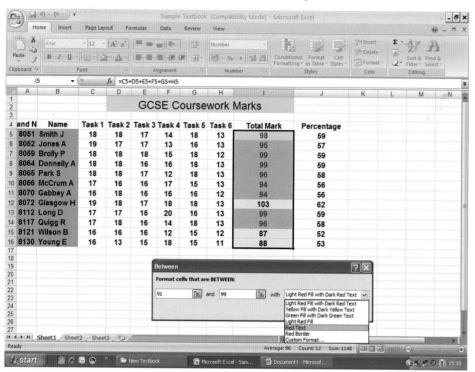

3 Once you have selected your colour click **OK**.

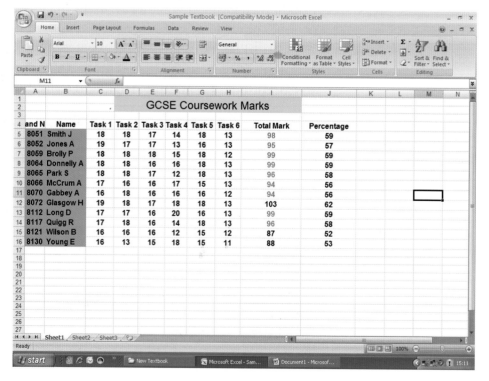

Data validation in spreadsheets

It is possible to control the value input into a given cell(s) by selecting the **Data Validation** menu.

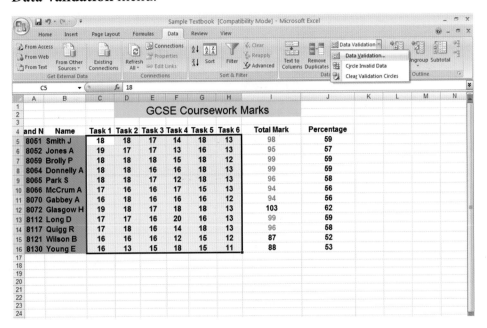

Consider all tasks in the spreadsheet and that each task has a maximum mark of 20. We need to consider a range check where the values lie between 0 and 20. You can also define the data type. In this case the number will be defined as a whole number.

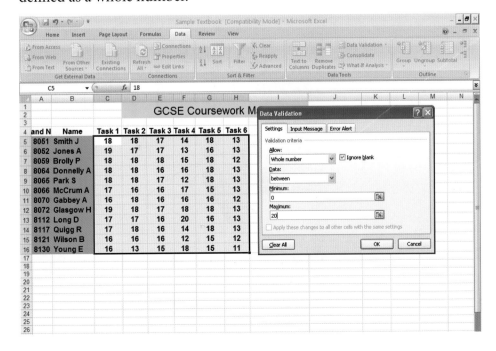

You can also enter a suitable message to guide the user by selecting the **Input Message** tab, and then entering your message.

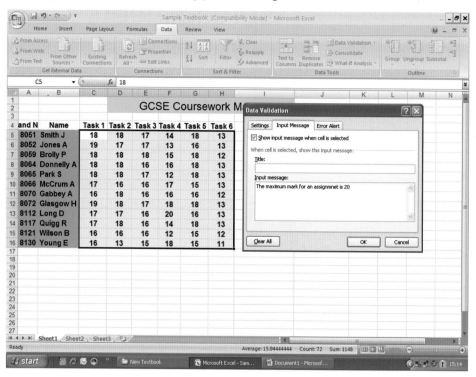

By using the **Error Alert** tab you can control the style of the error message by selecting **Stop**, **Warning** or **Information**.

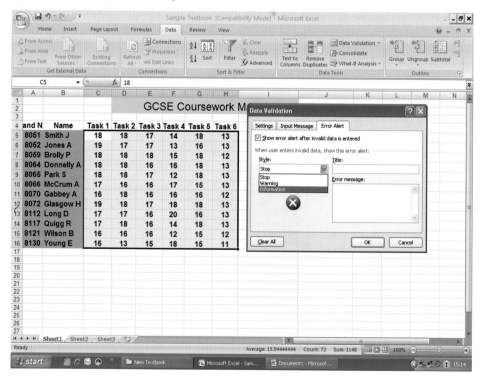

If we add a task score to the spreadsheet and input a higher value than 20 for task 1, the error message created will pop up in a dialogue box.

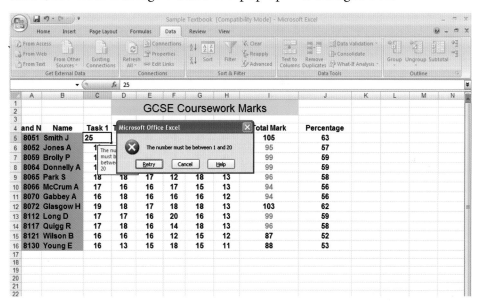

■ Using formulae and functions

SUM function

To enter a simple formula you start with an equals (=) sign followed by a formula or a function, such as =SUM(C5:H5), which will calculate a total score for Smith J for all tasks.

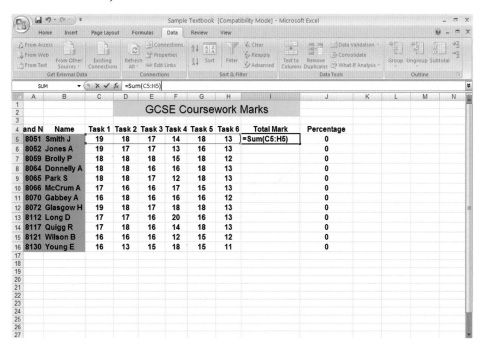

Selecting the **Fill** menu and the **Down** option allows the formula to be replicated in each cell in the selected column.

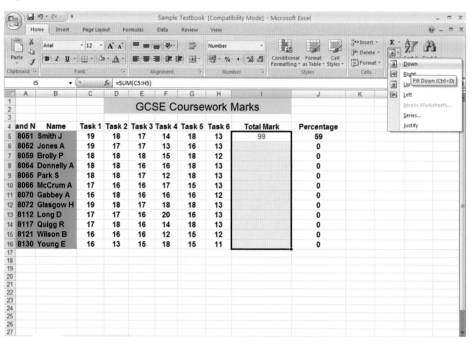

AVERAGE function

The AVERAGE function will automatically calculate the average of a group of selected cell values. In C19, type *=AVERAGE(C5:C16)* to calculate the average score. An alternative way of entering the cell range would be to click on C5 and drag down to cell C16.

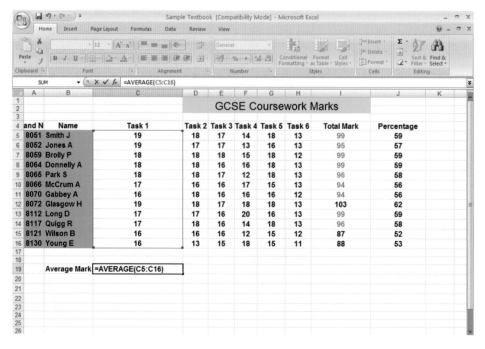

Selecting the **Fill** menu and the **Right** option allows the formula to be replicated in each cell in the selected row.

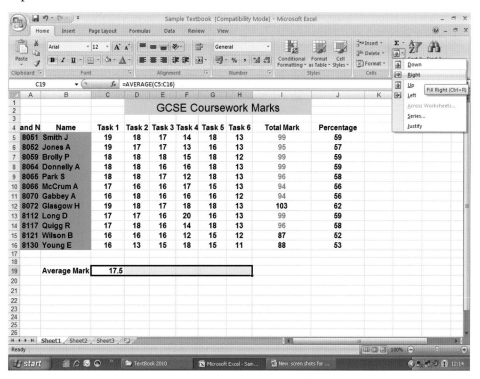

You can then set the value to a whole number in the selected range using the **Format Cells** option.

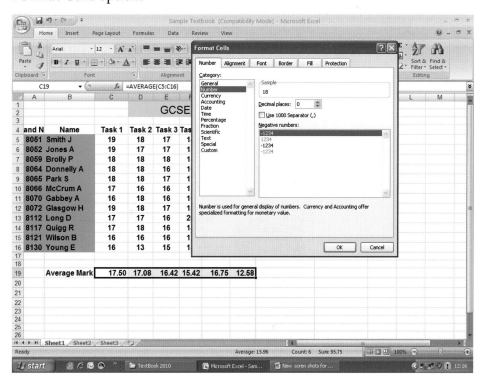

MAX function

The MAX function will automatically find the largest value of a group of cells. In C21, type *=MAX(I5:I16)* to return the highest total score in the class. An alternative way of entering the cell range would be to click on I5 and drag down to cell I16.

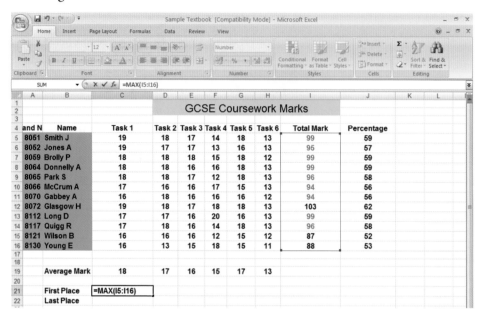

MIN function

The MIN function will automatically find the smallest value in a group of cells. In C22, type *=MIN(I5:I16)* to return the lowest total score in the class. An alternative way of entering the cell range would be to click on I5 and drag down to cell I16.

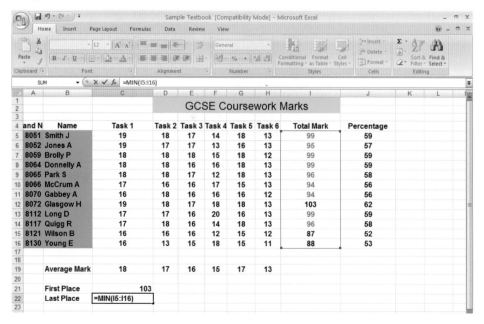

■ Complex functions

Using the IF statement

This function allows the user to examine a condition and return one of two actions. It can be thought of as:

IF condition is true **THEN** action 1 **ELSE** action 2.

In the example of coursework marks the teacher wants to give any score greater than 95 out of 120 a comment 'Excellent' and any score below 95 a comment 'Well Done'.

This can be thought of as:

IF *Grand Total* > 95 **THEN** *'Excellent'* **ELSE** *'Well Done'*

To translate this into a format understood by the spreadsheet, you need to select the **Formulas** tab and click on the option **Logical**. Then select the **IF** function.

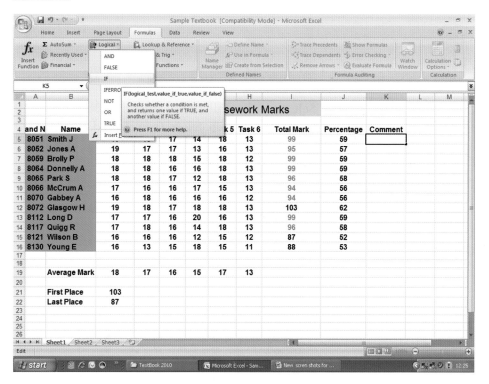

Then enter your condition and the actions required. Note, if you are using text statements in your actions they must be placed inside inverted commas.

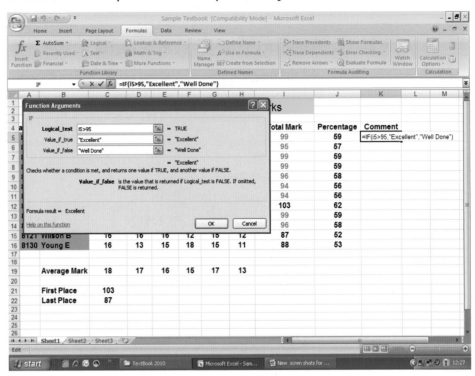

Selecting the **Fill menu** and the **Down** option allows the formula to be replicated in each cell in the selected column.

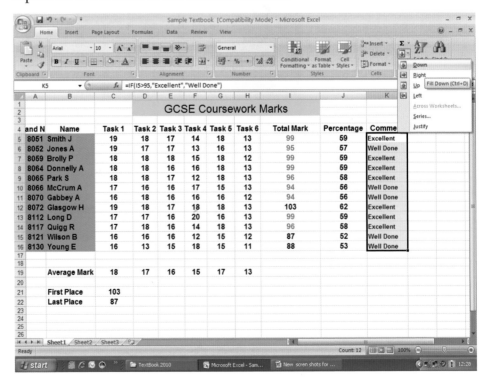

Absolute cell reference

If you do not want a cell reference to change when you copy a formula you can make it an absolute reference by using a $ sign such as I20, so the formula, when filled down a column or across a row, will always refer to the value in I20. In our example we will add a comment to all students, where the comment will depend on the score being 95 or over in all coursework tasks.

Using the VLookup function

This function will take a value in a selected cell and use a lookup table to find a match in a selected column of values (vertical lookup) and return a value in the next column in the same row. In the example of coursework marks the teacher will allocate a number 1, 2 or 3 to each Total Mark and a grade will be automatically placed in the appropriate cell.

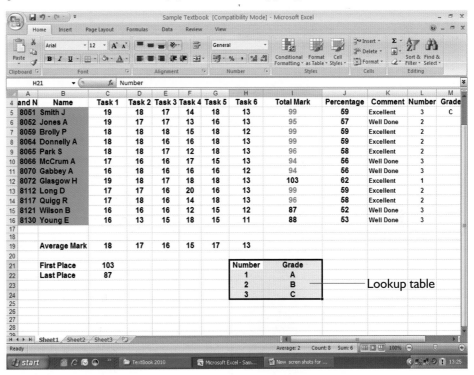

From the **Formulas** tab select the **VLOOKUP** function from the **Lookup & Reference** menu.

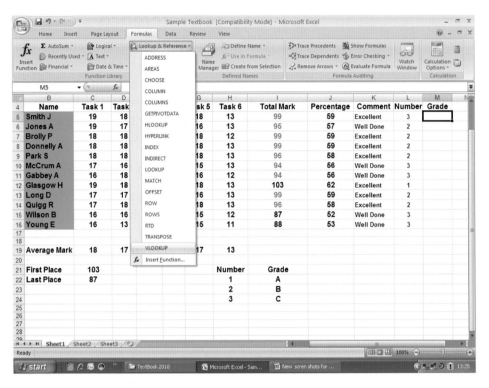

Then enter the cell reference that will collect the lookup value and the table cell references and the table column number where the value will be taken from.

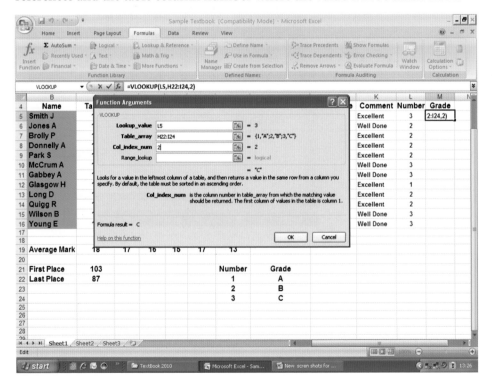

The value from the table will be automatically copied into the seleted cell.

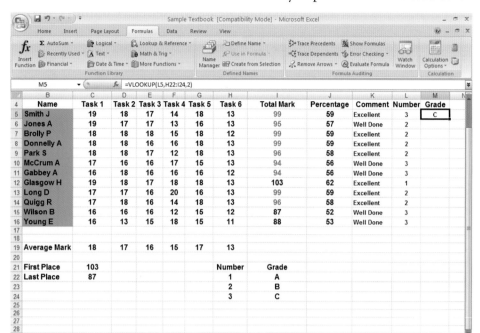

■ Using graphs to display results

1   First, select an area of the spreadsheet for consideration. In this example we will select Total Mark.

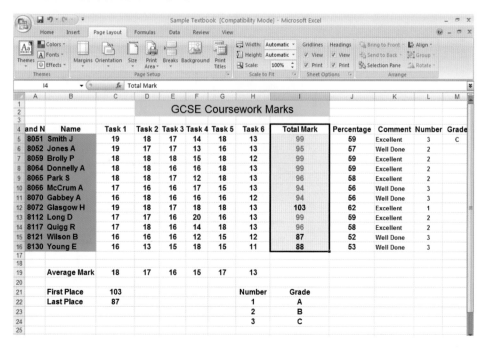

2   Then select the **Insert** tab and choose from a range of chart types. For this example we will select a **Column** chart.

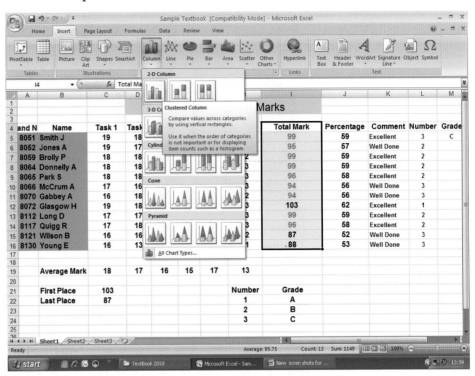

3   An outline graph is displayed, by **right clicking** on the graph you can select more data from the spreadsheet to add to the graph.

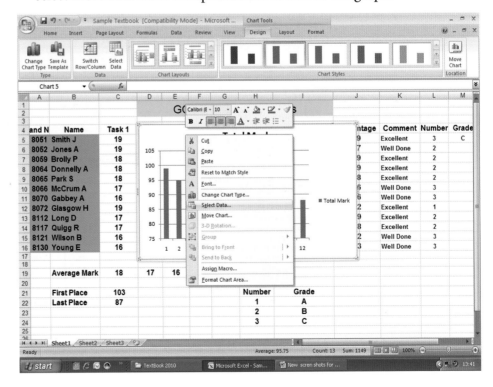

4 The vertical axis is the Total Mark but you need to **Edit** the **Horizontal Axis.**

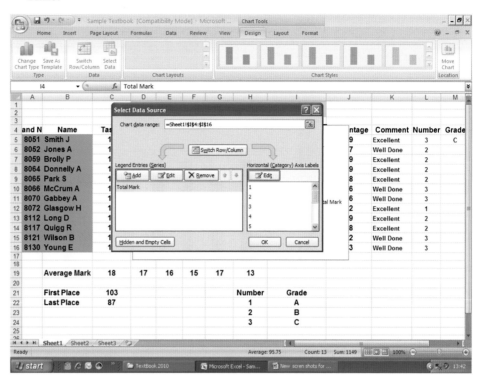

5 Select the names of the candidates from the spreadsheet to be placed on the horizontal axis.

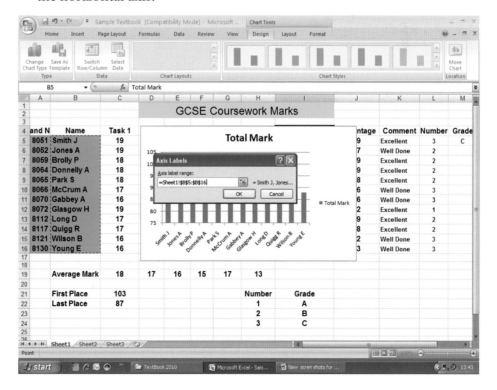

6   By selecting the **Layout** tab, you can add or edit more details on the graph.

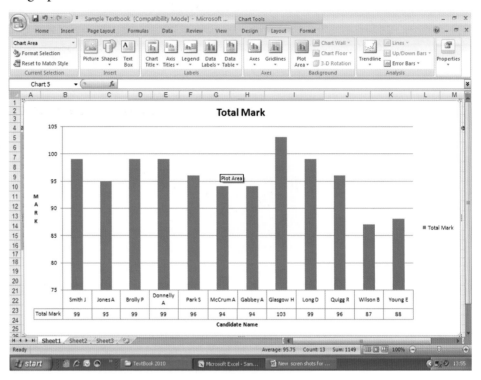

Questions on Unit 1 Tools and applications

1 Communication software

1 Expand the acronyms WWW and URL.
2 Apart from the feature 'Favourites', state **four** other features of a typical web browser.
3 Distinguish between a search engine and a web browser.
4 State **four** different search engines a student could use to search the internet.
5 State **three** different web browsers available to a user.
6 Explain how the use of 'wildcards' could help a student research a GCSE subject.
7 Design a suitable search for the following scenarios:
   a A tourist wants to rent an apartment in Spain but does not want to stay in a hotel.
   b A GCSE student wants information about pop music between 2000 and 2005 and female pop groups.
   c A Chelsea fan wants to find out about famous Chelsea footballers who are not from England or Ireland.
8 Distinguish between Cc and Bcc when referring to email software.
9 What is the purpose of an address book when using your email account?
10 Give **three** advantages of using email over using a Post Office.
11 What is the purpose of 'file attachment' in your email account?
12 A user can add message options before sending an email. Give **two** different message options available to a user.
13 State **three** advantages of using a VLE in teaching and learning.

2 Presentation package

1 What is the function of a storyboard when developing a multimedia presentation?
2 Explain the term 'multimedia'.
3 List **six** features that are unique to multimedia software.
4 How can a Slide Master improve the appearance of a multimedia presentation?
5 Explain the difference between linking and embedding objects in a presentation.
6 Alan is developing a presentation for his GCSE coursework. He is considering using a template.
   a Describe to Alan what a template is.
   b List **two** advantages of making use of templates when creating a presentation.

7 A presentation can include timings.

   a How do timings affect the presentation?

   b When would you recommend that timings be used within a presentation?

8 a What is a hyperlink?

   b List **three** ways in which a hyperlink can be used in a multimedia presentation.

9 John, a GCSE student, has added custom animation to his presentation.

   a What is custom animation?

   b List **three** ways in which an animation can be customised by a designer.

10 When creating a multimedia presentation for users, it should be tested and evaluated. Describe how you would test and evaluate a presentation.

3 Information handling package

1 a John has a large film collection. He owns DVD and HD disks. He is going to create a database so that he can keep track of the films in his collection.

   John will record the following data:

Film name
Director
Year of release
Number of minutes
Distributor

   i For each of the above fields suggest a suitable data type.

   ii Suggest **two** further fields which John could include in his database.

   b John has been told that he needs to include a key field/primary key in his database.

   i What is a key field?

   ii Suggest a key field for John's database.

   c John is unsure of how to structure his database. Explain the following terms to John:

   i Field

   ii Record

   iii File

2 Describe how John could use each of the following features in a database:

   a Query

   b Report

   c Form

3 A tennis club coach has set up a database for his members. The MEMBER table is structured as follows:

Field	Rules
MembershipNumber	Must be between 1 and 100
Surname	Must have a length greater than 1 character
Forename	Must have a length greater than 1 character
Gender	Can only be M or F
DateOfBirth	Must be at least 7 years old
TelephoneNumber	Can contain numbers and letters
EmailAddress	Must be present
Sport	Can only be Indoor tennis or Outdoor tennis
ClassNumber	Can only be 1–6

   a For each of the above, suggest a validation rule or an input mask.
   b The coach uses queries to search through the database. For each of the following state what criteria would be used:

Query	Criteria
Find all members who have membership numbers between 50 and 75.	
Find all female members who are aged 18 or over.	
Find all members who play indoor tennis and are under 12.	

4 The tennis coach adds the CLASS table to the database. It contains the details of all the classes.
   a Suggest a suitable structure for the CLASS table.
   b The CLASS table is linked to the MEMBER table, describe how this would be done.
   c What are the advantages of linking two tables together in a database?

5 What does the term validation mean?

6 List and describe **four** different types of validation checks that can be used.

7 A relational database prevents **data redundancy** and improves **data integrity**. State the meaning of each of the terms in bold.

8 A student uses a wizard to create a report from a database.
   a What is a wizard?
   b List **two** advantages of using a wizard when creating reports or forms.

9 Data can be shared between different applications. State **two** ways in which this can be done.

10 When creating a system for users, the system should be tested and evaluated. Describe how you would test and evaluate a system.

4 Spreadsheet package

1 Describe **three** features of a spreadsheet that would make it suitable to be used by a school tuck shop.

2 A cell can be formatted as currency. State **four** other methods of formatting a cell.

3 Define what is meant by conditional formatting.

4 Define what is meant by absolute cell reference.

5 Distinguish between MAX and MIN functions.

6 Consider the following spreadsheet. It shows monthly payments for a forthcoming school trip. The total cost for each student is £500. Students cannot pay in more than £100 per month.

	A	B	C	D	E	F	G	H	I	J	K
1	Forename	Surname	September	October	November	January	February	March	Total	Balance	Fully Paid
2	Joanne	Brown	£65	£75	£90		£85	£85	£400	£100	NO
3	Terry	Collins	£65	£95	£90	£100	£85	£65	£500	£0	YES
4	Norma	Anderson	£100	£60	£65	£55	£100	£90	£470	£30	NO
5	Heather	Browne	£75	£100	£85	£75	£55	£80	£470	£30	NO
6	Janet	Dennison	£65	£85	£65	£85	£100	£100	£500	£0	YES
7	Michelle	McKiernan	£85	£45	£90	£65	£80	£90	£455	£45	NO
8	Gavin	Palmer	£80		£90	£75	£75	£100	£420	£80	NO
9	James	Shelley	£75	£90	£90	£85	£100	£60	£500	£0	YES
10	Brian	Ferguson	£10	£100	£85	£85	£85	£90	£455	£45	NO
11	Anna	Galloway	£90	£55	£80	£80		£95	£400	£100	NO
12		Total	£710	£705	£830	£705	£765	£855			
13		Average	£71	£78	£83	£78	£85	£86			

a What is the value in cell C4?

b State a cell reference for a 'label'.

c Write down the formulae stored in the following cells

   i I4_____

   ii J2_____

   iii C12_____

   iv G13_____

d How could data validation be used with the data held in the cell range D2:D11?

e An IF statement is used in column K. Explain how the function is used.

f Write down **two** cell ranges used to create the bar chart below.

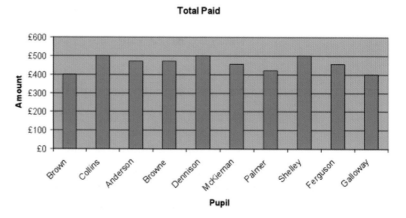

Total Paid

g A wizard was used to create the chart. What is meant by a wizard?

5 Using graphics

What you will learn in this section

In this section you will learn about:

- capturing and transferring images for further manipulation
- the importance of preparing graphics correctly for a specific purpose
- the difference between vector based and bitmap graphics.

Through the worked example you will gain skills which will assist in:

- creating and editing digital images
- applying effects to digital images
- the integration of images and text
- creating basic animated graphic images.

This is assessed through the following components:

Unit 3 Terminal Examination
Unit 2 Controlled Assessment Task 1
Unit 2 Controlled Assessment Task 2.

Acronyms:

- BMP
- GIF
- JPEG
- PICT
- PNG
- TIFF
- USB
- WWW

Keywords:

- Animation
- Bitmap graphics
- Bluetooth
- Compressed
- Crop
- Digital
- Fill
- Flash media
- Flip
- Infrared
- Memory card reader
- Pixel
- Resolution
- Rotate
- Scanner
- Stretch
- Tool palette
- Vector graphics
- Wi-Fi
- Zoom

■ Creation and manipulation of images

Digital still and animated graphics

GLOSSARY TERMS
Digital
Word art

The term graphic refers to any image-related file that is either still or animated. Digital still images can come in the form of clipart, **digital** photographs, **word art**, scanned images or images created using drawing tools in a graphics package.

Animated graphics are graphic images that move in some way. At the simplest level they may be clipart images with limited movement such as spinning or moving from side to side. More advanced computer **animations** include examples of animated movies such as *Shrek* or *Toy Story*.

Regardless of the complexity of the graphic it must be in digital format before it can be manipulated using a computer. For this to happen the graphic must either be created digitally or it must be captured using a specific hardware device and converted into digital format for use on a computer.

> GLOSSARY TERM
> Animation

Image capturing

Images can be captured in digital format using a variety of hardware devices:

- mobile phones
- digital cameras
- **scanners**.

> GLOSSARY TERM
> Scanner

Before these images can be edited using software, or imported into another application, they must be transferred from the hardware device used to capture them. This can be done by connecting the hardware device to a computer using one of the following methods:

- Uploaded via cable links, for example USB (Universal Serial Bus).
- Direct transfer from **flash media** via a USB port.
- **Memory card reader**/card slot.
- Wireless link – for example via **Bluetooth**, **infrared** or **Wi-Fi**.
- Email link – for example, the image could be emailed from a mobile phone and downloaded as an attachment from an email.

> GLOSSARY TERMS
> Flash media
> Memory card reader
> Bluetooth
> Infrared
> Wi-Fi

Features of graphics packages

All graphics packages have similar features. The table below illustrates some of the common features of graphics packages.

Feature	Detail
Draw lines	Lines can be straight, curved or freehand
Pre-defined shapes	Shapes such as rectangles and circles, can be drawn
Resize	Change the size of the shape (scaling the image)
Cropping	Cut out and discard part of an image
Stretch	Shapes can be stretched horizontally or vertically

> GLOSSARY TERMS
> Crop
> Stretch

GLOSSARY TERMS
Rotate
Flip

Feature	Detail
Rotate/flip	Shapes can be rotated through an angle either clockwise or anticlockwise. A shape can be reflected (flipped) horizontally or vertically
Colour	A paint palette can be used to change the colour of lines or objects
Fill	Allows areas/shapes to be filled with shading, patterns or images
Zoom	Allows an area of the image to be seen more closely
Clip art	A library of drawings that can be built into the package or sourced online
Tool palette	Shows the tools available for image manipulation using icons such as a brush or a magnifying tool
Text boxes	Used to add text to graphic images
Save As	Allows graphics to be saved in different formats depending on how they are to be used

GLOSSARY TERMS
Fill
Zoom

GLOSSARY TERM
Tool palette

Image compression

When we include graphics on web pages or we are transmitting graphics to someone else over the World Wide Web (www) it is important that those graphics can be downloaded in an acceptable time. When creating and editing graphics using image manipulation software it is important to take into consideration how the final graphic will be distributed before deciding what file format to save the graphic image in.

Bitmapped graphics

GLOSSARY TERMS
Bitmap graphics
Pixel
Resolution
Compressed

Bitmap graphics store details about every individual picture element (**pixel**) in the image. The higher the **resolution** of the device used to capture the device, the higher the quality of the image will be (this also means an increase in the file size). Bitmapped images can be **compressed** or saved in other file formats but this will mean a reduction in image quality.

Vector graphics

GLOSSARY TERM
Vector graphics

Vector graphics store information about the components that make up an image. They do not depend on resolution for quality, instead they store details about the shape of individual image components, their location in the image, their colour, and so on. This means they can be saved as smaller files and can be easily edited without loss of quality.

Image presentation

Images that have been edited using graphic manipulation software can often be saved in a variety of formats. The table below explains some of these file formats.

When selecting graphics for use in multimedia or gaming applications you should consider:

- the quality of the graphic
- the file size
- the file type.

The following compressed graphic file types are supported by web browsers and are therefore suitable when creating web pages: GIF, JPEG and PNG.

Gaming applications that are designed for web distribution should also use these file formats, otherwise most other formats will be appropriate, provided the graphic is suitable for purpose and audience.

File format	Detail
BMP	BMP (Bitmap) files store details about images at pixel level. Images saved using this file type therefore tend to take up a lot of storage so they are not a suitable file format for upload to websites as they can take up a lot of web space.
GIF	GIF (Graphics Interchange Format) files support compressed images. These file types take up little storage space so are suitable for inclusion on web pages. Animated GIFs combine a series of GIF images and display them one after the other.
JPEG	JPEG (Joint Photographic Expert Group) files also support the compression of images for storage. The level of compression can be selected by the user so they can determine the trade off between quality and storage. JPEGs are often used on web pages.
PICT	PICT files are the standard file format for Apple Macintosh graphics applications. They can support high-quality images but can also be compressed.
PNG	PNG (Portable Network Graphics) files allow for the compression of bitmapped graphics. PNG format was developed to support the sharing of graphics via the World Wide Web. Files in this format tend to take up slightly more storage than GIF images.
TIFF	TIFF (Tagged Image File Format) files store bitmapped images in a format that allows the image to be portable between a Windows and Apple Macintosh environment.

When saving an image it is important to consider how that image is going to be distributed to others before selecting the file format. Bitmapped images take up a lot of storage space and take a long time to load. This makes images that are stored in bitmap format unsuitable for distribution via the World Wide Web.

Animated graphics

Animated graphics are created by linking a variety of still graphic images together and presenting them in sequence at high speed. Animated graphics come in a variety of formats including GIF and Flash.

Image manipulation

Once an image has been uploaded and saved onto a computer it can be opened in an image manipulation application and edited. Online image editing applications are also widely available for those who do not have access to graphics editing software and many of these are free to use.

One example of an online graphics editing application is pixlr. It can be found at www.pixlr.com.

Creating images using an online graphics application – pixlr

Consider the following scenario

Philip organises guitar master classes and guitar recitals for the local school of music. He asks his friend Alex to design a logo that he can use on a website. Philip did not specify a text colour but the background colour of his website will be black.

He wants the logo to:

● Include his name: Philip Richardson.
● Include the words: Guitar Tutor.

Using the type tool in pixlr

This section is supported by the following digital media:

guitar logo.jpg

student 1.jpg

1 Go to www.pixlr.com and click on **Open image editor**.

2 Select **Create a new image**.

3 Name the image *PR Logo*.

4 Change the image **Width** to 640 pixels.

5 Change the image **Height** to 200 pixels.

6 Click the **Transparent** option box and then click **OK**. This means that the background colour or pattern on Philip's website can still be seen when the graphic is inserted.

Navigator panel shows a thumbnail of your graphic and allows you to zoom in and out of the image.

Tools commonly used in graphics packages. Click on any tool to select it. Place the cursor over icon to get a description of the tool.

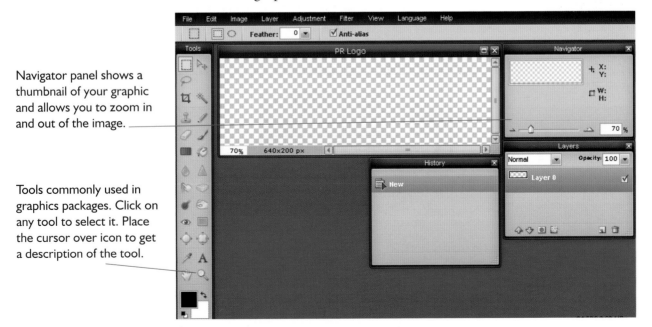

7 Click on the **Type** tool.

8 Click on the canvas called 'PR Logo'.

9 In the Text panel, type the words:

Philip Richardson

Guitar Tutor

10 Set the remainder of the panel up as shown. (Choose an appropriate text colour)

11 Click **OK**.

12 Click on **File** and select **Save** to save *PR Logo* to an appropriate location.

Editing existing images

1 Open the image called *guitar logo.jpg*.

2 Use the **Set foreground color** tool to select the colour black.

3 Use the **Paint bucket** tool to flood the red elements of the graphic with black.

4 Click on the **Filter** menu and select a filter to apply to the image. For example, the **Kaleidoscope** filter.

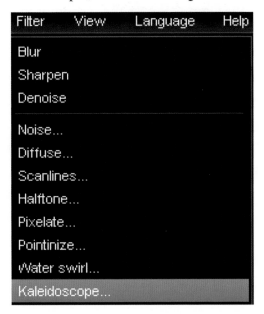

5 Click **OK** to view the impact this filter has on the image.

6 Click **Edit** and **Undo** if you are unhappy with the change and try another one.

Adding text to an image

Once you have edited the graphic and you are happy with the way it looks you can add text to it using the **Type** tool as shown on page 102.

Cropping an image in pixlr

1 Open the image *student 1.jpg*.

2 Click on the **Crop tool.**

Figure 1   Figure 2

You will use the **Crop** tool to edit the image so that it is altered from its original format in *Figure 1* to the image shown in *Figure 2*.

3 Drag the **Crop** tool over the section of image you want to keep. A grid will appear over the image.

4 Press the **Enter** key on the keyboard to confirm.

5 Save the new version of the image as *student 2.jpg*

Evaluating your graphic

Before using a graphic for any application you should evaluate the suitability of the graphic by considering:

1 Its suitability for the selected purpose and audience.

2 The quality of the graphic.

3 The file format (is the graphic in an appropriate format for the application?).

4 Is the graphic copyright protected?

Extension exercise

Use the tools available in pixlr to create a logo for Philip Richardson who is a guitar tutor.

The logo should include his name and an image of a guitar. He will use the logo on his new website. Save this file with an appropriate filename so you can use it in developing your website.

Creating animated graphics using an online tool

There are a wide variety of tools and applications available to support the creation of animated graphics. The most important thing to remember about creating an animated graphic is that it needs to be planned.

Animated graphics are best thought of as a series of still images that are presented to the viewer at high speed; much in the way that old-fashioned flip books create the impression of animation through the fast presentation of a series of images.

There are many tools available online to support the creation of animated graphics. Many of these tools are so user friendly that the most complex part of creating the animated graphic becomes creating the images that will form the animation. If the animation is to be high quality, many images are needed to help ensure the smooth progression of the animation.

> This section is supported by the following digital media:
>
> acoustic-guitar graphic.gif
>
> *acoustic-guitar graphic1.gif*
>
> *acoustic-guitar graphic2.gif*
>
> *acoustic-guitar graphic3.gif*

1 Open the image *acoustic-guitar graphic.gif* using a graphics package of your choice.

2 Edit the image, so you have four different versions of the image similar to those shown on page 105 (Or you can download and use the files named in the margin.)

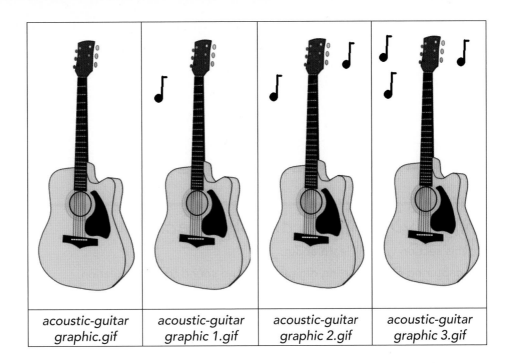

acoustic-guitar graphic.gif	*acoustic-guitar graphic 1.gif*	*acoustic-guitar graphic 2.gif*	*acoustic-guitar graphic 3.gif*

3 Save each version of the graphic separately and with a file name that indicates the sequence of each graphic in the animation.

4 Search the internet for a suitable website that will allow you to **create** your own **animated gif online**. (The words in bold could be used as the key words for your online search.)

5 Upload *acoustic-guitar graphic.gif, acoustic-guitar graphic 1.gif, acoustic-guitar graphic 2.gif, acoustic-guitar graphic 3.gif* in the appropriate sequence.

6 Create your animation.

7 A preview of the animation will normally be played online (it may take a while for this to be processed depending on the amount of detail in your individual graphics).

8 Play the preview and make any necessary amendments to the individual graphics.

9 Upload any amended graphics and preview your animation again.

10 When you are happy with the final animation save the animation to your computer in animated gif file format so you can use it in your own projects.

Hints for creating animated graphics

1 All graphics used in the animation should be the same size.

2 Individual graphics comprising the animation should be saved in gif format.

3 The smaller the difference between each graphic in a sequence, the smoother the animation will appear.

6

Using digital video and sound

What you will learn in this section

In this section you will learn about:

- capturing and importing digital video and sound for manipulation.

Through the worked example you will gain skills which will assist in:

- planning a digital video
- using specialised features to create a digital video
- adding audio effects to video clips
- preparing video and sound for sharing online and on DVD/CD.

This is assessed through the following components:

Unit 3 Terminal Examination
Unit 2 Controlled Assessment Task 1
Unit 2 Controlled Assessment Task 2.

Acronyms:

- 3G
- AIF
- AVI
- CD-ROM

- Codec
- DVD-ROM
- FLA
- HDTV

- MIDI
- MOV
- MP3
- MP4

- MPEG
- WAV
- WMA
- WMV

Keywords:

- Blu-ray
- Bluetooth
- Compression
- Decompression

- Digital
- Flash technologies
- Internet

- Microphone
- Optical storage media
- Optimise

- Upload

■ Digital video and sound

GLOSSARY TERM
Digital

Facilities for recording **digital** video and digital sound are now widely available. Most people have the facility to record digital video and sound on their mobile phones and most standard digital cameras can now be used to record and store short video clips.

GLOSSARY TERMS
3G
Upload
Internet
Microphone

Many **3G** phones and digital cameras now allow you to edit digital video clips stored on their memory chips. Videos created and stored on a mobile phone can now easily be **upload**ed to the **internet**.

Microphones can be used to input sound directly into a computer system. Sound input to a computer system this way is stored digitally and there are many applications available that allow you to edit these files both online and on your computer system.

Digital video and sound can be distributed to others in a variety of ways:

GLOSSARY TERMS
Optical storage
  media
Bluetooth
Flash technologies
Blu-ray

- **optical storage media** such as DVD or CD-ROM
- internet (email or publishing on websites)
- **Bluetooth**
- **flash technologies**
- **Blu-ray**
- HDTV.

The method you use to distribute your digital video file will have an impact on the way you save your file; for example, you would not place a 5 GB movie on an internet website as it would greatly slow down the loading of the webpage.

GLOSSARY TERMS
Optimise
Compression
Decompression

Before you can distribute a digital video or sound file you need to **optimise** the file. Optimisation involves reducing the file size. Codecs (**compression/ decompression** software) are used to do this. This means these files will take up less web space or storage space on the device you are using to distribute them. It also means that the digital video or sound file can be transferred across a network much more quickly.

Appropriate file formats for web distribution are:

Task

Research each of the file formats listed and expand each of the acronyms

Video	Sound
.fla	MIDI
.wmv	AIF
.mpg (mpeg)	WAV
.mp4	MP3
.mov	WMA
.avi	

Consider the following scenario

Philip organises guitar master classes and guitar recitals for the local school of music. He asks his friend Alex to plan and create a short digital video so he can add it to his website at a later stage.

■ Digital video planning

Before he can create the video for Philip, Alex needs to understand exactly what he wants the video to contain. Philip tells him he wants the video to be no longer than 20 seconds and it should include:

- a title screen and credits
- digital images of at least one of his students and comments they have made about their lessons with him
- a short video of him actually playing the guitar.

Before setting out to create the video Alex decides it would be best to create a storyboard. The storyboard will contain:

- details of any title or credit screens
- a description of any movie clips to be included and how long they will be
- a description of any still images to be included and how long each will appear for
- the name and duration of any sound tracks to be included in the movie
- any special effects applied to the movie.

Alex creates the following storyboard for the movie:

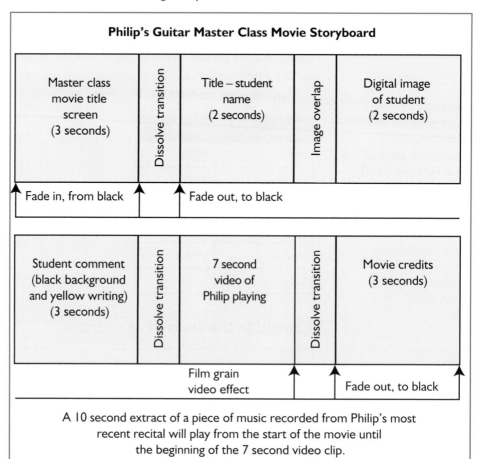

This section is supported by the following digital media:

Student 1.jpg

Video Clip 1.wmv

Sound Bite 1.wav

Sound Bite 2.wav

■ How to create a movie using movie editing software – Windows Movie Maker

This section is supported by the following digital media:

Student 1.jpg

Video Clip 1.wmv

Sound Bite 1.wav

Open Windows Movie Maker.

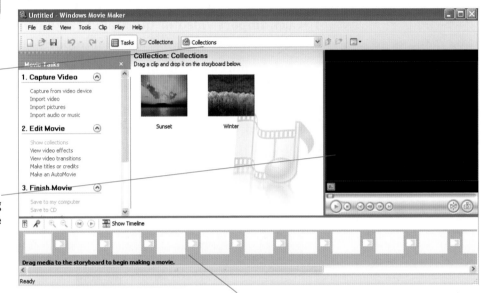

Collections refers to any graphic, video or sound file you have imported into Windows Movie Maker

Here you can preview any projects as you are working on them in Windows Movie Maker

The storyboard allows you to place items from your collections into your movie. Here you can reorder collection items and apply video effects and/or transitions.

To create a movie in Windows Movie Maker

A **project** contains all of the sound, video and graphic files in your movie. Save your work as a project until you have finished editing it. It is only when you are satisfied that your work is complete that you save it as a **movie** file.

1 Select **File** and then **New Project**.

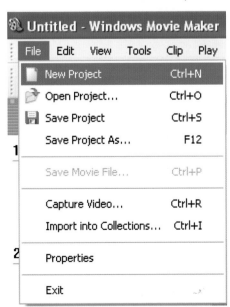

2 Import the following files to your project. You will use them to create your video:

Student 1.jpg
Video Clip 1.wmv
Sound Bite 1.wav

3 Click **Import pictures** in the **Movie Tasks** pane and then browse to the image *Student 1.jpg.* Click on **Import**.

4 Click **Import video** in the **Movie Tasks** pane and then browse to the videos *Video Clip 1.wmv.* Click on **Import**.

5 Click **Import audio or music** in the **Movie Tasks** pane and then browse to *Sound Bite 1.wav.* Click on **Import**.

6 To view all of the items you have imported, click on the **Collections** icon.

7 Click on the **Tasks** icon to begin creating your movie.

8 Drag *Student 1* and *Video Clip 1* to the storyboard in that order.

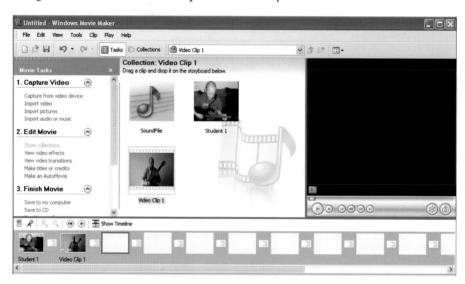

Editing individual video clips

1 Click on the **Show Timeline** icon.

2 Click and drag to trim the *Student 1* image so it plays for approximately 2 seconds (your cursor will change to a red cross hair).

3 Place cursor over *Video Clip 1* to see how long it is.

4 Trim *Video Clip 1* so it is 7 seconds long.

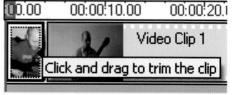

Adding titles and credits

1 In the **Movie Tasks** pane click on **Make titles or credits**.

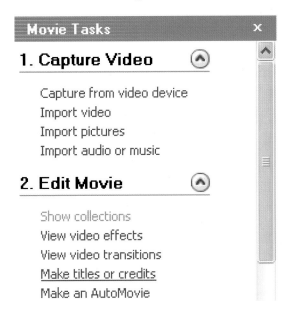

Choose **Add title at the beginning of the movie**.

2 Enter the text '*Philip's Master Class*' in the top text box.

3 Enter your name in the bottom text box.

4 Scroll down for **More Options** and change the title animation, font and colour to suit your own tastes.

Preview your titles and credits here

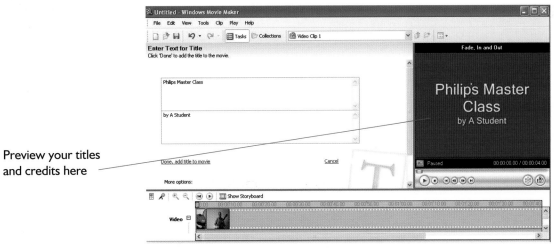

5 When you are happy with your title slide, click **Done, add title to movie**.

6 Click on *Student 1* image and then select **Add title before the selected clip in timeline**. Then add the text '*S Groves, Guitar Student*'.

Amend the animation, font and colour of the title slide.

7 Place another title after the *Student 1* image. The text here should read: '*Philip's lessons are at the right pace for me and he can teach classic and rock guitar.*'

Again change the animation, font and colour of the slide.

8 Add credits to the end of the movie with your name included.

9 Amend the length of each of the title slides to match Alex's storyboard.

Adding video effects and video transitions

1 Click on **View video effects**. You can add a video effect to any part of the movie by clicking and dragging the video effect onto the clip on the storyboard.

Add the **Posterize** video effect to the *Student 1* image by clicking and dragging it onto the image on the storyboard.

2 Video transitions affect how you move from one movie clip to the next.

Click on **View video transitions** and add the **Shatter right** transition to the clip containing the student's comments on Philip's lessons.

3 Add some video effects and video transitions of your own choice to the rest of the movie.

4 You can create a smooth transition between clips if the clips overlap. Use the storyboard to click and drag the *Student 1* image so it overlaps with the title screen containing the student's name.

On screen you will see a blue triangle which indicates how much the two clips overlap by

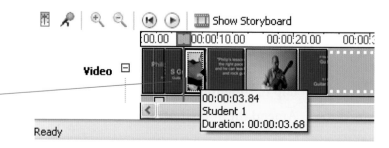

5 Continue editing the movie so all clips overlap in this manner. You may have to edit clip lengths to ensure the whole video remains 20 seconds in length.

Adding sound files to your movie

1 Click on the **Collections** icon.

2 Drag *Sound Bite 1.wav* from **Collections** onto the **Storyboard**.

The **Storyboard** will change to **Timeline** view.

Sound files are better added when you are happy with the duration of your movie. That way they can be easily clipped in length to suit your movie.

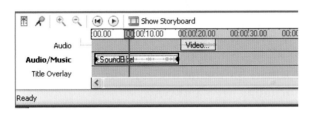

3 Trim *Sound Bite 1.wav* so that it stops before *Video Clip 1* starts playing.

4 Add *Sound Bite 1.wav* to the movie again so that it plays over the final credits.

Note: You may decide you want to include a voiceover for your own movie. You can do this in **Timeline** view by clicking on the microphone icon.

Saving your completed movie

You can use the **Save Movie** wizard to save your movie in a format suitable for the method of distribution you are planning to use, for example:

- playback on your computer
- CD distribution
- email distribution
- internet distribution
- digital video camera playback.

Save your movie for playback on your computer so you can upload it to your website at a later stage.

Export settings and file formats

When you save your movie it will be saved in WMV format and it can be played on any computer with the appropriate software.

When finishing your movie you can choose a variety of export settings depending on how it is to be distributed or played back. For example, if you are sending your video across the web you need to specify if it is being transferred via dial-up, ISDN or LAN, as different protocols are used for each.

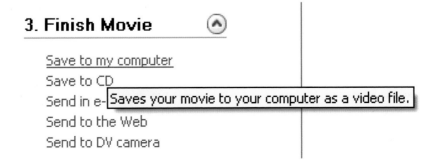

1 Click on **Save to my Computer**.

2 Enter an appropriate name and location for your movie, click **Next**.

3 Ensure **Best quality for playback on my computer** is checked and click **Next**.

4 Your movie will be automatically saved in WMV file format.

How to create and edit Sound files using Audacity

> An Audacity **project** contains all of the audio clips you have arranged onto tracks. It is not compatible with any other audio application. It is only when you are satisfied that your work is complete that you save it as an **audio** file.

Audacity is an application that is available for download from the internet. It allows you to create and edit sound files and save them in a variety of formats for digital distribution. Audacity can play a variety of file formats including MP3 and WAV.

Audacity can be used to create podcasts but can also be used to create sound bites for inclusion in web pages and other digital projects.

Audacity can be downloaded from http://audacity.sourceforge.net.

Open Audacity

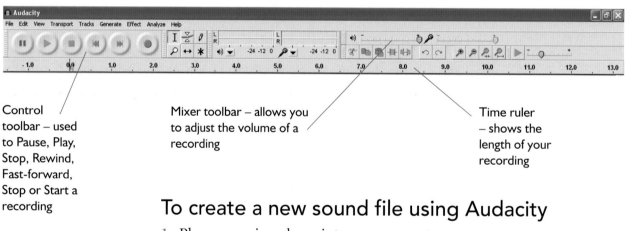

Control toolbar – used to Pause, Play, Stop, Rewind, Fast-forward, Stop or Start a recording

Mixer toolbar – allows you to adjust the volume of a recording

Time ruler – shows the length of your recording

To create a new sound file using Audacity

1 Plug your microphone into your computer.

2 Click on the **Record** button.

3   Start speaking and watch the sound wave develop on screen.

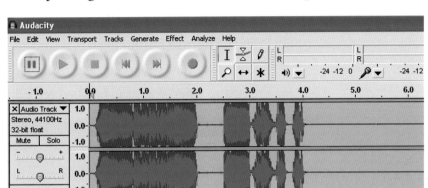

(A summary of your audio track appears to the right of your recording.)

4   Click the **Stop** button to end your recording.

5   Play back your recording by clicking on the **Play** button.

6   You can replay your recording from any point by clicking on the sound wave using the cursor.

7   Adjust the volume of your recording using the slider on the **Mixer** toolbar.

To delete part of a recording using Audacity

1   Use the cursor to highlight the part of the recording you want to delete.

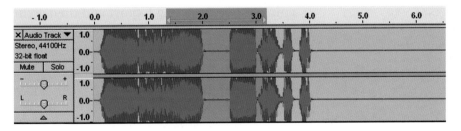

2   Press the **Delete** key on the keyboard.

3   The unwanted part of the recording is removed and the sound wave is automatically adjusted to make a continuous recording.

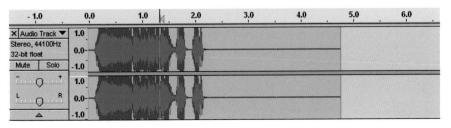

Adding sound to an existing recording.

1 Use the **Cursor** to select the start point for your new recording.

2 Press the **Record** button to start recording.

3 Record your new sound clip.

4 Press **Stop** when you have finished recording your new sound clip.

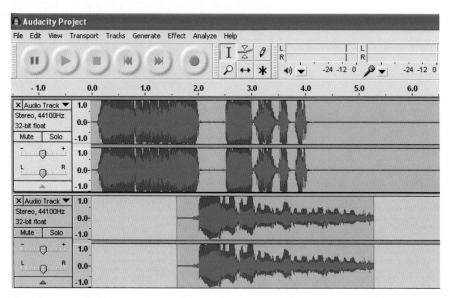

(Both sound clips are now shown in your Audacity project.)

Saving your recording

When you are happy with your recording you can save it as a WAV file by going to **File**, selecting **Export** and then giving the completed recording an appropriate name.

If you need to save your project before you have completed editing you must save it as an Audacity project. Do this by going to **File**, selecting **Save Project As** and then giving it an appropriate name and selecting an appropriate location. This way it can be opened and edited again in Audacity.

Extension exercise

Import the files *Sound Bite 1.wav* and *Sound Bite 2.wav* into Audacity and practise combining, deleting and adding effects to the sound files.

7

Games technology

What you will learn in this section

In this section you will learn about:

- trends in computer gaming
- game genres.

Through the worked example you will gain skills which will assist in:

- using storyboarding for game design
- the development of game proposals
- creating and evaluating computer games.

This is assessed through the following components:

Unit 3 Terminal Examination
Unit 2 Controlled Assessment Task 2.

Acronyms:

- 3D
- GoD
- MMORPG
- PDA
- PSP
- RPG
- WAP

Keywords:

- Action games
- Adventure games
- Altered reality gaming
- Apps
- Broadband
- Casual gaming
- Cheats
- Controls
- Feedback
- Game genre
- Game play
- Games console
- Haptic peripherals
- Interaction
- Interface
- Online gaming
- Puzzle game
- Role-play games
- Rules
- Scoring
- Sensory feedback
- Social gaming
- Storyboard
- Target audience
- Virtual reality
- Wi-Fi

■ Computer gaming

What is a computer game?

GLOSSARY TERMS
Interaction
Feedback
Haptic peripherals
Sensory feedback

A computer game can be defined as: an electronic presentation of a game that involves **interaction** with an electronic device containing a processor where **feedback** can be provided to the user. Feedback will at the very least be visual or auditory but the development of **haptic peripherals** (such as the peripherals used with the Nintendo Wii) now allow for the provision of **sensory feedback** through vibration.

Trends in computer gaming

Gaming has moved from being associated with arcade games, to being a popular entertainment activity that is no longer confined to a particular location. The technology associated with mobile phones and portable game playing devices means that computer game playing is now possible anywhere.

Computer games can be played on a variety of platforms including PCs, specialised **games console**s and mobile communication devices such as PDAs (Personal Digital Assistants) and mobile phones.

> **GLOSSARY TERM**
> Games console

Devices used to play games away from the traditional PC can be classified as console, or hand-held devices. Examples of these devices are:

Console	Hand-held
Dreamcast Nintendo GameCube Nintendo Wii Sony PlayStation (PS1, PS2 and PS3) XBox 360	iPod touch N-gage Nintendo DS Nintendo DS Lite PSP (Play Station Portable) (Most mobile phones can now also fall into this category.)

Developments in technology have led to an increase in processing power of games consoles and hand-held gaming devices. The resultant improvements in graphic **interface**s and the increase in game responsiveness have helped increase the popularity of computer gaming as a pastime.

> **GLOSSARY TERMS**
> Interface
> Target audience
> Game play
> Broadband
> Wi-Fi

The intuitive nature of the interfaces and peripherals associated with many of the gaming devices available today has helped widen the **target audience** for many game developers. One example of this is the Nintendo Wii. The popularity of this games console has increased due to the familiarity of the peripherals used to control it, in addition to the introduction of a social aspect to the **game play** of many of the activities available to the user.

The increased availability of internet connectivity through **broadband** in the home and **Wi-Fi** hotspots has not only extended the social element of gaming through websites such as Facebook but it has also led to a change in the way games are accessed and played by serious gamers.

High-speed internet access has allowed online game providers to provide Gaming on Demand (GoD) for subscribers, where games can be accessed and played as required. Gamers who want to access and play games this way no longer need high-speed processors on their home PCs to play complex and highly graphical games. Instead, all of the processing occurs on the game provider's server, interaction takes place via a high-speed broadband connection and feedback is provided to the user instantly, but without the need to invest in expensive computing equipment.

These developments have made the gaming industry an even more appealing investment for technology developers and programmers. It would seem apparent to developers today that the more realistic the game

GLOSSARY TERMS
Virtual reality
Online gaming
Role-play game
Social gaming
Altered reality
 gaming
Apps
Casual gaming

interface the more popular it will be. As such, the next generation of gaming devices are attempting to incorporate elements of **virtual reality** into the experience.

Gaming companies are becoming more aware of the needs of their target audience when producing games for widespread distribution. The target audience is the group of people the game is aimed at and their needs greatly impact on the type of graphics and the language used in the game and the speed of interaction required in the game.

As the size of the target audience increases so do their demands, and there are a number of different trends developing in the gaming industry today.

Trend	Explanation
Games consoles	Eighth-generation games consoles are slimmer and faster than their predecessors and include higher-quality graphics cards where gamers can look forward to 3D graphics in consoles such as the Nintendo 3DS. Hand-held consoles such as the PSP and Nintendo DS Lite remain popular but larger consoles still take a large share of the market for example, Xbox 360 and Playstation 3.
Online gaming	Game players play games online with other gamers across the world. Access to online gaming can be via PC, hand-held games consoles such as PSP or Nintendo Wii, among many others. High-speed internet access is required to facilitate the transmission of graphic and sound data to support the game play.
MMORPG (Massive Multiplayer Online **Role-Play Games**)	A feature of many online gaming websites, for example *World of Warcraft* which has over 11 million subscribers. Subscribers take on roles associated with fictional societies and act out scenarios often with people they have never physically met.
Social gaming	Has been made popular by social networking sites such as Facebook. Unlike MMPORG it is more likely that you will compete in the game against people you know.
Mobile gaming	The increased availability of free games has given developers cause for concern. The advent of the iPhone and its associated **Apps** has appeal also to the hobbyists that develop computer games in their spare time. The availability of WAP and Bluetooth connectivity also facilitates online game play.
Altered reality gaming	While virtual reality in its true form is not yet available to the mobile gamer, altered reality gaming such as that made available on the PSP console through games such as *Invizimals* marks a step in the right direction.
Peripheral-free game play	More and more research is being carried out into the use of hand gestures to control hardware devices. The incorporation of such an interface would open gaming up to an even wider audience, much in the way the Nintendo Wii has already done.
Casual gaming	Games stations such as Nintendo Wii opened gaming up to all generations and many developers are now also capitalising on this move with the continued development of casual games, such as *Bejeweled* for games consoles and PCs.
Training games	Games with high-quality and very often 3D graphics can be used in simulations to facilitate training in dangerous situations where human life may be put at risk or where it may be too expensive to provide access to actual equipment used in the real-life scenario.

GLOSSARY TERMS
Game genre
Rules
Storyboard

Developing computer games

Large teams of individuals are typically involved in the design, development and testing of computer games. Before games can even be considered for development it is important that the **game genre** and game play is clearly identified and presented to investors for approval. Game play can be explained through the identification of the **rules** of the game, an explanation of the various pathways through the game and a detailed outline of the script of the game (most obviously through the use of a **storyboard**), in addition to the way the user interacts with the game.

Following approval of the game for development a large team of professionals is assembled, including:

- musicians for the development of the soundtrack for the game
- artists to develop game graphics
- programmers to develop the actual application
- and perhaps hardware developers to develop any specialised peripherals required to operate the game.

Game genre

Computer games, regardless of the technology used to play them, can be classified into a number of different genres. A genre identifies a type of game that shares a number of characteristics and game plays (or sets of rules). Some game genres include:

GLOSSARY TERMS
Action games
Adventure games
Puzzle game

Game genre	Explanation
RPG (role-play games)	The game player plays the game through the eyes of a character in the game scenario and all of their interactions with the game are in this persona.
Action	The game player interacts with the game using high-speed input signals in time-crucial scenarios where fast reactions are needed. Slow reaction times can lead to the game player losing points or lives depending on the game play.
Adventure	The game player is often asked to solve puzzles often with no time limit imposed (unlike action games). The game player's responses to scenarios can dictate their passage through the game.
Puzzles	The game player must solve a series of puzzles or answer quiz-type questions that may get more difficult as the game progresses.

Games today do not often fall into one specific category, however, and they often combine different game-play techniques.

Most games will, however, incorporate the following elements in their creation:

Game elements	Description
Rules	Rules identify the actions the game player must follow when they are playing the game. The rules will help determine how the game is played and how well the player accumulates points to be recorded in the **scoring** mechanism.
Scoring mechanism	The game player's score is recorded in this mechanism according to the rules of the game. The score is often displayed throughout the game so the player can evaluate how well they are doing. Depending on the game play (rules), points may be linked to time allocation or the successful completion of tasks.
Controls	Controls represent the way the game player interacts with the game. On PCs the controls may be keys on the keyboard while on portable consoles they may be dedicated keys on the console. The method of control used is also linked to how quickly the player is expected to react to the game scenario or how realistic the scenario is expected to be; for example, in many driving games the game player will be provided with a steering wheel and gear stick input device to provide a real-life experience.
Feedback	Information relating to the impact of user input on the game scenario is necessary if the game is to be played successfully. Every movement of the cursor in an adventure game, or every response entered in a puzzle game, will lead to feedback being generated. Feedback could take the form of sounds, an onscreen message or the manipulation of the scoring mechanism so the game player can see the impact of their action. The type of feedback is dependent upon the game genre and the game play.
Interaction	Game players interact with the gaming interface in an attempt to complete successfully tasks set for them by the game. The method of interaction will depend on the input devices used with the game and will always result in the generation of some form of feedback.
Cheats	Cheats are a series of keyboard shortcuts or another combination of input elements that will allow a game player to skip an element of a game they are having difficulty with. Cheats are written into game code on purpose to ensure players can experience all elements of the game. They are often made available through specialised gaming magazines or discussion boards.

GLOSSARY TERMS
Scoring
Controls
Feedback
Cheats

Computer game peripheral devices

The way users interact with computer games has progressed beyond joysticks and cursor keys on a generic keyboard. In a bid to enhance the game play associated with their products, manufacturers often provide game players with realistic peripherals that help enhance the real-life experience of their game play.

Games such as *Guitar Hero* and *Rock Band* provide users with specialised input devices such as guitars and drum kits to facilitate interaction with the on-screen game. Examples of other peripherals used for game interaction are:

- concept keyboards
- haptic peripherals
- joysticks
- QWERTY keyboards
- trackerball
- touch screens
- touch sensitive mats (dance mats)
- voice activation
- steering wheels.

What makes a good computer game?

Game developers, when marketing a new computer game, need to consider if the game is meeting the needs of their target audience. Games that include graphics, language or game play that does not meet these needs will not be successful. Regardless of the complexity of the program, graphics and game play, a game will only be considered good, or successful, if it can meet the following criteria:

- it is appropriately priced
- it is available on the correct platform (or a variety of platforms)
- the language is appropriate for the target audience
- the game play is appropriate for the target audience
- appropriate peripherals are available to enhance the game-play experience
- technical support is readily available (through user documentation, discussion forums, gaming magazines, etc.)
- the game is distributed using appropriate media, for example GoD, online for download, CD-ROM or DVD-ROM.

The competitive nature of the games industry means that gaps in the market can always be filled by another games console or game developer. As the competition continues, the game player continues to reap the rewards in an environment where the general gaming experience continues to improve. New technologies are developing constantly to enhance the game-playing experiences of the wider market and it is not unreasonable to expect that in the near future we may be faced with the idea of 'intelligent' games that learn from the experiences of the gamer and adapt the game play to suit the needs of the individual.

Consider the following scenario

Philip organises guitar master classes and guitar recitals for the local school of music. He asks his friend Alex to design and create a computer game that will allow his students to assess their knowledge of guitar technology and music.

■ Developing a computer game proposal

Before Alex can create a computer game for Philip he needs to develop a proposal that will include the following:

- a description of the target audience
- details of the game genre
- details about the game play
- storyboards for the various elements of the game.

Before he can create the game proposal and then the game for Philip, Alex needs to understand exactly what he wants the game to contain. Philip tells him he wants the game to include:

- two pathways through the game
- a **scoring** mechanism
- electronic help for the user
- an original animation
- user feedback
- user interaction via mouse clicks or rollovers.

Alex produces the following game proposal for Philip.

Game Proposal for Philip Richardson School of Music

Target Audience:

The age range will vary from teenager to adult but all users will have a basic understanding of guitar technology and guitar music theory. These are the areas to be assessed in the game.

Game Genre:

The game will take on a quiz format.

Game Play:

The user will have two options when they start up the game:

- Take the Guitar Technology Quiz or
- Take the Guitar Theory Quiz

In the Guitar Technology Quiz the user will be asked to identify various items of technology associated with guitar playing. For each item correctly identified they will score 1 mark and they will score 0 for each that is incorrectly identified.

In the Guitar Theory Quiz the user will be asked to identify a series of words that relate to guitar playing and theory. For each letter correctly identified they will score 1 mark and they will score −1 for each letter that is incorrectly selected.

The scores in the two games will not be linked.

The user should be able to exit the game at any time but they do not need to be able to save their progress. The user should also have access to a Help Screen at all times during the game.

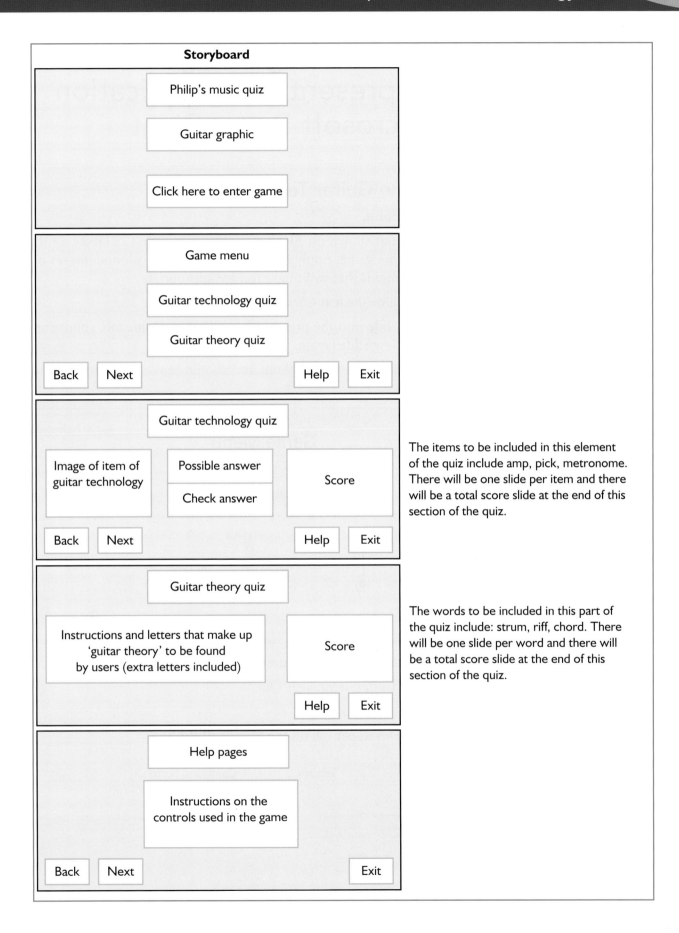

Storyboard

Philip's music quiz

Guitar graphic

Click here to enter game

Game menu

Guitar technology quiz

Guitar theory quiz

Back | Next | Help | Exit

Guitar technology quiz

| Image of item of guitar technology | Possible answer / Check answer | Score |

Back | Next | Help | Exit

The items to be included in this element of the quiz include amp, pick, metronome. There will be one slide per item and there will be a total score slide at the end of this section of the quiz.

Guitar theory quiz

Instructions and letters that make up 'guitar theory' to be found by users (extra letters included) | Score

Help | Exit

The words to be included in this part of the quiz include: strum, riff, chord. There will be one slide per word and there will be a total score slide at the end of this section of the quiz.

Help pages

Instructions on the controls used in the game

Back | Next | Exit

You should have revised the main features of Microsoft PowerPoint before beginning this task.

■ How to add gaming functions to a presentation application – Microsoft PowerPoint

Creating the Guitar Technology Quiz

1   Open **PowerPoint**.

2   Using the layout shown on Alex's storyboard on page 125 create a title page for Philip's game. Apply background images or colours, images or any other elements that you might feel are appropriate.

DO NOT include the text *Click here to enter game*.

3   Insert a new slide into the presentation. Click on **Home** tab, choose an appropriate **New Slide** layout.

This slide will be the Game Menu and should look similar to the one shown below.

This section is supported by the following digital media:

acoustic-guitar.jpg

amp.jpg

gibsonusapick.jpg

metronome.jpg

Game Menu

Guitar Technology Quiz

Guitar Theory Quiz

4   Insert a new slide for the first question of the Guitar Technology Quiz.

Add the title '*Guitar Technology Quiz*'.

Add the graphic *amp.jpg*.

5   Click on the **Developer** tab on the **Microsoft Ribbon**.

Remember an original animation is also needed in the game. You could add the animation you created in Chapter 5 to your slide.

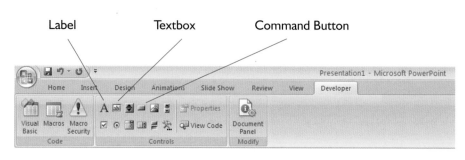

Label   Textbox   Command Button

6 Select the **Textbox** icon from the **Controls** panel.

7 Draw a **Textbox (ActiveX Control)** to the right of the graphic image.

8 Use a standard **Textbox** to add instructions to the user so your slide looks like the one shown below.

Standard **Textbox** from the **Insert** tab

Textbox Control from the **Developer** tab

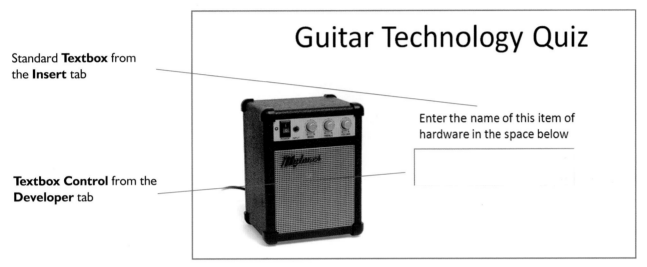

9 Use the **Label (ActiveX Control)** from the **Control** panel in the **Developer** tab to insert a field where the score can be stored.

10 Use a standard **Textbox** from the **Insert** tab to create a heading for the score label.

11 Use the **Command Button (ActiveX Control)** from the **Control** panel in the **Developer** tab to insert a command button the user can click to check their answer.

The game screen should now look like the one shown below.

Standard **Textbox** from the **Insert** tab

12 Right Click on **CommandButton1**, select **Properties** and change the caption to *Correct?*

If you click on **Correct?** at the moment nothing happens.

You need to use Visual Basic to tell PowerPoint what to do when the user clicks on the button.

Before we do this, set up the other three slides for this part of the game.

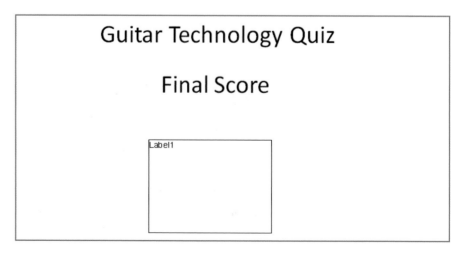

Edit **CommandButton2** and **CommandButton3** so that their captions also read *Correct?*.

Adding Visual Basic to PowerPoint to create gaming features

Each time the person playing the game answers a question, the score for that question will be held in the score label on that slide. The scores from all three questions are added up and a total score is given at the end.

1 Click on the first question slide.

2 Click on the **Developer** tab and select **View Code** from the **Control Panel**.

3 If the scores are to be passed from one slide into another they need to be declared as **Public** using Visual Basic. To do this type in the following code:

Public q1score As Integer
Public q2score As Integer
Public q3score As Integer
Public totalscore As Integer
Public wordscore1 As Integer (*used for the word search game*)

4 Each time someone starts the game it is important that the scores are initialised or reset to zero.

Add a command button to the title slide and change the caption to '*Click here to start the game*'.

In the **Developer** tab select **View Code** and type in the following code:

Private Sub CommandButton1_Click()
q1score = 0
Slide3.Label1 = q1score
q2score = 0
Slide4.Label1 = q2score
q3score = 0
Slide5.Label1 = q3score
totalscore = 0
Slide6.Label1 = totalscore
wordscore1 = 0
Slide7.Label1 = wordscore1 (*used for the word search game*)
ActivePresentation.SlideShowWindow.View.GotoSlide (2)
End Sub

5 The user needs to be able to check their answers and record their score now if they get the question correct. To do this we need to assign code to each of the command buttons.

Double click on the **Command Button** on the first question slide (this will also allow you to view the Visual Basic code).

> Remember Task 2 (a) requires you to add sound to your game!
>
> Carry out some research to find out how you can play a sound throughout your presentation.
>
> You could add a 'theme tune' to your game.

Type in the following code (this code checks that the user has entered 'amp' into TextBox1 and will update scores accordingly):

```
Private Sub CommandButton1_Click()
If TextBox1.value = "amp" THEN
   q1score = 1
   Slide3.Label1.Caption = q1score
   Slide6.Label1.Caption = q1score + q2score + q3score.
   MsgBox "Well done that is correct!"
Else
   MsgBox "Sorry that is incorrect!"
End If
End Sub
```

Add Visual Basic code to the Command Buttons on Slides 4 and 5 to allow the user to check their answers and update their scores.

The answer to slide 4 is 'pick'.

The answer to slide 5 is 'metronome'.

6   Slide 6 is used to add up the total score from the three questions.

The Label you created on this slide is automatically updated by the code you inserted into slides 3, 4 and 5.

Creating the Guitar Theory Quiz

In this quiz the user has to identify a word relating to guitar playing by clicking on the letters shown on the slide. For every letter correctly identified 1 mark is scored, for every incorrect letter, 1 mark is lost.

1   Insert a new slide into the game presentation.

2   The title of the slide is 'Guitar Theory Quiz'.

3   Set up the slide for the first word which is 'strum'.

Command Button (ActiveX Control) from the **Developer** tab. The caption of each button is edited to reflect the letter it represents

Textbox

Label (Active X Control) from the Developer tab

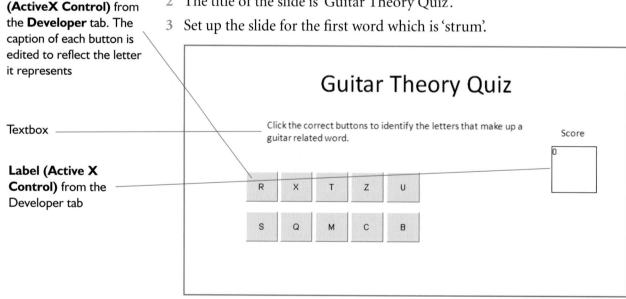

4 Use the **Developer** tab and the **View Code** option to add the following code to each **Command Button**.

Where a correct button is clicked the code is, for example:

Private Sub CommandButton1_Click()
wordscore1 = wordscore + 1
Label1.Caption = wordscore1
Slide7.Label1.Caption = wordscore1
End Sub

Where an incorrect button is clicked the code is, for example:

Private Sub CommandButton1_Click()
wordscore1 = wordscore1 − 1
Label1.Caption = wordscore1
Slide7.Label1.Caption = wordscore1
End Sub

Extension exercise

Continue to develop this game to include the two additional words in the storyboard.

Include a screen to record the total score for this element of the game.

Produce a short help system (no more than two slides) that describes the game to the user and explains the rules to them.

Apply what you already know about PowerPoint to add action buttons to allow navigation around the game. Your action buttons should allow the user to exit the game at any time. You should also have a link to your help file on every slide.

Saving your game

Ensure users can only navigate around your game using the controls you have put in place for them:

1 Click on the **Slide Show** tab in the **Microsoft Ribbon**.

2 Click on **Setup Slide Show**.

3 Ensure the **Browse at Kiosk** option is checked.

4 Click on the **Office Button** and select **Save As**.

5 Give your game an appropriate name.

6 Ensure you have selected **PowerPoint Macro-Enabled Presentation**.

7 Click **Save**.

Remember to create links to your planning and your evaluation on the start page of your computer game. Don't forget to complete your Game Evaluation Grid and include it in your evaluation document.

Creating a User Guide (Help Facility)

1 Ensure your User Guide (Help Facility) is available to the user at all times throughout the game.

2 Your User Guide (Help Facility) should at the very least include the following:

- the rules of the game
- how to control/play the game
- explanation of any feedback the user might get
- instructions on how to exit the game.

Testing your game

When you have completed your game you should ask another student to test it to ensure that at the very least:

- all pathways through the game can be accessed
- the scoring mechanism works correctly
- the feedback/instructions work correctly.

Evaluating the completed game

1 Complete the Game Evaluation Grid (this can be downloaded from www.ccea.org.uk) as part of your final evaluation of the game.

2 Your evaluation should include comments on:

a The suitability of the interface you designed for the target audience – for example, does the colour match their band or company logo? etc.

b How accurate the score counter was. It is OK to say at this stage that there were errors in your game. If errors have been identified in the score counter, perhaps suggest how they were or could be corrected.

c Was the help facility useful? This is where comments from someone else can help in the evaluation. Ask if they were able to understand how the game works based on the instructions in the help facility.

d The suitability of the graphics and language for the target audience – for example, if the game is aimed at small children, was the text large and easy to read? etc.

8

Using multimedia assets

What you will learn in this section

In this section you will learn about:

- using a web design package and designing a website.

Through the worked example you will gain skills which will assist in:

- designing a website
- using background colour or design
- including graphics
- creating links to pages and other websites
- including animation, sound and video.

This is assessed through the following components:

Unit 3 Terminal Examination
Unit 2 Controlled Assessment Task 1.

Acronyms:

- AVI
- FLA
- GIF
- HTML
- JPG
- MOV
- MP3
- MPEG
- PNG
- SWF
- WAV
- WIF
- WMA
- WMV
- WWW

Keywords:

- Breadcrumb trail
- Code view
- Design view
- Frameset
- Horizontal navigation
- Hotspot
- Hyperlinks
- Layers
- Optimised
- Preview mode
- Sitemap
- Tabs
- Thumbnail
- Vertical navigation

■ Some features of web design packages

Feature	Explanation
HTML pages	HTML is the language used for web pages. Web authoring tools will create HyperText Markup Language pages for you. Some people prefer to write the code themselves.

Hyperlinks	A hyperlink is a picture or text you can click on to take you to another web page either on the same site (an internal hyperlink) or on a different website altogether (an external hyperlink). Hyperlinks can also be used to open documents that are saved with the web page.
Design view	Design view allows the web designer to easily add text, graphics and other multimedia elements to the web page.
Code view	Code/HTML view allows the user to see the code used to create the web page and if they wish they can edit the code in this view.
Preview mode	Preview mode lets the user view the web page in a web browser so they can see how it will be viewed when it is opened on the internet.

Layout tools	**Framesets, layers** and tables can be used to control the way web pages and their content are presented to you.
	    A frameset is a group of pages that can be displayed at the same time. They appear as one page in the web browser even though each page is created and saved separately.
	    Layers are used to determine where text and other multimedia elements are placed on a web page. Layers can overlap and their location on a web page can be easily changed.
	    Tables can also be added to web pages and used to organise data in columns and rows.

Hotspots	A section on a large graphic that has been hyperlinked using a transparent graphic overlay.

GLOSSARY TERMS
Design view
Code view
Preview mode
Frameset
Layers

GLOSSARY TERM
Hotspot

■ Site management

Advice on creating and managing websites

- Folders for images and other multimedia elements help keep your website structured and easy to manage.
- Using straightforward and appropriate names for your web pages ensures you can easily locate an individual page for future editing.
- Calling your home page *index.html* will make it easy to locate.

Navigation

This allows the user to find their way around your website. The navigation section should always include links to the home page or index.

The increase in internet connectivity and developments in browser software have allowed web designers to take a more graphical approach to the production of website navigation. Previously, **hyperlinks** would have been text only to help ensure the fast download and presentation of the home page when the site was being accessed by a user.

Navigation can be presented to users either vertically, horizontally or via ordered lists.

GLOSSARY TERM
Hyperlinks

Horizontal navigation

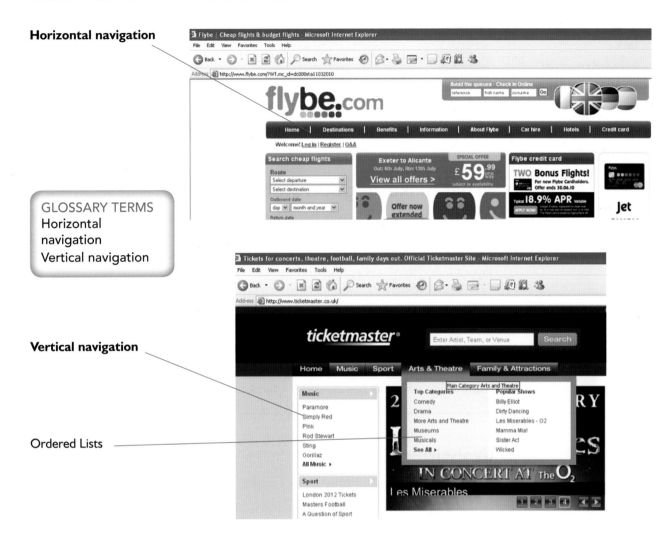

GLOSSARY TERMS
Horizontal
navigation
Vertical navigation

Vertical navigation

Ordered Lists

Alternative navigation styles include:

- **Tabs** – pages are categorised and listed under a general heading in the Tab menu.

GLOSSARY TERMS
Tabs
Sitemap
Breadcrumb trail

- **Sitemap**s – where another web page is used to list all of the other pages and external links in the website (like an index page).

- **Breadcrumb trail**s – here the user is provided with a list of pages visited and the sequence they have been visited in.

Multimedia components

Before any multimedia elements are included on a webpage for publishing it is important that they are **optimised**. This involves reducing the size of the multimedia file so that it loads quickly.

GLOSSARY TERMS
Optimised
Thumbnail

- Graphic elements – this can be done by creating a **thumbnail** of the image, cropping the image or by saving the image as JPG, GIF or PNG file types as opposed to BMP.

- Sound file formats – WAV, AIF, MP3 and WMA are appropriate file formats.

Task

Research each of these file formats and find out what each acronym stands for.

- Video file formats – AVI, MPEG, MOV, WMV and SWF file types all represent optimised video file formats.
- Animations – FLA or animated GIFs are appropriate animation formats.

Regardless of the file types you choose to use to display multimedia elements on your website, you need to make the appropriate plugins available for the web user.

What makes a good website?

A good website can be easily navigated and will load quickly. The inclusion of a large number of graphics, flash animation or video on the Home page will greatly slow down the loading time of a web site. Web users expect a consistent layout in terms of navigation and the look and feel of individual web pages.

Consider the following scenario

Philip organises guitar master classes and guitar recitals for the local school of music. He has decided to advertise his classes and recitals using a website which he has asked his friend Alex to plan and create.

Website planning

This section is supported by the following digital media:

student 1.jpg

philip 1.jpg

guitar logo.jpg

3D-Email.gif

Video Clip 1.wmv

Video Clip 1.swf

satriani.jpg

santana.jpg

sound bite 1.wav

abrsm_logo.gif

fender_logo.gif

avalon_logo.jpg

google-avalon.jpg

You should also use the logo you created in Chapter 5.

After discussion with Philip, Alex knows:

- his target audience is teenagers and adults who wish to take guitar lessons from beginner to master-class level
- he wants the site to look professional and be easy to use
- the website should include the following pages:
  - a home page which is the first page people will see and will include links to all other pages
  - a page about the classes that are available and fees payable
  - a page that details Philip's recital schedule and ticket prices
  - a page of comments from some of Philip's students
  - a page with links
    - to websites where students can enter examinations
    - to websites of guitar suppliers
  - a page with hints and tips for budding guitarists
- he wants to include a video clip on the website
- he wants to include a short sound file of him playing his guitar
- he wants people to be able to contact him from the website using his email address.

Alex creates the following planning document before starting to create Philip's website.

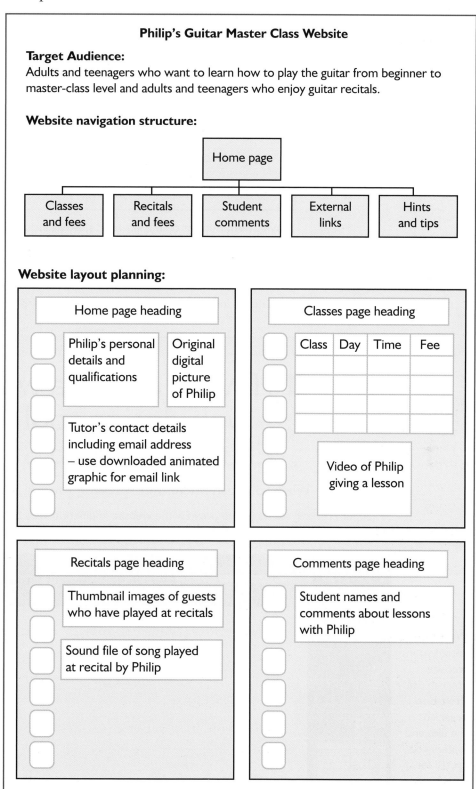

It is a good idea at this stage to identify your graphic sources so your teacher knows which graphics are original, downloaded or edited.

Remember including too many multimedia elements on one page/site can make it slow to load!

Philip's Guitar Master Class Website

Target Audience:
Adults and teenagers who want to learn how to play the guitar from beginner to master-class level and adults and teenagers who enjoy guitar recitals.

Website navigation structure:

Home page
- Classes and fees
- Recitals and fees
- Student comments
- External links
- Hints and tips

Website layout planning:

Home page heading
- Philip's personal details and qualifications
- Original digital picture of Philip
- Tutor's contact details including email address – use downloaded animated graphic for email link

Classes page heading

Class	Day	Time	Fee

Video of Philip giving a lesson

Recitals page heading
- Thumbnail images of guests who have played at recitals
- Sound file of song played at recital by Philip

Comments page heading
- Student names and comments about lessons with Philip

See page 106 for more details in video storyboarding and creation.

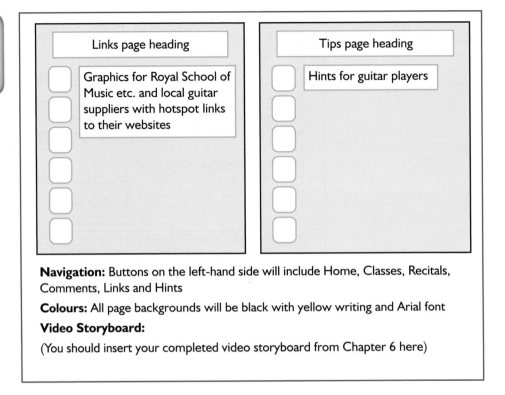

Links page heading	Tips page heading
Graphics for Royal School of Music etc. and local guitar suppliers with hotspot links to their websites	Hints for guitar players

Navigation: Buttons on the left-hand side will include Home, Classes, Recitals, Comments, Links and Hints

Colours: All page backgrounds will be black with yellow writing and Arial font

Video Storyboard:

(You should insert your completed video storyboard from Chapter 6 here)

■ How to create a website using a web design tool – Microsoft Expression Web 3

When you open Microsoft Expression you will see the following screen:

SP (Super Preview) allows you to preview the website in different web browsers. Why is this important when creating a website?

Use the Toolbox tab to add images etc. to your website

When you create your website you can use this tab to organise the files and folders you create for your site

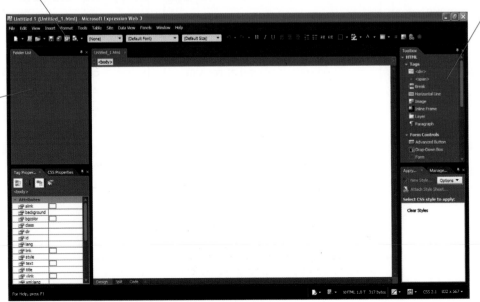

How to create a website

A website is a set of HTML (HyperText Markup Language) documents that can be viewed on the World Wide Web. The documents are normally linked together using hyperlinks. Hyperlinks are text or images that when clicked on will direct you to another web page or another website. HTML documents can contain a combination of text and other multimedia objects such as video, sound, animated images and digital photographs.

The layout of web pages can be controlled in a number of different ways. Some people use frames and some prefer to use tables. We will look at using tables to control the layout of our web pages.

To create a website in Microsoft Expression

1 Click on **Site** and select **New Site** or click on the **New Site** icon in the tool bar.

2 Select **Empty Site** in the **New** dialogue box that appears.

3 Use **Browse** to select an appropriate location for your website and name the site '*Philip's Website*'.

4 Click **OK**.

5 Select **Empty Site**.

6 Click **OK**.

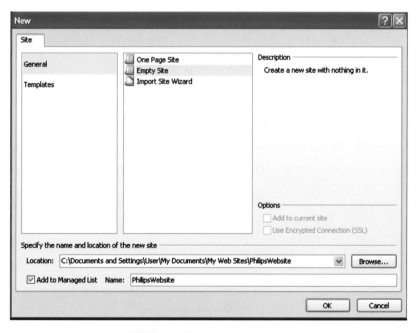

7 Your new website folder will appear in the **Folder List** tab.

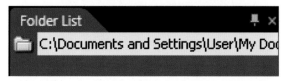

8   Click on **View**, **Site** and then **Files**. There are no pages in your website at the moment, so click **File**, **New**, **Page**, **General**, **Dynamic Web Template**, **OK**.

9   Set the page colour to black by clicking on **Format**, **Background**, **Formatting** tab.

10 Add a table to the web page with two columns and two rows.

Click on **Table**.
Select **Insert Table**.
Set the properties of the table as shown.

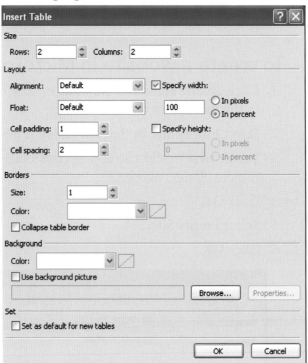

Hint

If you do not want to display your table borders on your website set the Borders size to 0.

11 Highlight the top two cells in the table.

Right click and select **Modify**. Select **Merge Cells**.
This row will hold the page title on all web pages.

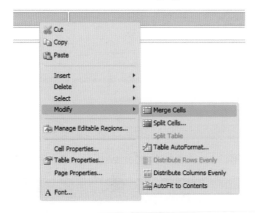

12 Resize the columns in the second row so they appear as shown

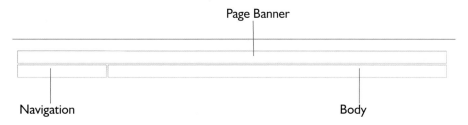

13 Right click on the first row of the table.

Select **Manage Editable Regions**.

Name this region **Banner**.

Repeat this process to create an editable region for the Body of the web page.

Adding navigation to the website

1 Click in the column to be used as the navigation panel.

2 Click on **Insert**.
Select **Interactive Button**.
Choose an appropriate button style from those available.

3 Set the text of the button to read *Home*.

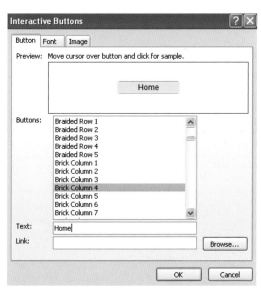

Repeat steps 1–3 to create buttons for the other pages:

Classes, Recitals, Comments, Links and *Hints.*

4 Right click on the cell containing the Navigation buttons and set the properties as shown.

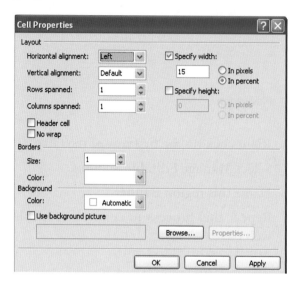

5 Use the text editing facilities to select an appropriate text font, size and style for the editable regions you created before saving the page.

Save the page.

Click **File**.

Click **Save As** and enter '*Philip's Template*' as the filename.

Creating the remaining pages from the Dynamic Web Template

Use the Dynamic Web Template to ensure that all pages have a consistent look. Any changes made to the .dwt page will be reflected in the pages linked to it.

1 Click **File** and **New**.

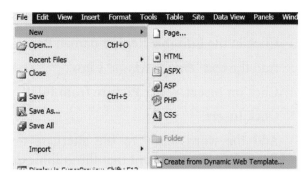

Select **Create from Dynamic Web Template**. Browse to the file called *Philip's Template*.

The first page you create will be the Home page for the website and must be loaded first by any browser being used to display it, so save this page as index.html.

2 Repeat steps 1–3 for the remaining pages:

Classes, *Recital*, *Comments*, *Links* and *Hints*.

Managing the site content

1 Click on the **Site View** tab to view the pages you have created.

2 Create folders to store any additional multimedia assets you are going to include in your website.

3 Click on **File**.

4 Click on **New** and select **Folder**.

Name the folder *Images*.

5 Create three additional folders called: *Videos, Sounds* and *Documents*.

6 Organise any sound, video or images folders downloaded into their appropriate folders before continuing.

Use the *Documents* folder to hold the final copies of the Games Proposal and Game Evaluation so they can be hyperlinked to the home page.

Placing content into the website

Before adding content to the web page, ensure you have any graphics or videos you wish to use saved in the appropriate folders.

> It is good practice to organise your assets as you add them to your website. That way they can be easily located at a later stage if you need to edit the site content.

1 Go to index.html and open the page.

2 Click in the **Editable Region** named **Banner**.

3 Add the text '*Philip's Master Class*'.

4 Click on **Insert**, select **Picture from File**.

5 Click **Insert**.

Add the word '*Logo*' to the alternate text field in the **Accessibility Properties** (in the event that the graphic does not load).

Click on **Browser** and browse to the images folder where you have saved the logo for Philip's Master Class (you created this in Chapter 5 or alternatively use *guitar logo.jpg*).

6 To edit the alignment of the object right click on the image and select **Picture Properties**.

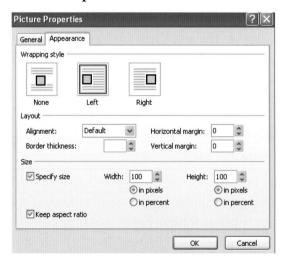

Click on the **Appearance** tab and edit the properties to ensure the graphic appears in the left-hand corner of the page banner.

Repeat this process to add the logo to the right-hand corner of the banner.

Animated graphics are inserted in the same manner – locate an animated gif on the internet and add it to the website Home page instead of the logo. Alternatively you could add the animation you created in Chapter 5.

Set the index page up so that it looks similar to the one shown:

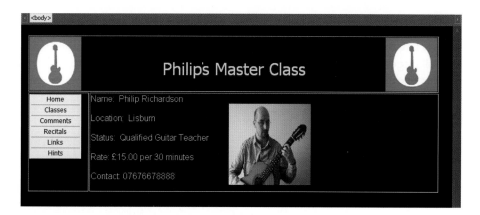

When you insert the picture you will find it is too large.

Right click and edit the **Picture Properties**.

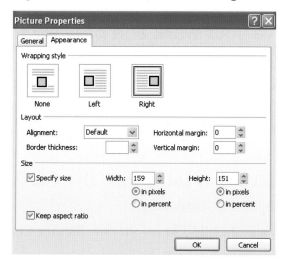

Note how this time the wrapping style has been changed.

Adding an email link to the Home page

1 Insert the graphic called *3D_email.gif* to the bottom of the Home page.

2 Centre the image.

3 Right click on the image *3D_email.gif* and select **Hyperlink**.

4 Select **E-mail Address**.

5 Enter your email address into the appropriate line so that you can be contacted via email using the website.

If you want the email link to appear on all pages, why not try editing the Dynamic Web Template to reflect this.

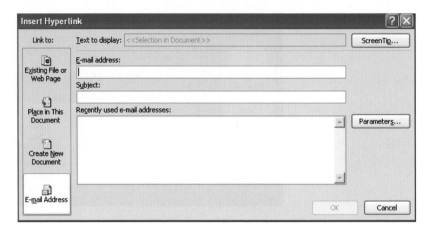

6   Click **OK**.

Save your work and preview the Home page

1   Click on **File** and select **Save All**.

2   Click on the **Preview in Microsoft Explorer** icon.

(Or press **F12**.) You will see that the graphic called *3D_email* is an animated gif.

Inserting a table into the Classes page

1   Open the Classes page.

2   Enter the title '*Classes*' into the **Banner** region

3   Place the cursor in the **Body** region.

4   From the **Insert** menu, select **Table**. The **Insert Table** dialogue box will appear.

5   Set the table properties as shown opposite:

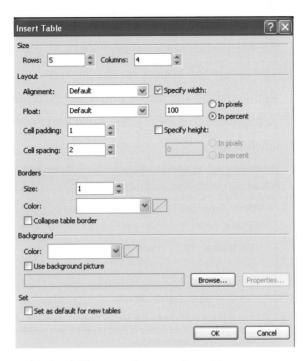

6   Add the following data to the table.

Class	Day	Time	Fee
Beginner	Monday	13:00–14:00	£30.00
Intermediate	Tuesday	13:00–14:00	£30.00
Expert	Wednesday	13:00–14:00	£35.00
Master Class	Thursday	13:00–14:00	£40.00

7   Centre the Time and Fee columns.

8   Use table properties to edit the background colour of the table to an appropriate colour.

Adding a video to the Classes page

1   Click below the table you have just entered.

2   Click **Insert**, select **Media**.

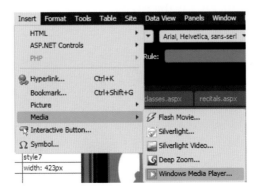

Note:

Some browsers do not support embedded WMV files.

Try converting your movie to SWF (Shock Wave Flash) and inserting it in this format instead.

3 Select **Windows Media Player**.

4 Browse to the movie called *Video Clip 1*.

5 The movie will appear on the page.

6 Right click on the movie and select **ActiveX Control Properties**.

7 Remove the check from the **Auto Start** option.

8 Click **OK**.

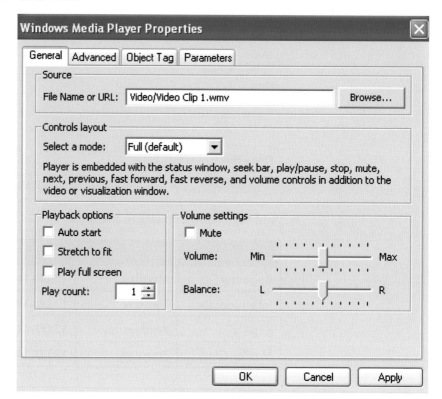

9 Press **F12** on your keyboard to preview your web page.

Adding thumbnail images to the Recitals page

1 Add the pictures called *Satriani.jpg* and *Santana.jpg* to the Recitals page.

2 Right click on each in turn and select **Auto Thumbnail**. (This is useful if you want to create a gallery of images and need to ensure the page still loads quickly for the user.)

Adding a sound that plays when the user enters the Recitals page

1   Right click on the page and select **Page Properties**.

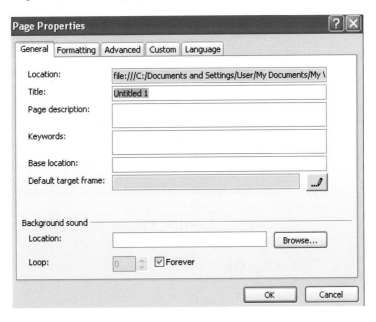

2   Browse to the file called *sound bite 1.wav* and uncheck the option to loop the sound forever.

3   Click **OK**.

When a sound is added to the page in this way, the user has no control over whether the sound plays or not. This could be very annoying if someone is visiting the site frequently.

Adding a sound file to the Recitals page using a hyperlink

By adding a sound file using a hyperlink the user can decide if they want to listen to it or not.

1   Add the following text underneath the thumbnail images:

    'To hear Philip playing guitar click here'.

2   Highlight the word *'here'*.

3 Right click on the word 'here' and select **Hyperlink**.

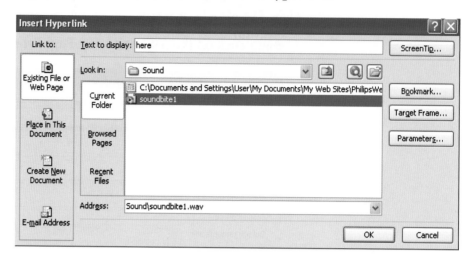

4 Click on **Existing File or Web Page** and browse to the file called *soundbite1.wav*.

5 Click **OK**.

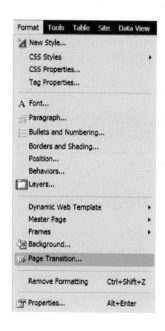

Inserting graphics and transitions to the Comments page

1 Add the graphic image called *student 1.jpg* to the Comments page.

2 Add the comment '*Philip ensures his lessons are at the correct pace for me. I have learned so much about music theory and practice in the six months he has been my tutor*'.

3 Click **Format**.

4 Select **Page Transition**.

5 Select an appropriate transition to add to the page on either **Page Enter** or **Page Exit**.

6 Click **OK**.

Adding external hyperlinks to the links page

1 Enter the following text to the links page.

'*To access any of the websites listed below please click on the appropriate Logo.*'

2 Add the words '*Royal Academy of Music*' to the links page.

3 Beside the text add the graphic called *ram_logo.jpg* (add alternate text for the graphic, for example '*Logo for Royal Academy of Music*').

4 Right click on the graphic.

5 Select **Hyperlink**.

7   Enter the address www.ram.ac.uk into the address field.

8   Click **OK**.

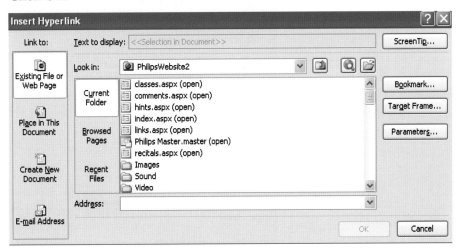

9   Repeat steps 1 to 8 to add the following hyperlinks.

Text	Graphic	Hyperlink from graphic
Associated Board of the Royal Schools of Music	abrsm_logo.jpg	www.abrsm.org
Fender	fender_logo.jpg	www.fender.com
Avalon Guitars	Avalon_logo.jpg	http://avalonguitars.com/

Add an appropriate alternate description as each graphic is inserted.

Adding a hotspot to the Links page

1   Underneath the Avalon Guitars link, add the text '*For directions to Avalon Guitars go to Google Maps*'.

2   Insert the graphic *google_avalon.jpg* (remember to add alternate text for the graphic).

3   From the **Drawing Toolbar** select the **Rectangular Hotspot** tool.

4 Drag a **Rectangular Hotspot** over the graphic and set up the **Insert Hyperlink** dialogue box as shown below.

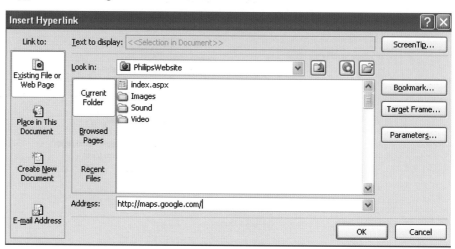

Adding text to the Hints page

1 Add the title '*Guitar Players Hints and Tips*'.

2 Add the following text to the body of the page.

i *Always ensure you are well rested before trying to learn a new piece of music.*

ii *Find a comfortable position for practising.*

iii *If you experience any pain when playing, take a break.*

iv *Being able to play lots of notes quickly does not make you good.*

v *Reduce feedback by rubbing a 'Bounce' sheet along your strings. Really!*

> Don't forget to complete your Web Evaluation Grid and include it in your evaluation document.

Creating document links on the Home page

1 Ensure the documents containing your Website Planning and your Evaluation are saved in the folder you created earlier called *Documents*.

2 At the bottom of the Home page type the words:

'*Click here to access the Website Planning document*'.

3 Highlight the word '*here*'.

4 Right click on the word '*here*'.

5 Select **Hyperlink**.

6 Select **Existing File or Web Page**.

7 Browse to the *Planning* document.

8 Click **OK**.

9 Repeat this process to link your evaluation document to the Home Page.

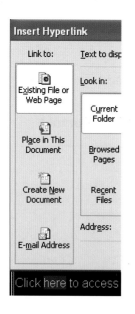

> Use hyperlinks to link your Game Proposal and Game Evaluation to your Home page. Remember to save one of these documents in PDF format and the other in an editable format.

Creating hyperlinks between each of the pages in the website

This can be done using the **Dynamic Web Template**. Any changes applied to the **Dynamic Web Template** will be applied to all pages linked to it.

1 Open the **Dynamic Web Template** called *Philip's Master*.

2 Double click on the button you created previously for the Home page.

3 Browse to the Home page.

4 Select the Home page and click **OK**.

5 Click **OK** to close the Interactive Buttons dialogue box.

6 Repeat steps 2–5 to add links to all of the navigation buttons on the **Dynamic Web Template**.

7 Select **File, Save All**. You will be asked 'Do you want to **Save Embedded Files**'. Click **OK**.

8 Select '**Yes**' in the next dialogue box.

Hyperlinks will now be created between all of the pages in the website.

■ Testing a website

It is best to take a logical approach when testing a website.

Plan your approach first and perhaps record the outcome of the tests in a table.

1 Click on the **Preview in Browser** icon.

2 Complete a testing table to ensure all elements of the website have been tested. For example:

Test item	Expected outcome	Result
Home button on all pages	Takes the user to the Home page from all pages	Yes
Comments button on all pages	Takes the user to the Comments page from all pages	Yes
Etc.		
Thumbnail image of Satriani	Opens larger image of guitarist	Yes
Etc.		

When your website is complete you should also ask another student to carry out the tests.

■ Evaluating your website

1 Ensure you complete your Web Evaluation Grid (available for download from www.ccea.org.uk).

2 Ensure you have completed a written evaluation that:

● makes reference to how long it takes for the website/pages to load

● includes a comment on how easy it is to navigate the website

● makes reference to any parts of the site that did not work and includes instructions to correct those errors

● includes how well you feel the website meets the needs of the target audience

● includes what you would improve upon.

5 Using graphics

1. Paul has a number of photographs on his mobile phone. He wants to transfer them to his PC. Identify two methods Paul could use to transfer the files from his mobile phone to his PC.

2. Select two file types from the list below that represent optimised graphics.
.mp3, .gif, .wma .bmp, .jpg, .wav

3. Many digital cameras come with USB cables so photographs can be copied directly onto a computer.
   a. Name **one** other way photographs can be transferred from a digital camera to a computer.
   b. List **one** disadvantage of using this method of transfer.

4. Amy has a number of photographs in hard-copy format. She wants to add them to a presentation. Identify **one** item of hardware she could use to input the photographs to her computer.

5. Tick **two** statements that are TRUE about bitmapped graphics.

Statement	Tick (✓)
Bitmapped images store information about the individual objects that make up a graphic image.	
Bitmapped images require a lot of memory when being stored because they contain animation.	
Bitmapped images require a lot of memory when being stored because they store details about each pixel comprising the image.	
Bitmapped images are high-quality graphic images that can be edited at pixel level.	

6. Identify **two** differences between bitmapped and vector graphics.

7. List **two** reasons why bitmapped images are not suitable for distribution via the internet.

8. When bitmapped images are optimised the quality of the image is reduced. Give **one** reason why this occurs.

9. a. Give **one** example of an application where bitmapped graphics might be appropriate.
   b. Give **one** reason to support your answer.

10. Simon wants to use MMS to send a photograph from his mobile to his friends. Identify **two** other methods that could be used in this situation.

11. Expand the following acronyms:
    a. GIF
    b. JPEG

12. Stewart want to remove an unwanted portion of a photograph he has input into a graphics package. What is the technical term for this process?

6 Using digital video and sound

1 Categorise the following file types in accordance to whether they are sound or moving image file types.

MPEG   MIDI   MP3   AVI   AIF   WMV

Video	Sound

2 a Pete is a music producer. A musician is emailing him a copy of a song they have recorded. Pete asks that the sound file be optimised. Why is this important?

b Give **one** disadvantage to Pete of receiving an optimised sound file in this instance.

3 Before a sound file can be stored on a computer it must be converted from analogue into digital format. Why is this necessary?

4 Expand the following acronyms:

a MIDI

b MPEG

5 Sean has created a two-hour-long movie as part of his A-level Moving Image project. He wants to send the movie to his friend in Canada. Identify a suitable means of distributing a movie of this size and give **one** reason to justify your answer.

7 Games technology

1 Alice has been asked by a primary school teacher to create a game that can help teach pupils the letters of the alphabet.

a Identify the target audience in this situation.

b List two ways Alice could help ensure her game is suitable for the target audience.

2 Casual gaming has become very popular. List **two** reasons why this is the case.

3 Game players no longer need a PC to play online games. Give **two** alternative ways of accessing online games.

4 List **one** difference between online gaming and social gaming.

5 List **one** difference between action games and adventure games.

6 Game developers need to take target audiences into consideration when developing game play and controls.

    a What is 'game play'.

    b How have changes in game controllers helped make games more accessible to a wider audience.

7 Feedback is very important to the user when playing any computer game. Identify **two** different types of feedback that can be provided to a user.

8 Games are widely used for entertainment.

    a Identify **one** other way computer games and simulations can be used.

    b List two advantages of using computer games in this way.

9 Identify **two** input devices commonly used with hand-held games consoles.

10 An online game developer wants to include a digital sound track throughout the game he is developing. Identify **two** problems associated with doing this.

8 Using multimedia assets

1 Brooklyn wants to add a graphic called castle.bmp to the home page of a website he is creating. Give **two** reasons why this would not be advisable.

2 Graphics should be optimised before being added to websites.

    a Explain what is meant by the word optimised.

    b Give **one** reason why this is necessary.

3 Rosa wants to include a photo gallery in the website she is creating. Her friend tells her to use thumbnail images in the gallery. Explain the term thumbnail image.

4 Caitlin has created a website with a sound file and a movie file on the home page. The sound file plays automatically in the background when the page is loaded. The movie file is played by clicking on a hyperlink which loads and plays it in a separate window.

    a Give **one** disadvantage of including the sound file in this way.

    b Explain what is meant by the term hyperlink.

Caitlin wants to include rollover buttons in the navigation bar of her website.

    c What is a rollover?

5 Aislinn wants to edit the HTML on the website she created. Expand the acronym HTML.

9

Knowledge of ICT components

What you will learn in this section

In this section you will learn about input devices, output devices, storage devices, memory and system software.

Acronyms:

- ATM
- CD-R
- CD-RW
- CD-ROM
- CPS
- CPU
- DAT
- DPI
- DVD-R
- DVD-RW
- EPOS
- Gb
- GUI
- JPG
- LCD
- Mb
- MP
- OCR
- PDA
- PPM
- PSU
- RAM
- ROM
- Tb
- USB
- VDU
- WIMP
- WORM

Keywords:

- Blu-ray
- Cache memory
- Character
- Concept keyboard
- External memory
- Function key
- Hot key
- Infrared
- Internal memory
- Joystick
- Magnetic disk
- Memory card
- Microphone
- Motherboard
- Mouse
- Multimedia
- Operating system
- Optical disk
- Pen drive
- Peripheral device
- Pixel
- Program
- Resolution
- Scanner
- Sensor
- Sound card
- Stylus
- Touch screen
- Tracker pad
- Transcription error
- User interface
- Video card
- Wireless link

■ Hardware

A typical PC has a number of hardware components. These can be put into the following categories:

- the processor (CPU)
- input devices
- output devices
- storage devices.

GLOSSARY TERM
Peripheral device

Peripheral devices are the devices that are connected to the computer externally, including input, output and external storage devices.

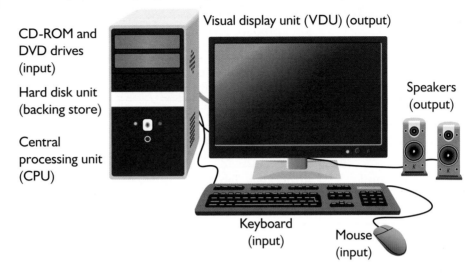

CD-ROM and DVD drives (input)

Hard disk unit (backing store)

Central processing unit (CPU)

Visual display unit (VDU) (output)

Speakers (output)

Keyboard (input)

Mouse (input)

The diagram below shows how the components are related:

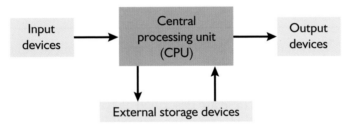

Input devices → Central processing unit (CPU) → Output devices

External storage devices

■ Input devices

Keyboards

A keyboard is a standard input device supplied when you purchase a computer. Manufacturers use a standard layout of keys (referred to as QWERTY) on their keyboards.

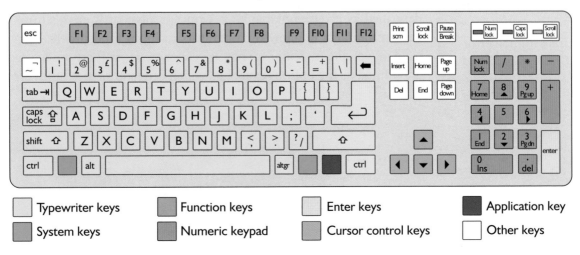

Typewriter keys   Function keys   Enter keys   Application key

System keys   Numeric keypad   Cursor control keys   Other keys

The table below summarises the types of keys on a standard keyboard:

Keys	Description
Alphabet	Keys produce lower case (small letters) or upper case (capital letters). 'Shift Lock' or 'Caps Lock' allows the user to type in upper case only.
Digits 0–9	Usually appear twice: once along the top of the keyboard and on a separate keypad to the right-hand side of the keyboard.
Alphanumeric	These can refer to letters and/or digits and combinations of these.
Other characters	Punctuation marks (, : ; ' ") Mathematical symbols (% $ £)
Cursor and control characters	Arrow keys, Tab, Page up/down Editing keys: Insert, Delete Control keys: Enter (or Return), Escape
Function keys	Labelled F1, F2, F3, etc… The function of these keys is normally set by the program currently being used.
Keys which change the function of other keys	Keys marked Shift, Caps Lock, Number Lock, Alt, Ctrl.

When using a keyboard the speed of input depends on the human operator. Compared to other input devices keyboards are considered to be slow. Owing to the amount of human involvement there is a tendency for errors to occur. These are described as **transcription error**s.

Some keyboards are specially designed for certain applications. The layout of keys is dedicated to the needs of the application such as automated teller machines (ATM), electronic point of sale terminals (EPOS) and 'chip and pin' terminals. These keyboards may have fewer keys with emphasis on numeric keys.

At home we use a lot of keyboard-type devices such as remote controls for televisions and burglar alarms.

In schools some teachers use **concept keyboard**s where the keys are described as pictures or words. Teachers can use overlays on concept keyboards to change the words and pictures. The keys are therefore sometimes described as programmable keys. Concept keyboards are also used in fast-food restaurants to allow the operators to input food orders. They are also used on vending machines. They are easier to use as there are fewer keys, but are limited by the options available, which can help reduce input errors.

GLOSSARY TERMS
Function key
Transcription error
Concept keyboard

Mouse

A **mouse** is also referred to as a 'pointing device'. It is designed to fit under the human hand and, when moved, controls the pointer on a VDU.

A mouse also includes two or three buttons which are used to make selections on the screen. The left-hand button is used to perform actions such as selecting options from menus, selecting icons and positioning the cursor on the screen. While the right-hand button is used to display a pop-up menu at the position of the cursor. The middle rotating button is used to scroll up and down the VDU.

This device is considered easy to use and inexpensive to purchase compared to other input devices. One drawback is that experienced users find it slow compared to using '**hot key**s'. For example, they prefer to press Ctrl and P to print rather than selecting menus and options.

Some mice use a built-in mouse ball, and built-in **sensor**s pick up the movements and send corresponding signals back to the computer. Other mice use technology such as **infrared** or **wireless link**s, which eliminates the need for the user to connect it to the computer by cable. A tracker ball is an alternative to a mouse. The user in this case will rotate the ball with their hand.

> **GLOSSARY TERMS**
> Mouse
> Hot key
> Sensor
> Infrared
> Wireless link
> Joystick
> Tracker pad

Joystick

A **joystick** is an input device that allows the user to control the movement of the cursor on the screen by manoeuvring a small lever in different directions. The lever can be moved in any direction including side-to-side, up-and-down and diagonally.

Similar to a mouse, it uses built-in sensors to convert the movements into co-ordinates on the screen. Joysticks usually have buttons to allow actions to be carried out. These buttons can be programmed to carry out certain actions. The main use of a joystick is in the playing of computer games (in this context it may be referred to as a games paddle). They are also used to move computer-controlled devices such as robots and hospital scanners.

Tracker pad

This input device is also known as a touch sensitive pad. It is used as an alternative to a mouse on a laptop computer due to space restrictions. The pad can sense pressure from your fingertip. Moving your finger on the pad allows you to control the cursor, which in turn will allow you to select options from menus, select icons and position the cursor. Double tapping on the touch pad is the same as double clicking the mouse buttons. The touch pad is very sensitive and therefore can be more difficult to use initially than a mouse. There are also buttons alongside or below the touch pad that operate in a similar fashion to those on a mouse.

Touch screen

GLOSSARY TERM
Touch screen

Touch screens work like a mouse. Touching the screen is the same as clicking your mouse at the same position on the screen. You can tap the screen twice to perform a double-click operation or you can also drag your finger across the screen to perform drag-and-drop operations.

The appearance of a touch screen is similar to ordinary computer screens but consists of a clear glass panel with a touch-sensitive surface. There are several different touch-sensing technologies in use today. Touch screens generally have an electrical current going through them and touching the screen causes a voltage change. This voltage change is used to determine the location of the touch on the screen. Built-in software is used by the computer to process the user request by manipulating the position on the screen that was touched. Touch screens are commonly used in banks, tourist offices, museums and information kiosks. Users do not require much ICT competence compared to using a mouse or a keyboard, which makes them attractive for applications in public places.

Microphone

This device is designed to input sound or human voice into a computer system (referred to as a voice recognition system). Voice recognition systems can convert sound to text or accept spoken commands. **Microphone**s are also used to record music and store it in digital format in the computer. The recognition rate can be low and inaccurate particularly if there is background noise.

GLOSSARY TERM
Microphone

Voice recognition can be successful when a user trains the computer to recognise their voice by storing words and phrases they use, which can then be recognised by the computer.

A microphone is used as an input device for voice mail which works like email except a voice message is left rather than a text message. It is also used in applications that only require a limited number of words/phrases such as telephone banking.

Scanner

A **scanner** can be used to input pictures and text from hard-copy format into a computer. There are two common types of scanners available. The most commonly used one is the flat-bed scanner where the user places the hard-copy document onto a glass plate. The other type, which is hand-held, is more portable and cheaper, but the image scanned is not as high quality as that scanned by a flat-bed scanner due to movement of the scanner over the object.

Flat-bed scanners are normally A4 in size but you can purchase bigger scanners that can scan images such as A3 size. Scanners work by passing beams of intense light over the image. The quality of the image scanned is measured in dots per inch (dpi). Cheaper scanners can scan 2400 × 4800 dpi but are limited to A4 paper size.

The greater the dpi, the greater the **resolution** or quality of the image scanned. The drawback of high-quality resolution scanning is that a greater amount of memory is required to store the image.

Once the image has been scanned it can be saved in a graphical format such as JPG. If text has been scanned it can be transferred and recognised as text in a word-processing package, using optical **character** recognition (OCR) software. The user can then format the text, edit the text and even email the text.

GLOSSARY TERMS
Scanner
Resolution
Character

Digital camera

The resolution of a digital camera is measured in mega**pixel**s, such as 10 MP. A digital camera can store many more pictures than a film camera. The picture taken by a digital camera is stored on a **memory card** as opposed to film. A typical memory card can hold 4 GB which allows around 1000 pictures to be stored in medium resolution or quality. Most digital cameras have a small liquid crystal display (LCD) screen which can display the picture(s) taken immediately. This allows the user the options of re-taking the picture, storing the picture or deleting the image taken.

Using a graphics software package, which normally comes with the camera, will allow pictures to be downloaded from the camera to the computer for editing, saving and printing. The user can purchase special photographic paper for producing high-quality hard copies of photographs.

Modern digital cameras can also capture short video clips that last a couple of minutes. Digital cameras are normally connected to the computer using a USB cable.

> **GLOSSARY TERMS**
> Pixel
> Memory card

Graphics digitiser

A graphics digitiser, also known as a digitising tablet, allows a user to hand draw images or pictures similar to the way we draw with a pencil on a sheet of paper. In some ICT applications they are also used to capture handwritten signatures. The device consists of a flat surface upon which the user draws using an attached **stylus**. The stylus works like a pencil. It allows the user to input data in a 'freehand' mode. The image does not usually appear on the tablet itself but is displayed on the VDU. The graphics digitiser can be used as an alternative to a mouse or other pointing devices.

> **GLOSSARY TERM**
> Stylus

■ Output devices

Output devices are used to provide results in a suitable format after data has been processed by a computer. Output formats are classified as one of two states: soft copy or hard copy. Soft-copy output is described as a temporary copy of information, such as information displayed on a screen, while hard-copy output is a permanent copy of information such as a printout.

Visual display unit (VDU)

Sometimes we refer to these devices loosely as 'screens', 'monitors' or 'display units' and formally as a visual display unit (VDU). Depending on the application, VDUs come in different shapes and sizes. For example, on portable devices the VDU is referred to as a liquid crystal display (LCD) screen. This type of screen is used on laptop computers and palm notebooks because it does not take up much space and is not heavy, which makes the computer portable. Apart from these advantages there are drawbacks. One drawback of LCD screens is that they are more expensive to purchase.

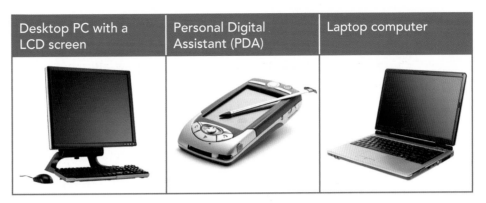

Desktop PC with a LCD screen	Personal Digital Assistant (PDA)	Laptop computer

VDUs differ from each other in size and resolution. The size of a VDU is measured in inches diagonally across the screen, while the quality of the image displayed is referred to as the resolution. Some applications use a monochrome VDU, while in other applications coloured VDUs are used. Monochrome screens can only display one background and one foreground colour such as black and white. Colour monitors can display from 16 to a million different colours. When we purchase a new screen, they are often referred to as **multimedia** VDUs because they are supplied with built-in speakers and even a built-in microphone.

The quality and detail of a picture on a VDU depends on the resolution.

GLOSSARY TERM
Multimedia

In Windows the advanced user can control the appearance of their VDU by going to 'Display Properties'.

A pixel is square in shape and represents the smallest area on the screen the computer can change or that can be edited by the user. Resolution is measured in pixels. High-resolution VDUs have a greater number of pixels than low-resolution VDUs. Modern VDUs have a built-in filtering system to help with the problem of eyestrain. The higher the resolution, the bigger the VDU size, and the more money it will cost!

Printers

There are a range of printers available. ICT users will purchase a printer depending on their needs. Typically a printer for a home computer costs less than £100. Apart from cost, a user will consider other factors when purchasing a printer such as:

● quality of print (dots per inch)

● speed of the printer (characters per second/pages per minute)

● colour or black and white printing capability

● ability to print text and graphics

● size of paper that can be used, such as A4 and A3

● type of paper that can be used, such as photographic paper

● volume of printing required

● cost of the consumables, such as the replacement ink kits.

Impact printer

Dot matrix printers are known as impact printers due to the striking action when in operation. The print head is made up of a series of pins laid out in rows and columns. Typically a dot matrix printer has 24 pins whereby each character is formed as a pattern of dots. The dots are created by pins striking a ribbon and leaving an image of a character on the page.

Dot matrix printers are not as popular since the development of ink-jet printers but are still used when organisations need to produce carbonised printouts (multi-part stationery) such as invoices and payslips. The advantage of this is the cheap cost of printing multiple copies of data. Compared to other printers they are cheaper to operate but the quality of output is low. The more pins in the print head, the better the quality of the printout.

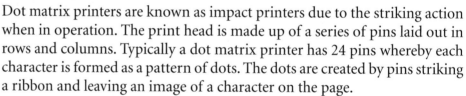

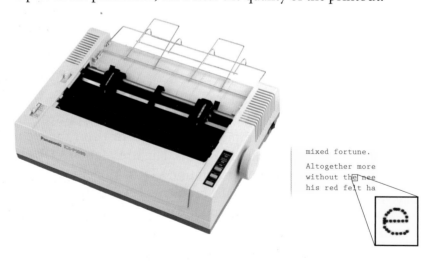

```
mixed fortune.
Altogether more
without the nee
his red felt ha
```

Laser printers

These printers are used on school networks and in offices. They resemble photocopiers in appearance and they produce high-quality output of both text and graphics. A reasonable laser printer will print around 20 pages per minute in a quiet fashion. For this to happen, laser printers contain their own memory where pages can be temporarily stored before printing. Although laser printers are more expensive to purchase than ink-jet printers, they are suitable for large volumes of data. The ink is powder based and is supplied in the form of a toner kit. Some laser printers can also print in colour but these are more expensive.

Ink-jet printers

These types of printers are mainly used in conjunction with a home PC. They give the user good quality text and graphic output for less than £100. They also allow the user to print in colour onto different types of media such as photographic paper, envelopes, labels, card and acetate. The cost of replacing the ink can be expensive as the user normally has to buy both black and colour cartridges.

An ink-jet printer consists of a print head which contains many nozzles (typically 64). Jets of ink are sprayed from each nozzle onto the paper. A bubble-jet printer is an ink-jet printer that operates by heating the ink before spraying it. Sometimes, if the printer is not used for a period of time, the nozzles on the print head get blocked, which means the user has to use a head-cleaning utility **program** to clear the nozzles.

> **GLOSSARY TERM**
> Program

Plotter

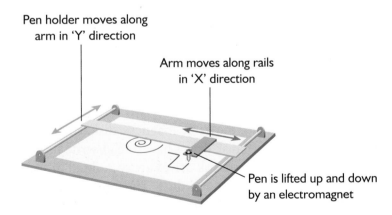

Pen holder moves along arm in 'Y' direction

Arm moves along rails in 'X' direction

Pen is lifted up and down by an electromagnet

The use of plotters enables very accurate, high-quality diagrams to be produced. Some plotters use special pens to produce drawings using a variety of colours. The pens are inserted into pen holders and move across the paper using the principle of (x, y) co-ordinates. Some plotters are described as 'penless' plotters (raster plotters) and work similar to laser printers. These plotters are used when high-density drawings are required such as maps and circuit diagrams. They can print in colour or black and white.

Speaker

Computers are fitted with a small internal speaker as a standard output device. They allow use of sound output when designing multimedia solutions. The speaker is also used when the computer is communicating with the user, such as producing beeping sounds to alert the user if an error occurs. To improve the quality of sound, external speakers can be plugged into the speaker interfaces. To allow sound to be outputted through external speakers, a **sound card** needs to be fitted inside the computer. Speakers can output music as well as the spoken word. Users who are visually impaired find speakers useful so that text or figures can be spoken by the computer.

> **GLOSSARY TERM**
> Sound card

■ Data storage devices

Data storage can be divided into two categories:

- **internal memory** (RAM and ROM)
- **external memory** (magnetic and **optical disk**s).

> **GLOSSARY TERMS**
> Internal memory
> External memory
> Optical disk
> Magnetic disk

External data storage devices allow programs and data to be stored permanently. Programs and data held on external storage devices must be transferred to RAM to allow the user to have access.

External storage devices are grouped into four categories:

- **magnetic disk**s
- optical disks
- magnetic tape
- USB flash drive.

Hard disk

> **GLOSSARY TERM**
> Operating system

The hard drive is the main storage device in most computer systems. A typical hard disk drive consists of a number of rigid disks stacked on top of each other. Each disk has two surfaces. The surfaces of the disks are magnetised, hence the name magnetic disk. Each surface is laid out in tracks and sectors. Hard disk drives have a read/write head for each surface.

Hard disk drives are contained in sealed units to protect against damage from dirt and dust. The read/write access speeds are much greater than a CD drive. The hard disk differs from the other external storage devices in three ways: size in gigabytes (GB) or terabytes (TB) (usually bigger), access and retrieval speeds (usually faster), and permanence (unlike other storage devices it is not removable whereas a CD is). Hard disks are mainly used to store the **operating system** such as Windows, applications software such as Microsoft Office and users' data/files.

Optical disks

This type of storage media includes:

- CD-ROM
- CD-R
- CD-RW
- DVD
- Blu-ray.

Read-only CDs

These are formally called CD-ROM (compact disk read-only memory). In appearance they look like ordinary music CDs. They are purchased with the information already on them and are read only. This means no new information can be saved and no existing information can be erased.

Data is burned on to the surface by a laser beam which makes small indentations known as pits. This means the data on the disk cannot be deleted or edited in any way. Since the data is packed closely together CD-ROMS have a huge capacity. A typical CD-ROM holds around 650 MB. This makes them suitable for multimedia applications. They are used for:

- storing archive material
- encyclopedias
- distribution of software by software companies.

Writeable CDs

These are classified into two types:

- CD-R (CD-Recordable)
- CD-RW (CD-Rewriteable).

The CD-R is a blank CD that can be written to only once but can be read many times. Therefore it is often referred to as a WORM (Write Once, Read Many) disk. Whereas CD-RWs can be written to, erased and rewritten many times just like a magnetic hard disk. They are more expensive than CD-R disks and can only be used in a suitable drive which is called a CD-RW drive. Both these media can store around 700 MB of data.

DVD (digital versatile disk)

Similar in appearance to CDs, DVDs are mainly used at home as a replacement for video tapes. They are sometimes referred to as DVD-ROMs as they were designed to be read only. In more recent times DVD-R has been manufactured which allows for recording onto a blank DVD. The DVD-R works on the principle of write once read many (WORM). DVD capacity is greater than a CD-R or CD-RW at around 5 GB.

DVDs also require a DVD drive to read and write (these drives can also read CD media). They are mainly used to store full-length feature films.

Blu-ray disk

This is an optical disk, named Blu-ray due to 'blue' for the colour of the laser that is used, and 'ray' for the optical ray used to read and write. **Blu-ray** disks have a much larger storage capacity than a DVD. There are more advanced features with Blu-ray including recording high-definition television without loss of quality. You can also record one program while watching another on this medium. Disks store digitally encoded video and audio information in pits (spiral grooves) that run from the centre of the disk to its edges. Blu-ray disks hold up to 50 GB of information (about ten times the amount of information that can be stored on a DVD).

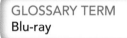

GLOSSARY TERM
Blu-ray

Magnetic tape streamers

These are also referred to as digital audio tapes (DAT). They are similar to magnetic and optical disks in that they store data permanently. Data is stored in blocks and between each block there is a gap on the tape known as the interblock gap.

Magnetic tape works on the principle of serial access, which means all data before the required item must be accessed, before the required item is read.

Magnetic tape can store huge amounts of data cheaply and is suitable as a backup to a hard disk. On a school network you will find a magnetic tape streamer attached to the file server. At the end of each school day it is used to backup the hardware as a security measure, in case the hard drive fails.

The magnetic tape streamers use magnetic tape cartridges which can have the same storage capacity as a hard drive. At the end of each day a backup program is run which will backup all work onto the tape streamer. The magnetic tapes are stored off-line and are used if the main hard drive fails.

GLOSSARY TERM
Pen drive

USB flash drive

These are sometimes referred to as 'memory sticks' or '**pen drive**s'. The pen drives are so named because of their size and shape. A pen drive is also referred to as a USB flash drive and is plugged into a USB port on a laptop or desktop computer. The USB (universal serial bus) pen drives are 'plug and play' devices, as they do not require special software to be installed to allow them to work. Pen drives are very compact in size as compared to CDs and DVDs. The capacity of a pen drive can range from as low as 32 MB to as high as 128 GB. The pen drives can be read as well as written to. Pen drives consist of a USB connector and a printed circuit board. The main advantage of a pen drive is its size and portability. Other advantages include the high speed of data transfer to or from the pen drive and the low power consumption. Most standard operating systems can support and detect pen drives.

■ Overview of the internal components of a computer

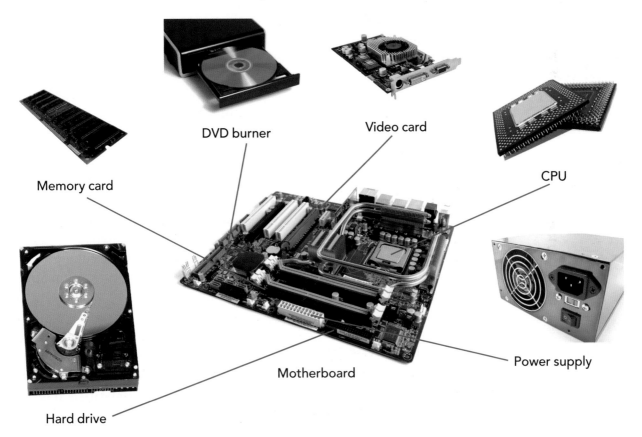

Memory card

DVD burner

Video card

CPU

Hard drive

Motherboard

Power supply

There are a number of hardware components inside a computer.

Power supply unit (PSU) – this provides the correct voltage and current for all the various internal components.

Motherboard – this is the main electronic circuit board. All components connect to the motherboard.

GLOSSARY TERMS
Motherboard
Video card

Video card – this is also known as a graphics card and is needed to connect the VDU to the motherboard.

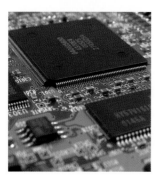

The CPU is sometimes referred to as the 'brain' of the computer. Although, unlike the human brain, it cannot think for itself. It requires humans to supply programs and data before it can process. One of the main components of the CPU is the memory.

The main memory is divided into categories:

- RAM (random-access memory)
- ROM (read-only memory)
- **Cache memory**.

> **GLOSSARY TERM**
> Cache memory

RAM (random-access memory)

This type of memory can be read from or written to. It is volatile, which means the contents of the memory are lost when the machine is switched off. The contents can be changed as the need arises such as the user using a different type of application program. It is used to hold programs and data that the user is currently working on such as Windows, Microsoft Word and an ICT assignment. All programs and data including those currently in RAM are held in permanent memory such as on a hard disk. Typical RAM size is 512 MB. The size of RAM can influence the speed of the processor, so the larger the RAM capacity, the faster the processor.

ROM (read-only memory)

This type of memory can be read from but not written to. Programs stored on ROM are permanent, which means the contents cannot be altered. Therefore if we describe RAM as volatile then ROM is non-volatile. They are used to store programs that are frequently required by the computer such as the 'booting up' program for Windows. This program runs automatically when the computer is turned on to load the operating system (such as Windows 7).

Cache memory

Cache (pronounced 'cash') memory is a type of memory used by the CPU and is similar to RAM in that instructions can be read or written. It is small in capacity compared to RAM but offers faster access speeds. Its purpose is to store frequently accessed program instructions, so when these instructions are required again, the processor will first search cache memory and thus the speed of processing is much faster compared to searching RAM.

Operating system

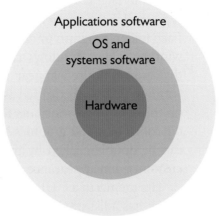

System software refers to the programs that help the computer run smoothly. This software allows applications software to be installed and used with computer hardware. A special type of systems software is called the 'operating system'. The main features of a typical operating system include:

Feature	Description
Interface	Communicates between the user and the computer. It will allow the user to perform activities on the computer system and also allow the computer system to communicate with the user such as through error messages.
Memory management	Allocates internal memory (RAM) to programs and data that the user is currently using. It will also manage the retrieving and storing of data on the external memory devices.
Resources	Controls all peripheral devices (input/output devices) and handles requests from the user such as a request to print their work.
Execution	This involves 'booting up' the computer when it is switched on, after which the user can carry out their requirements.
Errors	Deals with errors that occur when programs are running and communicates the responses to software developers and also to the user in user-friendly language.
System security	This involves checking and controlling user access to programs and data to prevent unauthorised access.

GLOSSARY TERM
User interface

Graphical user interface (GUI)

This interface is referred to as a 'Gooey' interface. The main features of a typical GUI are referred to as WIMP (Windows, Icons, Menus and Pointer). Each folder, program or document opened by a user is displayed in a separate window. These windows can be minimised or maximised. The windows that are minimised appear along the taskbar of the desktop, whereas the window that is maximised is described as the 'active' window. Icons reside on the desktop as shortcuts to folders, programs or documents and they are described as small graphics that represent the target program or file. They can be double-clicked by the mouse to select and open. Icons can also be customised in appearance and arranged by size or date modified.

The menus in a GUI are described as 'pull down' or 'pop up' menus. Each menu has a list of options available for the user to select from. Menus can be customised to show a full list of options (full menu) or a smaller list of options (short menu). The user will normally use a mouse to select a menu and then an option. Some options will lead to further menus. Experienced users prefer to use 'hot' keys as an alternative to menus, whereby they select a combination of two or more keys such as Ctrl+P to print a document. The user will also use a mouse to control a pointer on the screen. The user will move the pointer over an icon and then use the buttons on the mouse to select and open. The pointer can also be used to control the position of the cursor on the screen. Apart from these main features other features of a typical GUI include dialogue boxes, toolbars, buttons and tool tips.

Data and information

What you will learn in this section

In this section you will learn about data and information. You will also learn how to collect data using well-designed data collection forms and how to ensure that the data collected is valid and accurate. You will examine the advantages and disadvantages associated with data capture techniques. You will look at different file formats and how they can be used.

Acronyms:

- ASCII
- CSV
- GIF
- HTML

- JPEG
- MIDI
- MP3
- MP4

- MPEG
- OCR
- OMR
- PDF

- PICT
- RTF
- TIFF

Keywords:

- Check digit
- Data
- Data compression
- File

- Form design
- Information
- Length check
- Lookup table
- Pixel

- Portability
- Presence check
- Range check
- Type check
- Validation

- Vector graphics
- Verification

■ Information and data – what is the difference?

GLOSSARY TERMS
Data
Information

An information system, consisting of hardware and software working together, takes **data** as input and converts it into **information**.

An information system processes the data to produce information.

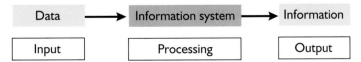

Data	Information system	Information
Input	Processing	Output

Information and data

Data is raw facts and figures which have not been given a meaning. For example, the following list could be described as a set of data:

85, 60, 65, 90, 70, 50, 40, 77, 60.

The data could be given a context or meaning. This can be done by describing the data.

For example, the following is a list of student marks, as percentages, for this year's French examination:

85% 60% 65% 90% 70% 50% 40% 77% 60%.

> GLOSSARY TERM
> Processing

The data has now become information since it has been given a meaning. Information can also be produced by **processing** the data. Processing the data means to take the values and manipulate them to produce more information.

What information could be produced by *processing* this data?

The *average class mark* for French could be calculated.

Question

1 What is the average mark for this class?

2 How can this information be useful to the teacher or her pupils?

3 What other information could be produced from the data provided on the sheet?

If the average mark for this class is calculated, the data has been processed to give the teacher useful information. ICT systems produce information which has been formatted so that an end user can make good use of it. This information could be paper based, for example a report, or digital in the case of output which is sent to a computer screen. Before producing information it is necessary to record the data. This is known as data capture.

Teacher Mark Sheet	
Subject: French	Class : 9B
Teacher: Mrs Black	
Name	**Mark (%)**
John Jones	85
Mary Smith	60
Anne Cleese	65
Hannah Greer	90
Giles Clarke	70
Alan Gray	50
Mark Black	40
Ellen Roddy	77
Jack Smyth	60

■ Gathering data

Form design

> GLOSSARY TERM
> Form design

Most of the time a business, school or organisation will use a form to collect data. In order that the information is collected effectively, thought must be given to the design of the form. Some questions to be asked by the person designing the form are:

- How will the data be collected?
- Who will provide the data?
- How will the data be used or processed to give information?
- How much data will be collected?

There are a number of ways in which data can be collected:

- paper-based forms
- computer-based forms
- automated data capture.

Paper-based forms will be used to collect data from people and then the data will be keyed in to the computer.

Screen-based forms are developed to be filled out online or on a computer screen. The advantage of using a screen-based form is that data is typed directly and does not have to be transferred from paper. This cuts down on the possibility of human error when entering the data.

In the case of a form, it is important to consider the design features. The design quality of the form will have an effect on the quality of the data captured. For example, if the form is difficult to fill out, people will not want to complete it. The quality of the data collected will have an effect on the information produced. Designers should ensure that forms have clearly presented instructions and sufficient space to enter the required details.

A form should include:

- a title suitable for the purpose of the form
- a logo (if appropriate) representing the company or organisation collecting the data
- a prompt which represents each item of data to be collected
- a suitable space to enter each item of data (the space can be on a line or in the form of a box, tick box or radio button)
- suitable instructions should accompany the form or instructions should be included on the form
- suitable text on the purpose of the form.

When designing a form the following should be considered:

- the font chosen should be suitable for the form's intended audience
- the font should vary in size to emphasise sections and headings
- colour should be used to enhance the form where appropriate, for example to break it into sections
- images such as company logos should be included but should not obscure areas of the form
- instructions should clearly explain the purpose of the form.

Forms should ask clearly for the data required and should not ask for any more than necessary. The completion of a form should allow users to make selections using tick boxes or radio buttons, this will cut down on incorrect data.

A good form is easily completed and collects the correct data. A form is useless if it collects only part of the required data. This will impact on the quality of the information produced.

Data capture – reducing human error

Another method of entering data into a computer is by direct data capture. This is when the data is not entered or typed in by an operator, but is read directly into the computer using a special method and reader. Two methods of data capture are optical mark recognition (OMR) and optical character recognition (OCR).

OMR – optical mark recognition

This method of data capture scans forms which have been filled in using marks or ticks. The documents have empty boxes printed onto them. OMR uses light to detect the position of marks on paper. The marks on the paper must be placed accurately to ensure that the data being input is read accurately. The OMR technology converts information about the presence or absence of marks into digital data. It enables high-speed reading of large quantities of data by the computer without using the keyboard. The OMR reader scans the form, detects the presence of marks and passes the information to the computer for processing by applications software.

OMR is used for the National Lottery. Players of the lottery fill out their number choices onto a form which has preprinted boxes used to select the numbers. The document is then scanned using an optical scanner. The data is read from the paper and a ticket is produced which has the selected numbers printed onto it. This acts as a receipt and is used by players to check off their numbers to see if they match the winning numbers.

OMR is also used on answer sheets for multiple-choice tests. This means the tests can be marked automatically using the OMR scanner. In some schools pupil attendance is recorded on OMR sheets. At the end of each session (morning and afternoon) the attendance sheet is read using the OMR reader and student attendance is recorded.

Advantages of using OMR:

- Fast – inputting large amounts of data can be done quickly as OMR allows many documents to be processed one after the other. The data on the document does not have to be typed, it is read directly by the optical mark reader.

- Accurate – because data is read directly from the document, it eliminates the possibility of typing errors made by humans.

- Data input to a computer using OMR can be analysed to produce high-quality information quickly.

- Staff will need minimum training in system use as documents are simply passed into a scanner.

Disadvantages of using OMR:

- The cost of buying OMR equipment could be high.

- Documents used must be kept in good condition. The system may not be able to read creased documents.

- OMR input is paper based. The cost of producing specially designed forms could be high.

- Unless the forms are recycled after input, it may not be the most environmentally friendly solution.

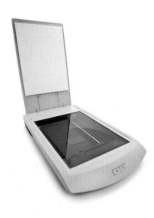

Flat-bed scanners can be used to scan a paper version of a document.

GLOSSARY TERM
File

OCR – optical character recognition.

This is the method used to take paper-based documents and transform them into editable computer **file**s. Let us say you need a digital replica of a document such as a magazine page, newspaper, fax, or printer output. You may try to retype a document from scratch, but this could take a long time. OCR provides the best alternative to manual typing. This technology makes use of an optical scanner.

Optical scanners will scan any page, placed into the scanner, as a picture. Most scanners have an OCR program included with them. An OCR program can look at the 'picture' of your document, 'read' the document, and convert it to text. This text is editable in a word processor. When a document is scanned using the OCR facility it is saved as an RTF (rich text file).

Where a high level of accuracy is required, or where a scanner is required to tell the difference between images and text, complex software and specialised hardware is required.

OCR is being used by libraries to digitize and preserve old documents and books. OCR is also used to sort the mail. Millions of letters are sorted every day by OCR machines, considerably speeding up mail delivery. Royal Mail use the postcode handwritten on to a letter to help sort mail.

BT31 2YZ ✓	Correct segregation of characters	
BT31 2YZ ✗	Unable to segregate characters – could be misread as BBI 2YZ	
BT31 2YZ ✗	T overlapping character space of 3. Unable to separate characters	

The picture above shows a postcode which is readable by an OCR device with Royal Mail and two that aren't.

Advantages of using OCR:

● Large quantities of text can be input to the computer quickly.

● An electronic copy of a paper-based document can be created without re-typing it.

Disadvantages of using OCR:

● Documents which are dirty or marked will not be read accurately.

● Systems that are highly accurate are expensive.

● OCR systems might not produce accurate results when required to scan forms (especially with boxes and check boxes), very small text, poor-quality photocopies, mathematical formulae or handwritten text.

■ Data checking – verification and validation

GLOSSARY TERM
Verification

Have you ever had to change your password on the computer system? Why do you have to type the new password twice? This is a form of data **verification**.

When a paper-based form is used it is necessary to take the data from the form and enter it into the computer. A computer operator will enter the data from the form. It is important that mistyped data is detected by the computer system. In order to detect this type of error verification of the data input is performed.

Data verification is carried out to ensure that data keyed into a computer has been accurately transferred from a paper-based form. The most common way of performing verification is to key the data twice. Data is keyed into the computer system by two different computer operators and then the computer system compares the two sets of data. Any mismatching data is rejected. Any rejected data is re-entered. This ensures that data is transferred accurately and correctly. Another method of verification is proofreading. Documents once typed can be proofread to ensure that they contain correct and accurate information.

Using computer-based forms

Most systems allow the collection of data using a form. This means that the data is keyed into the computer directly with no paper-based form being completed. Online forms are an example of this. When we book flights or buy tickets for concerts, data is entered directly onto the computer screen. The data is then processed to see if the flights or tickets are available.

Data collected using a data entry screen must be checked by the software, before it is accepted by the computer system. Checking data to ensure that it is acceptable and sensible is called **validation**. Validation of data ensures that the data is present, of the correct type, in the correct range and of the correct length. These checks can be made on data to be entered into the system. A validation check is made automatically by the system and generally an error message is displayed if data is incorrect. There are a number of different types of validation checks.

An online form that is completed by passengers booking a flight with easyJet

Presence

A **presence check** will ensure that data has been entered into an area on the form. This check means that data which must be entered is not omitted. You can see examples of this type of check when you fill out an on-screen form. On-screen forms are used:

- on websites – presence checks ensure that data has been entered in particular fields

GLOSSARY TERMS
Validation
Presence check

- for entering data for use in an ICT system, which is common in database applications.

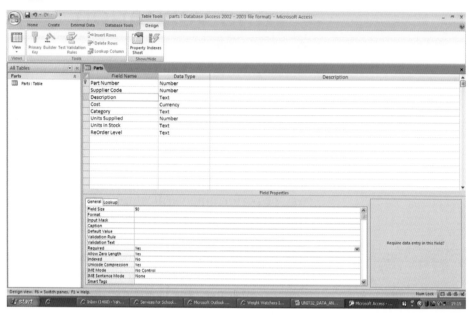

The above design view of a database table shows that a presence check will be carried out for the field Description, because Required is set to *Yes*. This is sensible because we would not want to enter a new product without giving a description for it.

This shows the error message that will be displayed if a user tries to enter a Part Number without entering the Description for it.

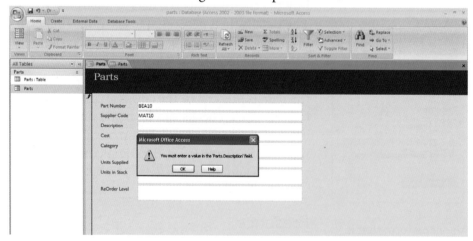

Length

GLOSSARY TERM
Length check

A **length check** will ensure that data entered is of the correct length. For example, the Part Number in the above database may have a length check to ensure that it is six characters long.

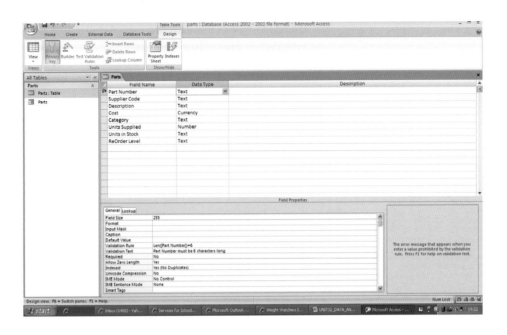

Data type

GLOSSARY TERM

Type check

A data-**type check** is used to ensure that the data entered is of the correct format. There are several data types. When defining data we usually give it a type and a valid range. Examples of data types are:

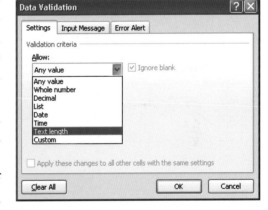

- Numeric – data takes on a numeric value and such data can be used in calculations.

- Text – data can be made up of letters or letters and numbers.

- Date – data takes on a value which is formatted as a date.

- Boolean – data which can have only two values, normally yes or no.

- Currency – data which represents money values.

Some spreadsheet applications allow cells to be validated by allowing only certain data types to be entered. Above we can see some of the different data type checks which can be made on data entered.

Type checks can be implemented in a variety of ways, here are some examples:

Format

Some database packages allow the user to specify exactly what format the data being entered should take. In the example below, the field Supplier Code is assigned an Input Mask, which requires that three letters followed by three numbers are entered (AAA000). The database will not allow data to be entered in any other format.

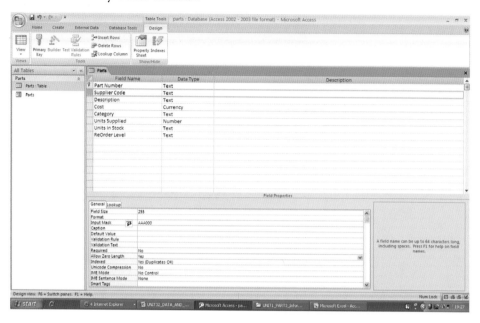

Range

GLOSSARY TERM
Range check

A **range check** ensures that data entered is within a given range. For example:

- Customer number can take on values between 1 and 500.
- Student grades can take on values between 'A' and 'E'.

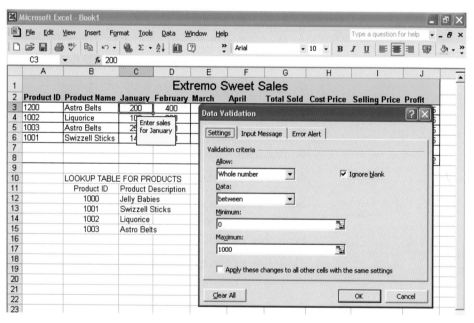

This data validation has set a range check to ensure that values entered into cell C3 are in the correct range, that is 0–1000.

Lookup tables

Lookup tables or lists hold valid values for data. When data is entered, the Lookup table is checked to ensure that the data is within the allowable list. These can be used very successfully in a spreadsheet application.

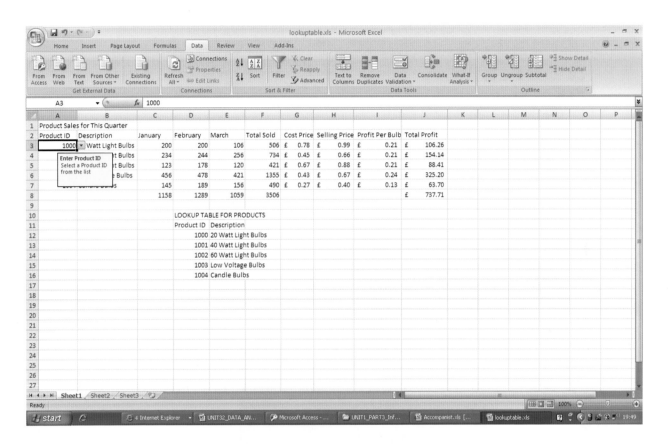

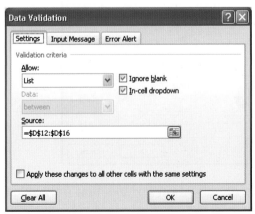

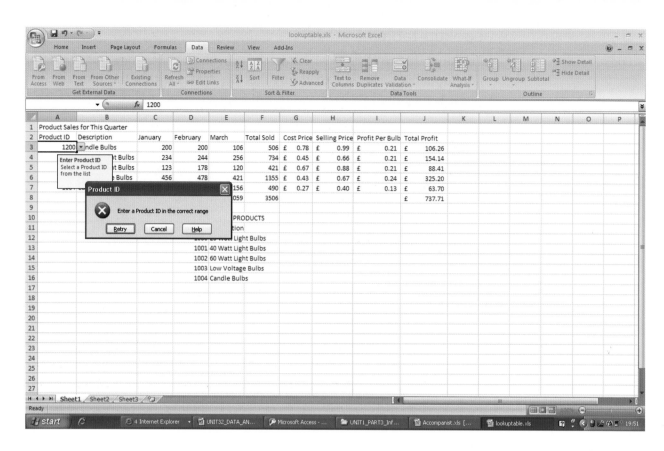

Here you can see that cell A3 has been validated so that only values in the Lookup table can be selected. The resulting error message comes from the data validation set in the box below. The lookup values are located in cells D12 to D16.

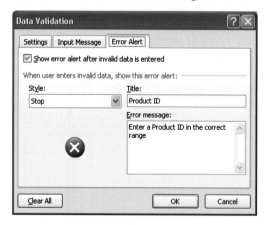

This form of validation ensures that only values in the Lookup table are acceptable.

Check digits

GLOSSARY TERM
Check digit

Check digits are characters that are added to the end of a code. The check digit is compared with the results of a calculation using the code. If the results of the calculation do not match the check digit, the code has to be input again. They are commonly found on ISBN numbers at the back of a book. They are also found at the end of the Universal Product Codes (UPC) or barcodes on items in supermarkets.

ISBN is the abbreviation for the International Standard Book Number. ISBNs are 13 digits in length and are usually of the form XXX-X-XXX-XXXXX-X. Here is a sample barcode with the ISBN displayed below it:

Check digits provide another form of validating data.

Barcodes also use check digits. In a supermarket a barcode is read from an item and a calculation similar to that for an ISBN is carried out.

The methods of validation and verification ensure that data entered is as correct and reliable as possible. However, the fact that data entry is carried out by a human operator means that it could be entered erroneously, even if it is valid. Operators can enter data incorrectly.

■ Data portability

GLOSSARY TERM
Portability

Data **portability** is the ability to transfer data from one system or software application to another without having to re-enter the data. The format in which data is held will indicate whether or not that data is portable between different software applications and different computer systems.

Comma separated variable (CSV) files

Using a range of software such as Microsoft Notepad or Microsoft Word a CSV file can be created. The file created below contains four fields separated by commas. The field names are entered first. Each record in the file is on a new line.

The file has been saved as *weather.csv*.

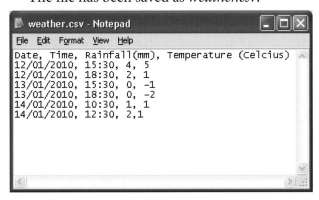

This file can then be opened using a spreadsheet. The contents will appear as follows:

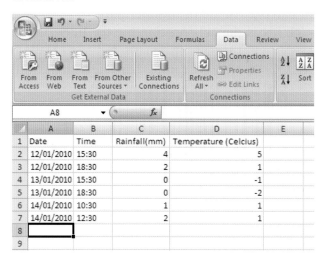

Once the data is available in the spreadsheet, it can be manipulated and graphs can be drawn.

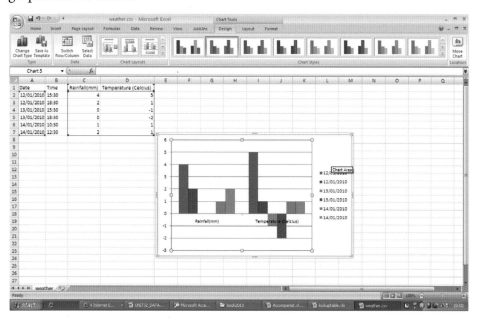

CSV files are produced from data-logging equipment. Can you see how we can take the data produced and import it into an application which can convert data to information?

Now using a database application import the contents of *weather.csv* (available at www.hodderplus.co.uk/cceaictgcse) into the database.

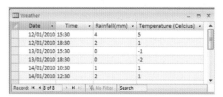

This is a simple example of data portability. The CSV file format allows the data to be used in a word processor, a database and a spreadsheet.

File formats

The format in which a file is stored will determine the portability of the file. Files can be made up of text or graphics. Each type of file can be stored using different formats.

CSV – Comma Separated Variables

Files of this format hold data which is separated by commas. In general a comma separates a field value, and a single line in the file normally represents a record. CSV files can be imported directly to spreadsheets or databases as rows and columns.

RTF – Rich Text Format

This file format allows users to transfer data between different applications. For example, a user of Word 2007 could save a file as .rtf and send it to someone using a different word processor. Both should be able to use the file. Documents scanned using the OCR facility of a scanner are usually saved as RTF documents. This means that the document can be opened using a variety of word-processing applications.

JPEG – Joint Photographic Experts Group

Any graphic image file produced using the JPEG standard. This group of experts develop standards for compressing images. JPEGs are commonly used on web pages and are normally small files. If a file is stored as a JPEG it can be used on any document on a number of different operating systems. For example, JPEGs can be opened in the Windows and Apple Macintosh operating systems. This makes them highly portable.

MPEG – Moving Picture Experts Group

Any moving picture produced using the MPEG standard. This group of experts develop standards for compressing digital video. This is a compressed file format.

MPEG-3 (MP3)

MP3 is a file format used for compressing sound or audio files. The music files are CD-quality compressed recordings that are about ten times smaller than the equivalent CD WAV/AIFF file. MP3s are reduced in size by filtering out all noise that is not detectable to the human ear. This file format is used by iTunes when music is being downloaded and for podcasts. The compressed file format decreases download time.

MPEG-4 (MP4)

MP4 file format was created specially for video files. MP4 is used for compressing files which contain video, sound, text and pictures. Video files and DVDs can be compressed using MP4. This means that high-quality video can be viewed using portable MP4 players and across the internet.

Both MP3 and MP4 have changed the face of entertainment. Most people now download music electronically onto their computer or MP3 player. MP4 has improved the portability of video.

PICT

PICT files are the Macintosh native picture format. PICT files are used by Macintosh graphics applications, they can support high-quality images and can be compressed.

TIFF – Tagged Image File Format

This is a graphics file format and stores bitmapped images. The graphics can be black and white, greyscale or coloured. This file format is portable between different applications and different types of computers. It can be used in Windows and Apple Macintosh environments.

GIF – Graphic Interchange Format

This graphics file format supports compressed images. They are usually small in size and are suitable for inclusion on web pages. Colour quality can be a problem.

TXT – text file (also called ASCII TXT files)

Most text files use ASCII (American Standard Code for Information Interchange) codes for characters. This is a simple text file which will hold letters and numbers but not formats such as bold and italic.

ASCII files can be imported into a word processor but the ASCII file may not appear in its original format. Each word processor will apply its own page layouts to ASCII files. ASCII files are highly portable and are supported by almost every application.

MIDI – Musical Instrument Digital Interface

These files are produced when digital musical instruments are connected as input devices to the computer. They are sound files.

PDF – Portable Document Format

This file format was developed by Adobe to allow files to be viewed on different computers. A PDF file can be created from a range of files, for example a Microsoft Word document or a PowerPoint presentation. The PDF file generated is usually smaller than the original file. In order to view or print the PDF file a special piece of software is required. This is called Adobe Reader and can be downloaded free from Adobe's website. The main advantage is that the PDF file can be viewed on any computer which has the free reader installed. Special software like Microsoft PowerPoint or Word is not required.

HTML – HyperText Markup Language

Web pages are usually designed in HTML (HyperText Markup Language) format. Browsers are programmed to interpret the HTML in order to display the contents on screen.

A section of HTML code which is interpreted by the browser software.

■ Data compression

GLOSSARY TERM
Data compression

Digital data is not always stored efficiently. Normally it is stored in the default format saved by the software used. When there is not a lot of storage space, data can be compressed. **Data compression** is used to convert digital data to as small a size as possible without losing any of the information contained in a file.

Why compress data?

When we transmit images over the internet it is important that they can be downloaded in an acceptable time. Data which has been compressed can take less time to upload and download. For example, a TIFF file of 600 KB when converted to a GIF file will contain approximately 300 KB of data. The same TIFF file converted to a JPEG will contain about 50 KB of data. Download time will be reduced significantly if we choose the GIF or JPEG format of compression.

Bitmapped graphics

GLOSSARY TERM
Pixel

Graphic compression can be done using a graphics package. The graphic can be saved using the specified format to a given resolution.

Bitmapped graphics depend on resolution for quality. The resolution of a graphic is the number of **pixel**s used to represent the image. A pixel is the smallest unit editable in a graphic. These graphics are made up of a grid of pixels. The more pixels in the grid, the higher the resolution of the graphic. This will make the graphic bigger in size and of better quality. They cannot be stretched without losing image quality.

Graphic image which has not used enough pixels

The same graphic at a higher resolution

Bitmapped graphics can be compressed or saved in other file formats, for example .gif, .jpg to reduce their size.

Vector-based graphics

GLOSSARY TERM
Vector graphics

Not all graphics are dependent on their resolution for clarity. Vector-based graphics are formed from vector objects, like the lines on a 'join the dots' image. They can be stretched or shrunk without losing the quality of their image. **Vector graphics** do not depend on resolution for quality. This means that no matter how many dots per inch you're using on screen or in print, your image will look the same. Because of their structure, they can generally be saved as smaller files than bitmaps.

Data compression tools

Tools to compress data are available. WinZip is one example. It will compress files to a fraction of their size. Files which have been compressed in this way are called ZIP files. These files are compressed before being transferred and must then be decompressed at their destination before they can be used.

Data compression tools can also compress full folders of information and store them as a single file for emailing or transporting. The destination computer must have the data compression tool so that the ZIP file can be extracted or unzipped.

Some compression tools allow users to create self-extracting files. These files automatically decompress once they have been downloaded onto a computer system.

Data compression tools are useful:

● when a folder of information is to be emailed as a single file

● when a user wants to email a large file, it can be reduced in size by compressing it

● when a file is too large for a particular storage media, although this is happening less and less because storage media capacity is increasing

● to reduce the amount of storage space taken up by files as they can be stored in compressed format.

Data files can be compressed by saving them using a particular file format:

● Graphics can be compressed using JPEG or GIF format.

● Music files can be compressed using MP3 format.

● Video files can be compressed using MPEG format.

In all cases the purpose of compression is to make the files smaller in size to facilitate the efficient digital transmission or storage of the data.

Digital communication systems

What you will learn in this section

In this section you will learn about how computers are linked together to form networks. You will see that networks can exist in a single building or over a large geographic area, and examine the different measures that can be taken to protect information systems from misuse. You will explore the use of wireless/mobile technologies and evaluate the technologies which support these devices. You will learn about the internet and the technologies and media used for communicating online.

Acronyms:

- ADSL
- HTML
- ISDN
- ISP

- LAN
- PC
- PDA
- PSTN

- URL
- VoIP
- WAN
- WAP

- WWW

Keywords:

- 3G
- Analogue
- Backup
- Bandwidth
- Bluetooth
- Broadband
- Browser
- Electronic mail
- Encryption

- Fibre optic
- File server
- Firewall
- Hub
- Internet
- Internet Service Provider (ISP)
- Intranet
- Network

- Network interface card (NIC)
- Password
- Protocol
- Router
- Search engine
- Spam
- Spyware
- Switch

- Video-conferencing
- Virus
- Wi-Fi
- Wireless technology
- World Wide Web

■ Data networks – LANs and WANs

GLOSSARY TERM
Network

A **network** consists of a set of computers which are linked together. Computers which are linked together can share resources such as printers and software; they can also communicate with each other.

Networks can be made up of a few computers linked together on a single site in a local area network (LAN) or they can be linked via powerful computers over a large geographic area in a wide area network (WAN). A WAN is a collection of networks connected using a telecommunications link. Most WANs make use of the public switched telephone network (PSTN). The **internet** is a WAN.

GLOSSARY TERM
Internet

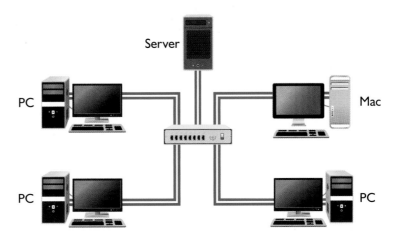

The main differences between a LAN and a WAN

LAN – local area network	WAN – wide area network
Spread over a small geographic area usually one or two buildings.	Spread over a vast geographic area over countries or the world.
Computers on a LAN can be effectively linked together using copper cabling.	A WAN is a network of networks, the most effective way to link networks together at a distance is by using a **fibre optic** cable, or a wireless link, like satellite.

GLOSSARY TERM
Fibre optic

■ Local area networks – LANs

This type of network is used in places like schools and offices. It is spread over a small geographic area such as one or two buildings. The network links computers in the buildings together using different types of network cables or through wireless connections. The data is transmitted from one computer to another along the network cables or the wireless connection. Computers on a LAN can be networked in different ways.

Most organisations have networked computers rather than stand-alone computers. When computers are networked together there are several advantages:

- Expensive peripherals can be shared between a number of computers. For example, one printer, one fax machine or one scanner can be used by several computers in a room or building.

GLOSSARY TERM
File server

- A single copy of the software is stored on the **file server** and this is shared by all the computers on the network.

- Networked computers allow users to communicate with each other. This can be done using email, broadcasting messages or electronic conferencing on the network.

- Users can share files and work on joint projects using shared resources and folders on the network.
- Users have flexible access, that is they can log on at any computer and access their files.

Computer networks are constructed using a combination of the following components.

File server

A file server is the main computer on the network. It is more powerful than all of the other computers with a large amount of RAM and hard disk space. Most servers will have multiple hard drives. A typical server will hold:

- network operating system software, such as Microsoft Windows Server
- application software, such as Microsoft Office
- user files created by the users on the system
- system software which will manage the network resources and security
- utility software, such as a virus checker.

> **GLOSSARY TERM**
> Password

The file server manages file and network security across the network and makes sure that only authorised users log on to the system. The log-in process makes use of usernames and **password**s.

Network interface card (NIC)

Each computer must have a network card so that it can communicate with the file server and all other computers on the network. The network card provides a 'port' for the network cable. You can see this in the picture below.

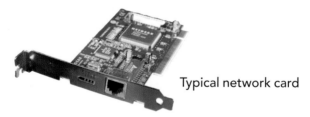

Typical network card

The network cable is inserted into the port shown. This connects the PC to the file server. Ask your teacher to show you where the network cable is on your PC.

Network interface card (NIC)

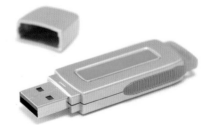

USB wireless adapter

A wireless **network interface card** (W**NIC**) may already be installed in a computer or laptop when it is bought. Such a computer is 'wireless enabled' and can connect to a wireless **router** providing mobile access to a network. Alternatively, a WNIC or USB wireless adapter can be added to the computer to enable wireless access to a network.

Network cables

A typical data cable with RJ-45 connector

> **GLOSSARY TERMS**
> Network interface card
> Router

The network cables plug into the back of each computer and link the computers together. These cables plug directly into the network card contained inside each computer.

Generally, cables are made of copper and the data travels along the cables to and from the file server. In a STAR network each computer has its own cable linking it to the server.

Switches

A **switch** is a single connection point for a group of computers. The switch shown allows 22 computers to be connected to it directly using network cables. The switch is connected to the file server and organises communication between the file server and the computers connected to it. A switch will send data to a particular computer which is connected to it. Not all networks use switches; some use **hubs**. A hub will send data to all of the computers that are connected to it.

> **GLOSSARY TERMS**
> Switch
> Hub

Network software

When a computer is part of a network, the network software must be installed on it. This allows it to communicate with the file server and other computers.

Router

Wireless router

A router is a piece of networking equipment that shares a network connection between devices. A router can be wired or wireless.

A wireless router or wireless access point can allow a computer to connect to a LAN. Many schools have wireless laptops which allow pupils mobile access to the school network. Wireless routers also enable home users to connect to the internet without the inconvenience of cables. Computers which connect to a wireless router or wireless access point must contain a wireless network interface card or must be wireless enabled.

A router enables a LAN to connect to the internet and allows the two networks to communicate with each other. A router may have a security feature like a **firewall** integrated into it.

> **GLOSSARY TERM**
> Firewall

A router is used if LANs are to be connected to the internet or to a WAN. The router will translate information from the internet so that the computers on a LAN can understand it. It will translate information coming from the LAN to the internet and will find the shortest route to send data across the network.

The need for communications protocols

Computers and networks which communicate with each other must send and receive data using the same format and method. They must 'speak the same language' and use rules for transmitting and receiving data. For example, if one computer is transmitting data and the computer which is meant to receive the data is also transmitting, then data could be lost.

A communications **protocol** is an agreed standard or set of rules for sending or receiving data on a network. If a computer receives data on a network, it must support the communications protocol of the sending computer. There are many different types of communications protocol which are defined by organisations who sell network hardware and software.

The protocol used on the internet is TCP/IP. Transmission Control Protocol/Internet Protocol makes sure that data is not lost as it travels from one computer to another. The protocol used to transmit data around a LAN may be different. If your school network is connected to the internet then the computers must be able to understand the TCP/IP protocol. The router used to connect the two networks (the LAN and the internet) together will perform a translation function and allow computers of differing protocols to communicate.

> **GLOSSARY TERM**
> Protocol

■ Digital communication security

Why secure the network?

The network must be protected from:

- viruses such as Trojan horses and worms
- unauthorised access by users or hackers
- authorised users who might damage important files
- unexpected breakdown resulting in the loss of data
- physical damage.

The network must protect:

- user data
- the software on the file server
- the resources which are shared between users.

■ Basic network security measures

Usernames and passwords

Each user on the network is given a unique username. The user can decide on a password which only they will know. When a user wants to use the network they must log on. Logging on involves entering the username and the password.

The username can be seen but the password appears in asterisk or dot format. When the user clicks on the login button, software on the file server checks to see if a username with the password entered exists. If the password and username do not match, the person will not be allowed access to the network. This is one way of stopping unauthorised users from getting onto the network. Some networks only allow users a limited number of attempts at logging on and disable the username for a period of time after unsuccessful login attempts.

Users set their own passwords. A good password will help reduce the possibility of someone accessing your account. Here are some of the features of a good password.

It should:

✔ be a combination of letters, numbers and other characters

✔ have a minimum number of characters, for example some school networks require passwords to be at least 8 characters long

✔ be changed regularly

✔ be kept confidential.

It should not:

✘ be your username, pet's name or family name

✘ be a word (once you say it someone can remember it and use it when you are not there)

✘ be written down anywhere.

Levels of access

Another way of keeping the network secure is to limit the things which users can do on the network. This is done by giving users different levels of access. For example, in a school, pupils, teachers and the system manager have different levels of access.

The login information on the left shows that a member of staff is currently logged on and that the person has advanced access rights.

A pupil can:

- access software
- use the internet
- change the content and location of their user files
- change their password
- select a printer to print work
- connect and use portable storage devices.

A teacher can do everything that a pupil can and also:

- give students printer credits
- reset their passwords
- monitor their activity using special software
- set up shared folders for pupils to use.

The system manager can do everything a teacher and pupil can do and also:

- set up new users and delete or disable existing users
- change the amount of disk storage space that each user is allocated
- copy files between users
- allocate network resources such as printers
- connect new devices to the network
- install software such as printer drivers.

Each group of users has a different level of access. This protects the network from damage by users.

Encryption

GLOSSARY TERM
Encryption

Data which is being transmitted across a WAN or a LAN could be intercepted and read by unauthorised users. To prevent this data can be encrypted.

Encryption is the process of encoding data which is to be sent across a network, making that data unreadable to anyone who intercepts it. Only a user with the encryption key software can read the data when it arrives at its destination. This is one way of keeping data secure whilst it is travelling on the network.

Data can also be stored in encrypted form. This means that users can only read the data if they have access to the special software which will decrypt or decode the data.

■ Measures that can be taken to prevent information systems from misuse

An information system includes all the components used for the input, output, storage and processing of data. The entire information system must be protected.

Virus protection

GLOSSARY TERM
Virus

A **virus** is a computer program which is designed to damage some aspect of an information system. These viruses generally need to attach themselves to a document or program so that they can infect computers.

A worm is designed to spread and does not have to be attached to any document or program. It spreads by replicating itself. This can cause problems on a network as the worm will slow down processing whilst reproducing.

A Trojan horse gains entry to a user's computer 'in disguise'. The user may think that it is a useful program. Instead it provides hackers with an entry point to the user's computer.

Information systems are under constant threat from viruses, worms, Trojan horses and other such computer programs. Any computer system will need virus protection software installed to prevent these attacks. This will protect the data and the computers on the network from virus infection. The virus protection software on most networks is automatically updated at least to take account of any new viruses. Viruses can enter the network in many ways, for example:

- from a portable storage device like a flash memory stick

- through the internet

- by email.

On a network, the virus protection software will scan all of the linked computers each day to ensure that there are no infections. When a user connects a USB storage device, such as a flash memory stick, to the computer, it is automatically scanned to make sure it is virus free. If the device contains a virus, the user and system administrator will be notified.

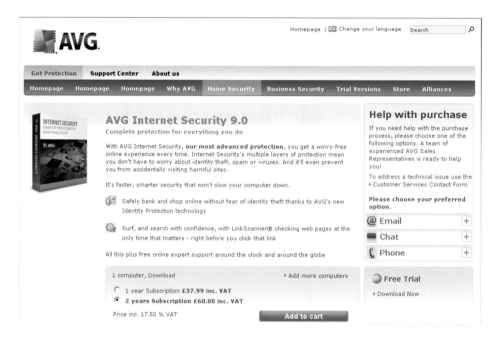

Spam and spyware

GLOSSARY TERMS
Spam
Spyware

Spam and **spyware** also create problems for users of information systems. Many anti-virus products provide protection against these and other threats.

Spam could be described as the bulk sending of electronic messages to people who have not requested the information. Many internet users receive this in the form of junk email which can fill their inbox.

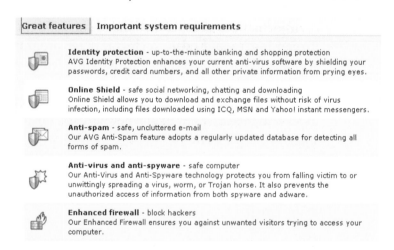

Spyware is malicious software (malware) which is secretly installed on a user's computer. It collects pieces of information about the user such as the websites they have visited. Spyware can also allow other programs to be installed, which could change computer settings or even monitor keystrokes so that passwords can be captured and used by criminals. Running anti-spyware software has now become a part of ensuring that a computer system is kept secure.

Firewalls

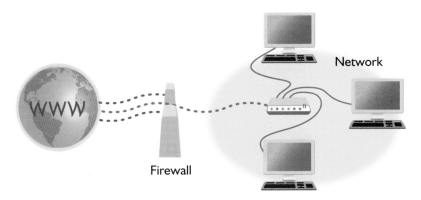

A firewall can be integrated into a hardware device or a software program. It will filter information coming from the internet to the computer network. The firewall will prevent a variety of activity from affecting the network. It can prevent:

- hackers from entering the network via the internet
- viruses and spam from entering the network via the internet
- users/computers within the network from uploading data onto the internet.

Backing up data on a LAN

GLOSSARY TERM
Backup

User data on the LAN must be protected. If data is lost, the system must have some method of recovering the data. Most network systems use a **backup** process to make sure that there is a copy of the data that can be loaded on to the system if the original data is lost.

Backup copies of data are stored on a variety of media.

Hard disk backup

Network-attached storage (NAS) devices

This is a hard disk storage system, which is connected to the network through a network point. It is not part of the main server. When a backup is scheduled, all of the files from the file server are copied onto the NAS. An NAS device can share data with other servers and devices on the network.

Direct-attached storage (DAS) devices

This is a hard disk storage system which is connected directly to the main computer in the network. Backups are scheduled and all of the data on the server is copied to the DAS. A DAS device cannot be accessed through other devices on the network.

Magnetic tape

Backup to magnetic tape has become less popular. The tape is stored in the tape drive on the file server and a backup of the system is taken at regular intervals. A backup is usually taken every day using a different tape. Backup activity may slow the network down as it uses system resources. Backup is done regularly, when the computer system is not busy, for example during the night. Tapes are kept for an agreed period before being reused.

Data backup on a PC

Users of standalone PCs should also keep regular backups of data files. This prevents accidental loss of data or software. Windows operating systems include a special utility that makes it easy for users to backup data.

Users are prompted using a wizard and guided through the steps leading to the backup of their data.

Back up can be done on the existing hard disk or to a removable storage medium with suitable capacity, such as CD-R, CD-RW or DVD. The advantages of using CD or DVD are:

- high capacity
- low cost
- portability.

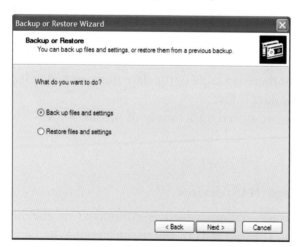
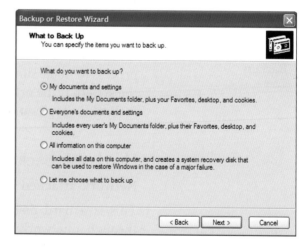

A high capacity external hard drive can be attached to a computer and files can be backed up to it. The hard drive is generally connected using a USB cable.

Online storage can be used for LAN or PC

Using this method, data is uploaded to a location on the internet. This can be scheduled to be completed automatically, depending on the website used. Files stored in this way can be accessed from anywhere and can be shared easily. However, if the company is unreliable the data may not be held securely. Also, some companies hold sensitive data and it may not be acceptable to store that data on the internet.

Vstuff is provided by Virgin Media for PC home users as part of their internet services. This facility allows users to backup important files to a secure server online.

■ Mobile digital communication

GLOSSARY TERMS
Wi-Fi
3G
Bluetooth

The emergence of **Wi-Fi**, **3G** and **Bluetooth** wireless technologies have increased the use of mobile devices. These devices are used for a wide variety of activities depending on which of the wireless technologies are being used. Most mobile devices feature at least two of the three technologies mentioned. Some wireless technologies use radio waves to transmit data.

Wi-Fi (Wireless Fidelity)

Devices connecting to a Wi-Fi network must have a wireless adapter to enable them to communicate with the wireless router. Wi-Fi networks can be protected and may require the user to provide a password in order to log on. Wi-Fi hotspots can be found in many hotels or city centres. (Here tiny antennae are installed on streets, lamp posts and even street signs.) In these locations, free wireless internet access is provided and a password may not be required. In many airports, computer users can buy a voucher which will enable their device to connect to the Wi-Fi network and internet. They enter the voucher number and are allowed access until the voucher runs out. Using Wi-Fi, data can be transmitted at speeds of 54 Mbps depending on the standard of Wi-Fi being used. A wireless router providing access to the internet at home makes use of Wi-Fi.

Advantages of Wi-Fi:

✔ Users can log on in any location using a wide range of devices.

✔ Wi-Fi devices are widely available.

✔ Networks can be set up without wires.

✔ Prices for Wi-Fi are decreasing.

✔ Wi-Fi networks can be protected to ensure only authorised users can log on.

✔ Wi-Fi allows devices to roam from one network to another.

✔ Wi-Fi has a recognised standard created by IEEE.

Disadvantages of Wi-Fi:

✘ Wi-Fi networks are limited by their range – devices will lose connection with the wireless router after a certain distance.

✘ Signal strength can vary according to how close you are to the wireless router.

✘ The connection may not be as secure as traditional wired connections.

✘ Interference from other wireless sources may distort data signals.

✘ Wi-Fi may be affected by weather conditions.

GLOSSARY TERM
Wireless technology

3G (Third Generation)

3G is another **wireless technology** which makes use of the mobile phone network. Many new mobile phones are 3G enabled. In order to use 3G a subscription to a service provider is needed. This is usually the mobile phone company who provided the phone and SIM card. A subscription or network tariff provides access to the internet from any location which has network coverage. Users pay for using 3G services through their network plan or by paying for the amount of data downloaded. This can be expensive especially if it is done using a different network. Smart phones like the one shown allow users to connect to the internet using 3G data services.

3G data speeds can reach 14.4 Mbps; however, unlike Wi-Fi, there is currently no standard definition of speed. The 3G speed can be affected by the numbers of users using the network cell.

Advantages:

✔ Mobile phones can also be used for voice calls and a range of other data services.

✔ Video calling is possible.

✔ Map and positioning services are available.

✔ Can be used where normal broadband is not available.

Disadvantages:

✘ Data transfer can be expensive.

✘ Increased power consumption means that mobile phones need to be larger to house the high capacity batteries.

✘ Activities requiring high **bandwidth** cannot be carried out using 3G, a Wi-Fi connection is required. For example, watching TV programmes is not always possible using 3G.

✘ Performance is affected by network coverage and the strength of the signal.

✘ Download times can be affected by the number of users in a network cell and the amount of data being downloaded.

GLOSSARY TERM
Bandwidth

Bluetooth

Bluetooth is a short-range wireless technology. This means that the devices communicating must be relatively close together. The signal will not travel for a long distance. Bluetooth uses less power than other wireless technologies and is much cheaper to use. Bluetooth-enabled devices can connect directly together without the need for a router or a provider at no cost. This technology is targeted at voice and data transfer applications. Versions of Bluetooth offer data transfer of 24 Mbps.

Advantages:

✔ Can penetrate solid objects.

✔ Does not need line of sight.

✔ Low cost.

✔ Less power used.

✔ Easily connected to other Bluetooth-enabled devices.

Disadvantages:

✗ Lower-level security.

✗ Data transmission rate is lower than other wireless technologies.

✗ Short range.

■ WAP (Wireless Application Protocol)

WAP-enabled mobile phones can be used to access the internet. WAP is Wireless Application Protocol and was designed to allow handheld devices access to the internet. WAP is a communication protocol and it is used to access network services and information using mobile devices. WAP-enabled mobile phones use micro-**browser**s to display information.

GLOSSARY TERM
Browser

■ Mobile communication devices

Devices making use of mobile technology are being used more and more. Mobile technology provides a high level of flexibility for users. They can communicate, access information, use the internet and talk whilst on the move. Businesses, schools and the health service make use of wireless-enabled devices.

Mobile phones

The mobile phone uses radio frequency to transmit data. Its size means that it can be carried around easily and used anywhere that there is network coverage. This mobile communication tool means that people can be contacted 24/7. The mobile phone is a highly personal device and most people now have their own mobile phones.

Short message service (SMS)

This is the text message facility associated with a mobile phone. Users can send messages to other mobile phones on any network. This is done instantly. A text message can get through even when a call is in progress. A text message goes to a central message centre and it is forwarded as soon as a transmission space is available. Many mobile phones can be used to take digital photographs or short movies. These can also be sent to other mobile phones through the message centre. The message function can also be used to send emails and fax messages.

Email

Email can be sent by SMS through a gateway. The gateway converts the SMS to email format and the provider will forward the email to the recipient. Email can also be sent from mobile phones using 3G and Wi-Fi technology.

Roaming

Mobile phones can send and receive data and telephone calls whilst in another country or anywhere in the world. This is useful if people are away from work or home and they can keep up to date on all current information.

Voicemail

Voicemail enables callers to leave a message if the owner of the telephone is not available or is on another call. This means that no calls will be missed.

Smartphones and Personal Digital Assistants (PDAs)

Devices which combine internet services and mobile phone functions are called 'smartphones'. Handheld devices such as Personal Digital Assistants (PDAs) and smartphones are used to access the internet and can receive full email attachments. These include Blackberry and iPhone products. Such devices allow users to make use of Wi-Fi and 3G technologies to communicate. They also operate as a mobile phone and will provide many if not all of the functions of a mobile phone.

The table below summarises how some devices use wireless technology.

Device	Technology available	Possible uses
Laptop	Wi-Fi	Connecting to a wireless LAN via a router. This allows the laptop to access the server and all peripherals available to network users.
	Bluetooth	Connecting to other Bluetooth-enabled devices such as printers, other laptops, cameras.
Mobile phone	Bluetooth	To connect to other mobile phones and transfer pictures or MP3 files.
	3G and WAP	To connect to the internet and download web pages in a suitable format.
Smart phone/ Personal Digital Assistant (PDA)	Bluetooth	Connecting to hands-free or Bluetooth headsets. Transferring photos or music from one phone to another.
	Wi-Fi	To access internet services on the move. For example, to connect to a wireless network in a hotel or airport.
	3G	When Wi-Fi is not available, 3G technology allows users to access internet services.

■ The internet and intranets

GLOSSARY TERM
World Wide Web

Firstly consider the difference between the internet and the **World Wide Web**.

The internet and the World Wide Web are two separate things, although each requires the other. The internet is the network of networks, that is all the computers connected together. The internet does not contain information but provides transport links for information to pass between computers. Users on the internet can make use of different services. Typical internet services are:

GLOSSARY TERM
Electronic mail (email)

- **Electronic mail** (**email**) – allows you to send and receive mail.
- Instant messaging – allows you to communicate online by text.
- WWW – the World Wide Web.

The World Wide Web is an application which runs on the internet and is the largest and most used service on the internet.

Features of pages on the World Wide Web:

- written using the programming language HTML
- viewed using a browser
- contain hypertext which provides the user with clickable links to other pages on the web
- can contain sound, video, animation, graphics and hypertext as well as simple text
- uses HyperText Transfer Protocol to send pages across the internet.

For this reason the WWW could be described as a multimedia service on the internet. The URL of pages on the WWW usually begins with http://, indicating that the page uses the HyperText Transfer Protocol.

The difference between an intranet and the internet

GLOSSARY TERM
Intranet

An **intranet** is a private network website used within an organisation. The website uses the same protocol as the WWW, that is TCP/IP. An intranet is not accessible to the general public. Only authorised users can log on and use an intranet.

In larger organisations users can log on to the company intranet from home. Security software called a firewall will protect the intranet from being accessed by unauthorised users.

Intranet users need a browser to view pages. Like the internet, intranets are used to share information, to communicate and to facilitate discussion through bulletin boards and messaging facilities. This will cut down on the amount of paper produced by an organisation. If information is stored and displayed in one location it means that employees can access the information at any time. This will improve the company's internal communication.

Some schools have an intranet which is used to communicate with both staff and students.

Through a school intranet, teachers can:

- develop departmental websites which contains notes about topics being studied, homework and provide feedback on tests undertaken
- communicate with pupils and other staff within the school using the email facility
- share exemplary student work with the school community
- share resources with other subject teachers.

Through an intranet, students can:

- use the notes and materials to work independently
- communicate digitally with teachers about problems or difficulties with homework
- email homework to teachers
- find out about general school information.

A major advantage of having an intranet is that once the information is uploaded it can be viewed by everybody within the organisation at any time. Good communication builds good communities; the use of an intranet will improve communications within an organisation and so improve every employees' view of the organisation's vision and strategies.

■ Connecting to the internet

Internet Service Provider (ISP)

GLOSSARY TERMS
Internet Service
  Provider (ISP)
Search engine

An **ISP** sells internet access to companies or individuals. The ISP provides web servers which connect to the **search engine**s on the internet. An ISP will provide the user with a range of services.

Typical services provided by an ISP

- a variety of bandwidth options
- a variety of usage options
- an email service
- a security package, which can include protection against hacking, viruses, spyware and identity theft
- web hosting service which allows users to upload their own web pages
- online and telephone assistance
- junk mail blocker
- pop-up ad blocker

- website filtering which will filter out unsuitable content
- telephone package
- mobile broadband – users buy a dongle so that broadband can be accessed in a variety of locations.

When a user selects an ISP they must install the software for that ISP on their PC. This enables the PC to communicate with the modem/router provided and ensures that it connects to the correct internet file server, enabling the user to 'surf the net'. This comes on a CD-ROM and will install automatically. It contains drivers for the modem which is to be used and connection settings for the PC.

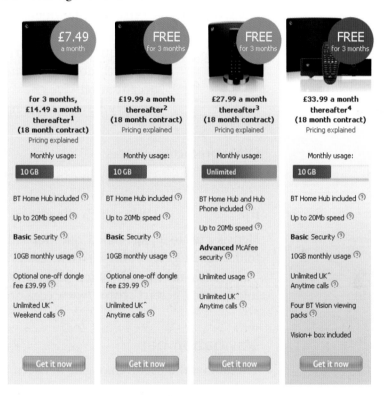

Above you can see an online advertisement from BT showing the features associated with BT Broadband.

Browser software

This software allows users to view and use the web pages on the internet. These are usually in HTML format.

It is important to note that web browsers can be used to view any HTML pages whether users are online or offline.

There is a wide variety of web browsers available. Some of the most widely used include Microsoft Internet Explorer, Mozilla Firefox, Google Chrome, Apple Safari and Opera.

Features provided by a typical web browser

Address bar

This allows the user to enter the web address or URL of the website they wish to visit. Smart address bars will suggest sites already visited if the user types the first few letters of the URL.

A URL is a **Uniform Resource Locator**, this is just another name for the website address. For example the URL for for the CCEA website is http://www.ccea.org.uk

http://	HyperText Transfer Protocol – the protocol used to exchange information
www.ccea.org	Domain name which includes the name of the host server. ccea.org is called a second-level domain name. It must be unique on the internet. (On its own **.org** is known as top-level domain name indicating the purpose of the organisation.)
.uk	country-level domain name in this case United Kingdom.

Other protocols

mailto:	URLs which can be used to invite a user to write an email message to a particular email address.
ftp:	URLs which allow users to upload files to servers.

Here is a url to a page called 'questions.html', the page is contained within a folder called 'gcseict': http://www.ccea.org.uk/gcseict/questions.html

Here is a url to a file called 'computer.gif' , the file is contained within a folder called 'gcseict': http://www.ccea.org.uk/gcseict/computer.gif

Navigation bar

This allows the user to navigate between the web pages visited.
A user can:

- go back and forward to previous web pages using the **Back** and **Forward** buttons

- reload a web page using the **Refresh** button – this is useful if the web page does not look as though it has fully loaded

- set a home page. This page will load automatically when the default browser opens. The user can return to this web page at any time by pressing the **Home** button.

GLOSSARY TERM
Uniform Resource Locator (URL)

Bookmark or Favourites option

A user can keep a list of their favourite websites by adding the URL of the website to a list. This list is kept by the browser and when the user clicks the **Favourites** button, a clickable list of web addresses appears in the side window of the browser.

Search engine

Most browsers provide a search engine facility. The user enters text into the search engine box and the search engine will scan the internet for other web pages containing the text that the user has entered. When it finds matching information, the web addresses of these pages are displayed in a list. The user can click any of the returned web addresses to visit the pages. Remember that the browser is not in itself a search engine, it includes a search engine for user convenience.

A user can use the address bar to enter the URL of a search engine and go directly to it.

Some search engines use a spider or webcrawler. This programme 'crawls' through the web and constructs an index of pages. When a user wants to search for a topic using the internet, the index of topics, made by the webcrawler, is used. It is the job of the webcrawler to ensure that the index is up to date. Different search engines will search different file servers to make up the index of pages. This is why a search on different browsers might give different results.

Meta tags allow people who create web pages to specify special words in the heading of the HTML page. These words will help the search engine categorise the page and decide whether or not to include it in the results for a particular search.

Using a search engine to search for information can give a large number of results. Users can be confused when a lot of web links are returned. Before searching, think carefully about keywords and refine your search to return the most relevant websites.

History button

The browser will usually keep a list of web pages visited in previous days and weeks. If the user clicks on the **History** button, these web addresses will be displayed. The user can set the number of days that web addresses are stored in the History list.

Browser settings and internet options

Browser software will filter content based on the settings provided by a user. The user can:

- provide settings for content and language
- give a list of websites which may not be viewed

● set the home page and decide how long the history pages will be kept.

Some browsers also provide:

● a button which takes the user directly to their email home page

● a button which will open an interactive chatroom

● a button which will print the page being viewed.

Tabs

A browser with four tabs opened.

This is a feature which allows users to browse a number of web pages in the same browser without opening a new browser window. Users can move from one web page to another using the Tab feature.

Private browsing

Users can turn on a private browsing option. This means that any websites visited are not stored in the history list. Internet files and cookies are not stored on the computer when a user browses in this mode. This mode could be useful when using computers in a public place and users do not want to leave personal data behind.

Accelerators

The Accelerator icon available in Internet Explorer reduces the number of clicks required to do a particular task, making navigating the internet faster.

The user can highlight (or copy) text and make use of the appropriate accelerator by right clicking.

Customisation options

Users can personalise the browser using customisation options. They can add toolbars to the browser, for example the Google Toolbar, or set the appearance of the browser and manage security settings.

■ Bandwidth and its impact on internet access

In computer networks the bandwidth tells us the rate at which data can be transmitted down the communications line in a given period of time. Normally it is the number of bits (binary digits) per second. The higher the bandwidth, the quicker data will flow along the line. This normally means that with a higher bandwidth:

● web pages are loaded more quickly, giving the user a better experience

● large multimedia files can be downloaded faster

● connection to the internet will be quicker

● network traffic will not be congested

● response time on a network will be better.

There are a number of different connection types available and each will provide differing bandwidths and features.

Connection type	Features
PSTN Public Switched Telephone Network	• Uses the traditional telephone system to allow access to WANs and the internet. • Low bandwidth 28 kbps (kilobits per second) up to 56 kbps. • Dialup connection.
ADSL Asymmetric Digital Subscriber Line	***ADSL provides high bandwidth – this is known as broadband.*** • Transmits digital information at high bandwidth down a telephone cable. • It is permanently 'switched on', there is no need to dial up. • Telephone or fax messages can be received or made while the user is online. • ADSL provides high-speed internet access. • Generally upload speed is much slower than download speed. This is because users tend to download much more information than they upload. 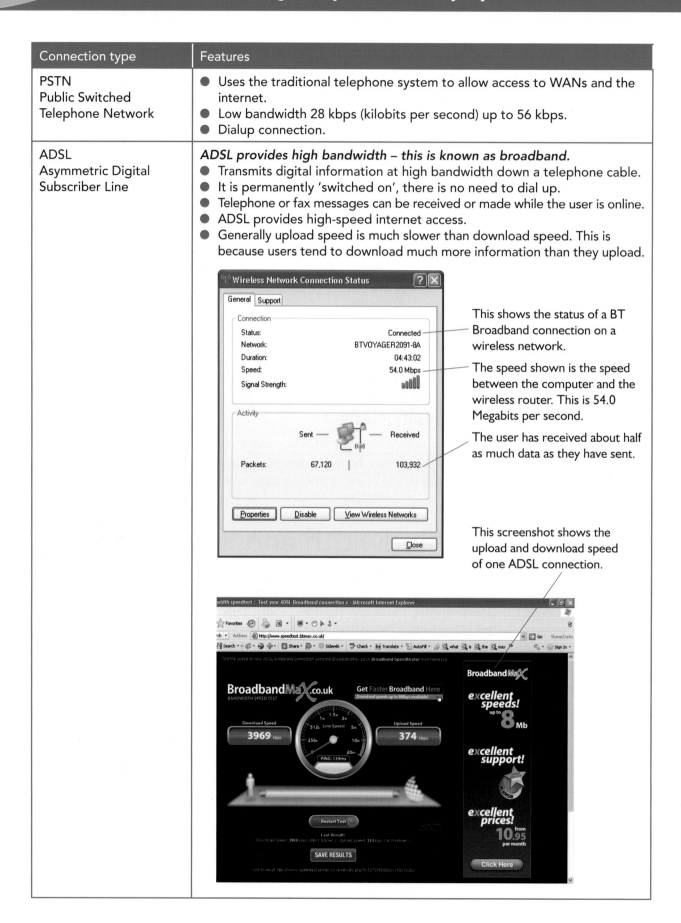 This shows the status of a BT Broadband connection on a wireless network. The speed shown is the speed between the computer and the wireless router. This is 54.0 Megabits per second. The user has received about half as much data as they have sent. This screenshot shows the upload and download speed of one ADSL connection.

Fibre optic cable	<ul><li>Fibres of glass or perspex used to carry signals (as pulses of light) which can be voice data or computer data.</li><li>Very high bandwidth.</li><li>Data can potentially be transmitted at the speed of light.</li><li>Lighter and thinner than copper cabling.</li><li>Immune to interference by radio signals, etc. and so is more secure.</li><li>They are expensive.</li><li>Specialised skills required to join cables together.</li><li>Used to connect telephone substations.</li></ul>
Cable	<ul><li>Customers must be in an area where cable network is available.</li><li>Users who subscribe to a cable TV company such as Virgin Media can connect to the internet using their cable connection.</li><li>Digital TV and phone services can also be provided.</li></ul>
Satellite	<ul><li>A computer connects to the internet and receives and sends information via a satellite dish.</li><li>Useful in rural areas where the telephone system is not up to date and where there is no cable TV available.</li><li>Satellite connection is expensive.</li><li>Users must purchase a satellite dish.</li></ul>

A word about modems

Computer — Modem — Telephone network — Modem — Terminal

Modem is short for Modulator Demodulator. Modems were first created to convert the digital signals from your computer into **analogue** signals so that they could travel down the telephone line. At that time most telephones lines were analogue.

The digital signal from a computer was MOdulated and converted to an analogue signal to travel across the telephone network.

A modem at the other end DEModulated the analogue signal and converted it to a digital signal which the receiving computer can understand.

The speed at which the modem operates affects the download time of web pages and files.

People who still use a dialup connection may have a 56 K modem instead of an ADSL or wireless **router**. This means that data will travel at 56 kbps on the line.

Nowadays internet users can subscribe to **broadband**. This provides greater bandwidth and improved internet performance.

GLOSSARY TERMS
Analogue
Router
Broadband

Broadband lines can carry digital data, so no translation from analogue to digital data is needed. However an ADSL modem is provided to broadband customers. This modem has a slightly different function to the dialup modem.

An ADSL modem will:

● split the signal into two channels – one for voice and one for data transfer – users can use the telephone and the internet at the same time
● expand the bandwidth available for data transfer
● transfer data from the internet to your computer much faster than uploading data – making the assumption that most users download more data than they upload.

The hardware and software required to access online services

Single users can connect to the internet. In order to connect successfully a number of items of hardware and software are required. As well as a PC, a single user needs the items detailed below:

● Internet Service Provider (ISP)
● ISP software
● Browser software
● Telecommunications line (dialup, ISDN, ADSL)
● Modem/ADSL broadband modem/cable modem/ADSL wireless router.

To connect up using wireless technology:

1 Ensure your wireless router is switched on and the wireless function of your PC is on/enabled.
2 Open the web browser.
3 The router/modem converts the signals from your computer so that it can travel along the telecommunications line to your ISP.
4 The ISP provides a connection to the internet.

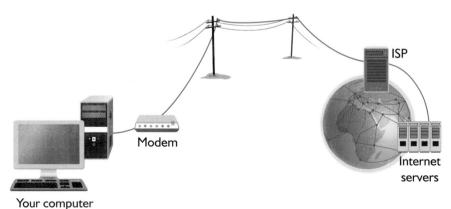

Modem

Your computer

ISP

Internet servers

■ Communications technology

The advance in communications networks has led to an increase in the number of widely available communications technologies.

Email

Email or electronic mail allows users to send messages from a computer across the internet at anytime. Emails can be read at any time by the recipient. In order to use email, users must have all of the technology required to connect to the internet.

Email allows users to:

- create messages
- reply to messages
- forward messages to other users
- send a message to a list of people
- send files of any format as an attachment
- save and print an email.

In order to send or receive email, users must have an email address.

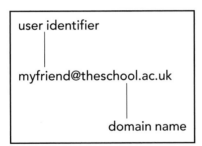

An email address is made up of the user identifier followed by the @ symbol then the domain name of the computer receiving the email.

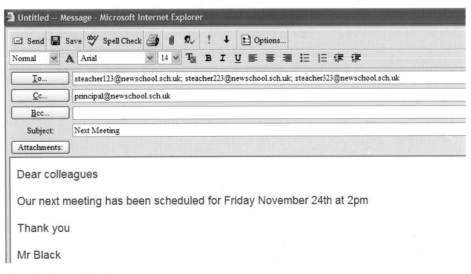

A typical email window

To...	The sender of the email enters the email addresses of the recipients here.
Cc...	Carbon copy: the sender enters the email address of people receiving a carbon copy of the email for information purposes only.
Bcc...	Blind carbon copy: the sender enters the email address of people receiving a blind carbon copy of the email. These recipients will not see any of the other recipients' email addresses.
Subject	The sender types a short description of what the email is about.
Attachments	The sender can attach files of almost any format to the email.

Advantages of using email:

✔ Flexible – can be sent anytime day or night. The recipient need not be at their desk; emails can be read when the recipient logs on.

✔ Easily managed – less paper is used and all emails arrive in the Inbox.

✔ Fast – delivered instantly to any location in the world and to any number of people.

✔ Inexpensive – compared to telephone calls, faxes and courier services.

✔ Filtering of email can be done easily – protecting users from inappropriate communication.

✔ Attachments – the sender can attach any type of file to the email. Sound, graphics and text files can be easily distributed.

✔ Secure and private – emails can be sent securely and privately unlike faxes and telephone calls.

Disadvantages of using email:

✘ Technology – the sender and recipient must have access to the internet.

✘ It is easy to insert a wrong address into the 'To…' box. A confidential email could be sent to the wrong person.

✘ Spam – unwanted emails selling or advertising products can be sent. This is like electronic junk mail.

✘ Users are not notified of new emails unless they are logged on to the email system.

Facsimile

GLOSSARY TERM
Facsimile (fax)

Facsimile (fax) machines work by making a digital copy of an image or text which is fed into the machine. This image is then transmitted to another fax machine via a telephone line. The receiving fax then prints an image based

on reconstructing the signals coming in via the telephone line. A fax machine is made up of a printer and an optical scanner. The advantages of modern fax machines include their ability to scan, print and copy documents as well as perform their fax function. Fax machines can transmit drawings and handwritten documents very accurately.

Fax documents can only be sent to one location at a time. Compare this to email where many people can be sent the same email at the push of a button. Another disadvantage of using a fax machine is that there may be a loss of quality during the transmission of a document. The copy of the document received is dependent on the original and will be of poor quality if the original is of poor quality.

Some of the disadvantages of using fax machines:

● Fax machines must be connected to a telephone line. Most offices have a dedicated fax line so that incoming faxes are not interrupted because of telephone calls.

● Most fax machines operate in black and white and produce hard copies of documents.

● They are expensive to buy.

● The running costs include toner cartridges for printing, electricity charges and the cost of telephone calls every time a fax is sent.

● If the receiving fax machine is not free to receive the document, it will have to be sent again.

■ Collaborating using communications technologies

Communications technologies provide a method for people to communicate instantly regardless of where they are in the world. They have changed the way we communicate and our expectations of the speed of reply. New technologies have shaped the way in which we communicate.

Voice over Internet Protocol (VoIP)

This technology allows users to make telephone calls over the internet. Users can download VoIP software and buy a telephone or headset which will allow them to make a telephone call. Calls can be made from a PC to a normal phone or from PC to PC. This is much cheaper than using a telephone company as users are making use of their broadband connection.

Skype is one example of a company which supports VoIP. Users of Skype can also make video calls if they have the correct equipment – that is a computer, microphone, broadband connection and a webcam.

Video conferencing

GLOSSARY TERM
Video conferencing

Video conferencing involves using the internet to transmit pictures and sound between computers. Video conferencing can be done by a single user on a desktop PC using a webcam or using specialist equipment with a group of users in a meeting room.

Transmitting pictures and sound together requires a communications line with high bandwidth. Normally a high-speed telecommunications line is used, such as broadband or ISDN. If the communications line is low bandwidth, images and sounds will not arrive together and the overall quality of the video will be poor.

In order to be able to video conference the following equipment is required:

● a video camera or webcam to transmit pictures

● microphone and sound system to transmit and receive sound

● a screen to view other participants

● a high bandwidth telecommunications line

● **video-conferencing** software.

Note that the video camera/webcam, microphone and computer can be replaced by a purpose-built video-conferencing system. The camera position, sound, view mode and number of connecting devices can be controlled by the user. These systems are expensive but have been installed in many schools, providing a portable solution to video conferencing. Only the device, a screen and a network point are required.

This technology allows people to see and interact with each other in real time at a personal level.

Many global organisations use video conferencing to enable people based in different locations to meet without travelling. This means that face-to-face meetings can be held with individuals from different points on the globe. The company saves money on travel and the workers can meet without the inconvenience of travel.

Advantages	Disadvantages
• Collaborate with team members without having to leave your desk. • Collaborate with people in the company and those from other companies. • Visual and audio contact means more realistic meetings. • Full multimedia presentations by using the application sharing tool. • Meetings can be set up on demand by connecting up to the videolink. • No travel costs for the company. • No travel time for the employee.	• High cost for initial set-up. • Specialist training may be required to make use of a purpose-built VC system. • Network performance may be poor when VC is in operation. • A high bandwidth is required to ensure good performance.

Video conferencing (VC) is being used more and more in schools. Some schools provide A-level subjects via a videolink to a tutor. The pupil and tutor log on together once a week and they communicate via email at other times. This allows pupils to study subjects that their school does not provide. VC links with experts in a variety of fields are set up so that pupils can question them directly. Pupils have the opportunity to share experiences with children from different parts of the country or the world. Sometimes universities teach students at different campuses who study the same courses using video conferencing.

Instant messaging

Instant messaging allows users to use text to communicate instantly with each other. When a user types a message, all of the users logged in can see the message instantly.

Bulletin boards

These provide text-based messaging but it is not instant or interactive. A user will log on to a bulletin board and 'post' a message. It may be a few hours or days before a reply is posted onto the bulletin board.

Internet services

The internet has evolved and now provides a wide range of services for work and leisure activities. Our lifestyle and the way we work has been transformed through services such as online shopping and banking, social networking and the ability to stream sound and video. These will be discussed in greater detail in the next section.

What you will learn in this section

In this section you will learn about applications of ICT (including electronic monetary processing, billing, virtual reality and simulation, computer control and data logging, education) and implications of using ICT (employment, leisure, health and safety, legal and environmental)

Acronyms:

- ADC
- ATM
- CAL
- CRT
- DAC

- EAN
- EFTPOS
- ELF
- EPOS
- HMD

- ICC
- MIDI
- PDA
- PIN
- POS

- RSI
- SET
- VLE
- WAN

Keywords:

- Analogue
- Batch processing
- Check digit
- Chip and pin
- Computer control
- Data collection
- Data controller
- Data logging
- Data subject

- Digital certificate
- Digital signature
- E-commerce
- Feedback
- Hacker
- Information Commissioner
- Interactive TV
- Intranet
- Magnetic stripe

- Master file
- Modelling
- Multimedia
- Podcast
- Sensor
- Simulation
- Smart card
- Software piracy
- Telepresence
- Teleworking

- Transaction file
- Validation
- Verification
- Video-conferencing
- Virtual reality
- Virtual world
- Virus

▌ Electronic monetary processing applications

There are many reasons why retail outlets have made widespread use of ICT. They have to keep the shelves well stocked with goods for customers to purchase otherwise customers may shop in other stores. They need to reorder stock that is low, preferably automatically, so that customers can always choose from the full range of goods. Customers get frustrated when shops run out of stock. Shop managers need to use computers to assist in deciding which goods are selling well and which goods are not selling well.

This means they can offer product promotions on the goods that do not sell well and also make sure that those goods that do sell well are always in stock. Some shops also like to offer customers loyalty cards to offer them rewards and at the same time track their shopping habits.

No matter whether a shop is small or large the manager needs to calculate what price to sell goods at and what profit can be made. Generally computers are very good at keeping track of information to assist managers and shop staff in decision making. The following points summarise why shops use computers:

- to assist in stock control
- to order new stock
- to calculate profit margins
- to assist managers in decision making
- to reward and track customer shopping habits.

EFTPOS systems in shops

An EFTPOS (Electronic Funds Transfer Point of Sale) terminal in a shop is a checkout connected to a computer with a barcode reader, and a **chip and PIN** terminal which can transfer money from a customer's account using a credit/bank card to the shop's bank account.

Try to imagine large shops without an EFTPOS. This could mean that some activities would take a long time to carry out and even introduce the risk of human error into their information system. For example, if the price of a product changes, it means having to change the price ticket on individual products. This in turn could lead to the same product with different prices, or even all products with the wrong price. If we investigate further you will find other drawbacks in shops such as the checkout operator keying in the wrong price of a product at the checkout, leading to human error and resulting in either undercharging or overcharging a customer.

For managers, stock control would be difficult because it would mean having to record stock levels manually. There is no easy way of recording the stock levels as purchases are made. Some shops like to use loyalty cards to monitor customer spending habits in return for customer rewards. Without EFTPOS, keeping track of customer spending and shopping habits would be impossible.

Some customers like to pay for their goods using credit/debit cards and if the shop did not have chip and PIN technology, purchases using credit cards and debit cards would be difficult, as the shop could not automatically check customer details, leading to increased security risks.

To summarise, the disadvantages to a shop without EFTPOS are:

- difficulty changing the price of a product
- increased risk of human error at the checkout

GLOSSARY TERM
Chip and PIN

- difficulty in carrying out stock-control activities
- difficulty of monitoring customer spending habits
- increased security risks of accepting customer credit/debit cards.

When using EFTPOS systems shops can overcome these problems and many more. Shops can make use of barcode readers to record stock purchases, to check the price of a product, to allow customers to 'self scan' as they shop and to allow staff to check stock using shelf-edge labels. These shops can also use **magnetic stripe** readers to automatically accept credit/debit card purchases and to allow customers to make use of loyalty cards. Using the computer system also allows for immediate updating of stock records, ordering new stock and assisting managers in making decisions.

> GLOSSARY TERM
> Magnetic stripe

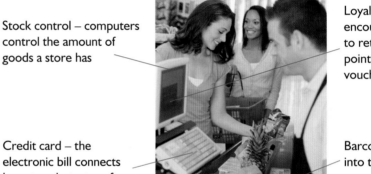

Stock control – computers control the amount of goods a store has

Loyalty card – encourage customers to return by awarding points, gifts and vouchers

Credit card – the electronic bill connects by networks to transfer money from bank accounts

Barcode is scanned into the computer

■ Components of a typical EFTPOS system

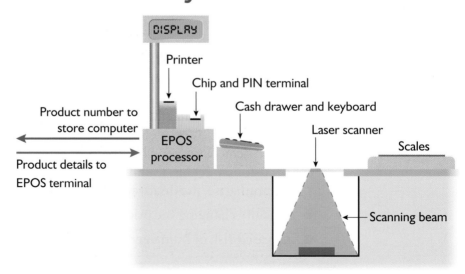

DISPLAY

Printer

Chip and PIN terminal

Cash drawer and keyboard

Laser scanner

Scales

Product number to store computer

Product details to EPOS terminal

EPOS processor

Scanning beam

Barcode readers

GLOSSARY TERM
Check digit

When products are delivered to a shop the manufacturer includes a barcode as part of the package. The bar codes are unique for each product and are registered under a European article numbering (EAN) system. Also, shops that supply their own products, such as fresh provisions, will use their own in-house barcode system. Each product contains a unique barcode. The information on a typical barcode includes a product code, manufacturer code, country of origin and a **check digit**. The layout of a typical barcode is:

The first two digits identify the country where the product was made →

The next five digits identify the manufacturer of the product

50 01935 01432 3 ←

The next five digits are the product code

The last digit is the check digit

When barcodes are created, digits are coded as a series of light and dark vertical bars of varying width. Although barcodes are not readable to us, such that we cannot determine a product from its barcode, the rate of accuracy from the barcode reader at the checkout is very high. The barcode can be read by a hand-held or a fixed laser scanner (normally at checkouts in supermarkets). The barcode reader uses laser beam light to read and enter the code details automatically. When a barcode (remember all barcodes are unique) is scanned, it is matched with a record held on the shop's computer system, where other data can be retrieved such as a product description and a price, which will allow the customer to receive an itemised receipt and also assist the checkout operator in verifying the scanned details. If a barcode is damaged, it cannot be read but it can still be keyed in by human operators.

Barcode scanning at a typical supermarket checkout

Each time a barcode is scanned at an EFTPOS terminal the following activities occur:

- The barcode scanner reads the barcode on the product.
- The barcode is sent to the computer (containing the stock database) by the EFTPOS terminal.
- The computer uses the barcode to search the stock file looking for a matching product.
- When the product is found, the product price and product description are sent back to the EFTPOS terminal.

- The branch computer updates the stock level for the product to show that one (or more) has been sold.
- The product price and description are displayed at the EFTPOS terminal and printed on a receipt.
- If a scanned barcode cannot be matched with any item in the stock file, an error message is displayed or a beep is heard through the speakers.

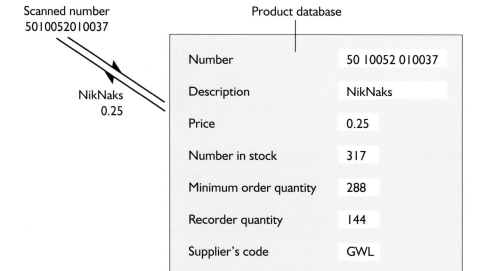

Product is scanned and barcode is matched with an entry from the product database

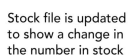

Stock file is updated to show a change in the number in stock

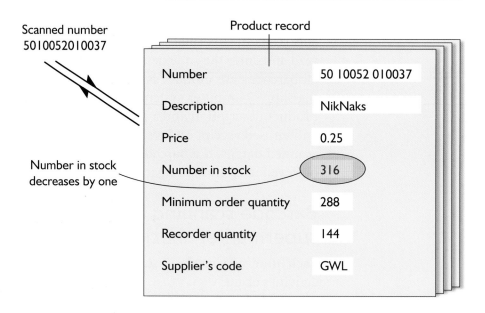

Advantages and disadvantages of EFTPOS

Advantages of EFTPOS to the customer:

✔ Less chance of theft because no cash is used.

✔ More secure when transferring large sums of money.

✔ Customers using debit/switch cards can also obtain cash at the checkout.

✔ Some customers feel they have more personal security if they don't have to carry large amounts of cash in their wallet/purse.

✔ Changing money into other currencies when abroad is not an issue.

Disadvantages of EFTPOS to the customer:

✘ Some people don't have bank accounts or prefer to use cash.

✘ Customers may have to pay a fee for each transaction.

✘ Cards are not practical for buying small items.

✘ It can become too convenient for unplanned or impulse buying, leaving the customer in serious debt.

✘ Customers are anxious about card fraud and may become reluctant to use EFTPOS.

Advantages of EFTPOS to the vendor:

✔ Payment into the shop bank account is guaranteed as long as the transactions are properly authorised.

✔ Cash must be manually counted by the cashier at the POS and counted again when the cashier finishes their shifts. This can lead to human error.

✔ Less paperwork for the shop to process as fewer cheques or less cash to pay into their bank.

✔ Improved security because less cash is held in the stores.

✔ Reduced concerns with forged money.

✔ The shop collects less cash so there is a reduced chance of theft.

✔ If the money is deposited immediately into the shop bank account, they may receive more interest.

Disadvantages of EFTPOS to the vendor:

✔ Shops are charged a percentage fee by the credit/debit card companies for each transaction which can lead to a decrease in profit.

✔ Initial set-up costs – the systems are expensive to install.

✔ System failures (part or whole) can cause major problems.

✔ If the wrong product price has been programmed into the computer, everyone buying it will be charged the wrong price.

Automatic teller machines (ATM)

Sometimes we refer to these loosely as 'hole in the wall' machines. Each bank operates and maintains their own network of ATMs. These networks are referred to as wide area networks (WAN). ATMs are normally located outside each main branch of a bank. Nowadays they are also found in large shopping centres and even in large supermarkets. They allow a customer to gain access to their account 24 hours a day, 7 days a week. In other words they never close. ATMs allow an increasing range of activities to take place, such as:

- withdrawing cash (with or without a receipt)
- ordering a bank statement
- ordering a new chequebook
- obtaining an account balance
- printing a mini-statement (usually the most recent transactions)
- lodging bank cheques
- informing customers of new banking services.

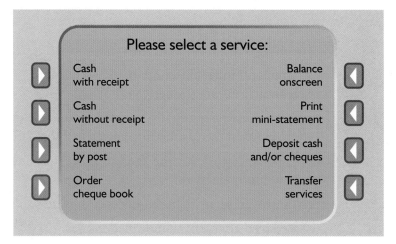

Operation of an ATM

To use an ATM the person needs a bank/credit card normally containing a magnetic stripe and a microchip. Information about the customer is stored such as:

- cardholder account number
- PIN – which is encoded onto the card for security reasons
- bank sort code
- cardholder withdrawal limit
- amount withdrawn so far that day
- maximum amount that can be withdrawn in a day.

When the bank card is inserted into the machine, the ATM automatically reads the customer account number embedded in the card. The ATM then becomes interactive by asking the customer a number of questions and responds to the customer's answers. It normally asks the customer to enter their personal identification number (PIN). This is a form of security designed to protect customer details against unauthorised access. To increase security, the customer may only be given a limited number of attempts to enter their PIN correctly (usually three). After the PIN is entered a number of options are given to the customer. If the PIN is incorrect the customer is asked to rekey their details.

If the PIN is correct, they are offered an on-screen menu with a number of choices. When the person uses an ATM that does not belong to their bank, the number of choices will be limited to only cash withdrawal with or without a receipt. On the other hand, when the person uses an ATM belonging to their bank, the number of choices is more extensive such as printed statements and balance enquiries.

When a person wishes to withdraw cash, a further check is made to ensure they have sufficient funds in their account at that time and that they have not exceeded their daily withdrawal limit. When cash is withdrawn, the customer account is usually updated immediately.

This is where the customer inserts the plastic card. The card must be inserted the right way round.

The customer is given step-by-step instructions on how to operate the cash dispensing machine.

This is the VDU screen where messages appear, such as 'Enter PIN number'. The screen gives instructions to the customer.

From here, the amount of money the customer has keyed in is released.

The keyboard (input device). The customer types information in here, including their secret number (PIN).

There are many advantages for both the customer and the bank of using an ATM machine:

✔ Banks need fewer employees behind counters, as there are fewer customers withdrawing cash hence reduction in staff wages.

✔ Customers have access to their accounts 24 hours a day and 7 days a week.

✔ This system makes it impossible for a customer to withdraw cash from their account unless they have sufficient funds.

✔ There is no need for customers to carry large amounts of cash, as ATMs are widely available, hence less theft.

✔ Using a PIN helps the bank deal with fraud.

✔ People can use ATMs that don't belong to their bank, which provides greater access.

✔ Customers do not have to live close to their bank.

Chip and PIN

Microchip

Mybank plc   VISA

4321 4687 3457 3336

Valid 02/01   Exp 02/03 V
MR M FOSTER-SMITH

GLOSSARY TERM
Smart card

The **smart card** was designed to replace the magnetic stripe. Although the plastic card is similar in size, it now contains a tiny embedded microchip. In a technical sense, it is referred to as an integrated chip card (ICC).

The microchip can store more data than a typical magnetic stripe. Banks and retailers have replaced magnetic stripe readers with smartcard technology, where credit/debit cards contain an embedded microchip and are authenticated automatically using a PIN. When a customer wishes to pay for goods they insert the card into a chip and PIN terminal. This will access the chip on the card allowing the customer to enter their 4-digit PIN, which is checked against the PIN stored on the card; if the two match, the transaction can then be completed, otherwise the transaction will be aborted. With the introduction of wireless technology came a wireless chip and PIN terminal, which means the customer feels safer as their card is never out of their sight. The terminal can be brought to the customer and they can insert their card, complete their transaction and then remove their card so it can not be copied or used for unauthorised transactions. This technology is also used in mobile phones (SIM card) and in satellite TV receivers to allow customers to access to television programmes they have subscribed to.

Online banking

As well as the flexibility of using the ATM, customers can access their bank account using the bank's secure website. This is known as online banking. Most banks allow this provided the customer registers with the bank for it. It involves the customer logging on to the website and entering their username and password. The customer may then be asked for certain verification data before being allowed to view the account details. Once online, customers can:

Welcome to Online Banking

Statements

Current-123

Statements
View up to 100 transactions on your accounts

- view recent transactions
- pay bills online from a list of approved billers
- transfer money from one account to another
- set up regular payments
- view related credit card balances
- search for particular transactions

- add or delete accounts from the online account (this is not equivalent to opening or closing accounts)
- view bank statements online.

What are the advantages of banking like this?

Advantages for the customer:

- ✔ The customer does not have to visit the bank. Transactions can be done at home, work or on the move using mobile technology like an iPhone.
- ✔ The website is available 24/7 and the customer is not concerned about opening or closing times.
- ✔ The website is available from anywhere in the world, even if the bank does not have branches in that country.
- ✔ Transactions made online can be transferred faster than some ATM and face-to-face transactions.

Advantages for the bank:

- ✔ Fewer branches and staff are required as customers do not need to visit the bank as often.
- ✔ Banks can have 'online only' products such as e-statements, which save on paper and post for them.
- ✔ A broader customer base may be made available through the website.

What are the concerns of banking like this?

Concerns for the customer:

- ✘ Customers may not have the necessary technology or equipment.
- ✘ Customers may not have the necessary skills to navigate the internet.
- ✘ Customers may not be confident and may worry about transactions not going through.
- ✘ Customers may worry about fraud and their details being stolen.

Concerns for the bank:

- ✘ The storage of so much personal data requires high-level security to prevent it being stolen.
- ✘ Specially trained staff will be required to maintain the website.
- ✘ As technology changes security procedures will have to be reviewed and updated.
- ✘ There is no direct contact with the customer therefore customer service cannot be monitored directly.

■ Utility billing applications

Electricity, telephone and gas bills are often described as utility bills. Some of these bills are sent on a monthly basis while others are sent on a quarterly basis (every three months). Although each household or customer may only receive one bill, if you consider all bills collectively you will realise that there is a huge volume of data processed. Large billing applications use powerful computer systems to process their data. The mode of computer processing for utility bills is described as **batch processing**.

GLOSSARY TERM
Batch processing

Batch processing

Batch processing involves collecting groups (or batches) of similar data over a period of time and inputting to a computer system. These batches of data are then processed collectively without human intervention or involvement. The idea behind this method of processing is to allow data to be collected over a period of time (such as a day/week/month) and then all the processing can be done at a convenient time (such as night time or at the weekend). Due to the huge amount of data it normally takes a long time for the computer to process the data.

This means the computer system cannot be used for any other activity while batch processing is taking place. Therefore, if the computer is tied up at night time, it can be available for another activity during the day, such as an enquiry system to answer customer billing queries. Batch processing only suits certain application types where data does not require immediate processing. It also suits applications with high volumes of data.

Applications that make use of batch processing include:

● electricity billing systems

● telephone billing systems

● gas billing systems

● producing a weekly/monthly payroll of a large organisation.

To illustrate batch processing we will consider a typical electricity billing system that is used to collect meter readings from your home and produce customer bills for electricity usage.

From previous bills the computer has almost all the information required to produce the next bill such as customer account number, customer name, address details, last meter reading, amount of electricity used over the past number of quarters and so on. This type of information does not change in the short term (from one billing period to the next) and is stored in the customer **master file**.

GLOSSARY TERMS
Master file
Data collection

Data collection forms in the form of pre-printed meter reading cards are produced for each customer, including their personal details such as their address, and are completed by an employee visiting each address. As an alternative to meter cards some companies use hand-held terminals to enter meter readings. The new information required to produce the bill is the current meter reading.

At the end of each day the meter reading cards are returned or the data from the hand-held terminals is downloaded, prepared for batch processing and details entered into the computer system as a batch at a convenient time. Only the customer account number and the meter reading are entered into the computer and a **transaction file** (or a temporary file) is created.

Using the customer account number on the transaction file and the same customer account number on the master file, records are matched to allow other customer details to be retrieved (such as customer name and address) and the calculation of the bills takes place.

The number of units used is normally calculated by subtracting the previous reading from the present reading. The bill can be calculated by multiplying the number of units used by the price per unit.

> **GLOSSARY TERM**
> Transaction file

Stages in producing the electricity bills

1 Meters are read by the meter reader and recorded onto the customer data collection form.

2 Customer meter readings are then placed together as batches.

3 These are then entered into the computer system.

4 The data is then checked, using data **verification** and data **validation** techniques.

5 At this stage any errors are notified such as the wrong number of digits in the customer account number and an error report is produced.

6 The valid data is then used to create a transaction file.

7 The transaction file is then sorted into the same order as the master file using the key field, which is normally the customer account number.

8 The sorted transaction file is stored and will be used to allow the matching of transaction records easily with master file records.

9 Both the master file and the transaction file are used to calculate and print customer bills.

10 The details on the transaction file are used to update the master file and this is saved as a new master file.

11 Customers are then sent their bill.

12 The new master file will be used to calculate the bill in the next quarter and the process continues.

> **GLOSSARY TERMS**
> Verification
> Validation

■ Virtual reality and simulation

> **GLOSSARY TERMS**
> Virtual reality
> Simulation

A **virtual reality** system enables a person to move through and react within a 'real' environment simulated by a computer. The **simulation** is a computer program that models a real-life situation. This involves putting values into a computer model to see how it behaves in different environments.

Car manufacturers use simulations during the design stage to test cars to see what happens when they crash. Architects use these systems to design new buildings and simulate strong winds or an earthquake to see how a shopping centre would react before it is built. Virtual reality and simulation assists designers before the real product is developed.

Simulations and virtual reality on computer systems are normally designed with computer-controlled graphics to generate realistic scenes with which the user can fully interact. These worlds are created using 3D **modelling** techniques. The person is given the impression that they are actually in the real-world environment created by the computer (**virtual world**). This is done by using specialised devices to help stimulate a range of the user's senses such as sight, sound and smell.

Devices used in virtual reality include stereoscopic helmets (HMD – head-mounted device) to allow 3D visual hearing, hand gloves for touch sensations to control the model and tracking devices or joysticks to navigate around the environment.

Examples of applications that use virtual reality include:

- training airline pilots
- training medical professionals
- gaming.

GLOSSARY TERMS
Modelling
Virtual world

Training airline pilots

Training a pilot to fly an aeroplane can be both dangerous and expensive. If a pilot were trained entirely using a real aeroplane, it would be expensive in terms of fuel costs and loss of possible air fares by taking a plane out of service. More importantly if the pilot makes a mistake, the plane may crash resulting in a loss of life. Therefore aircraft simulators can save money and are much safer to use in training new pilots. They also give the pilot an experience of a range of real environments.

Although the simulator does not look like an aeroplane in its physical appearance, it is a full size replica of a typical cockpit, but never leaves the ground. Computer screens replace the windows of the cockpit. The simulator is programmed to give trainee pilots all the experiences they may or may not encounter in the air. It is also used to allow for continuous training of experienced pilots. These experiences are based on real-life possibilities and include:

- turbulence, thunderstorms, snowstorms
- landing a plane on an icy runway
- flying a plane with only one engine working
- different types of faults on the plane to give the pilot the experience of dealing with emergencies
- flying a plane in thick fog
- landing at different airports around the world using high-quality graphics showing the layout of runways and the surrounding environment.

It creates the illusion of real flying using real airports. The inputs to the system will be the control devices in the cockpit and a computer would monitor the settings of these. All the pilot's actions would be recorded by the computer system and would be used to provide **feedback** to the pilot to help plan their future training needs.

GLOSSARY TERM
Feedback

Training medical professionals

In the medical world, body scanners are available to collect large amounts of data about a person's internal system and biological makeup. A computer can be used to produce a 3D model of the whole or part of the body, creating a 'virtual patient'.

This can be useful as it allows a surgeon to investigate a person's medical problem in detail before carrying out surgery. Surgeons can then plan and practise (simulate) a particular operation on the virtual patient in order to learn how to do this operation, before actually carrying it out on the real patient. This is sometimes known as **telepresence**. The surgeon can also consult with other specialists around the world by using computer technology such as video conferencing.

GLOSSARY TERM
Telepresence

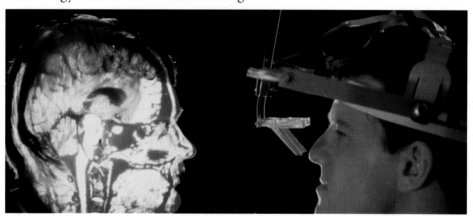

Another use of virtual reality in medicine is in the area of training medical students. An example of this would be to give the medical students an experience of what it is like to be exhausted from a medical illness such as undergoing chemotherapy to cure cancer. This would involve the medical student being placed on a specially designed chair with foot pedals and making use of a HMD. Using virtual reality they are placed into a virtual house, where they can see the layout of the house through the headset.

The computer makes the student carry out relatively simple tasks through simulations. An example could be the computer ringing the front door bell making the student move the pedals to move from a room to answer the front door. The pedals are designed to be difficult to move, giving the impression of how difficult it is for a patient to do this simple task. The image on the headset can also be continuously altered with different levels of vision from good vision to blurred vision, giving the impression of dizziness. This makes the new doctor aware of the problems patients will have.

Gaming

Many computer games are designed with virtual reality.

For example, when you play a football game on a computer, you are simulating a real game such as a World Cup final. On the other hand, you can also have simulations which do not involve a computer, such as Monopoly for buying and selling real properties.

Computer games involve the designer programming a set of rules (model) for the user to follow. These rules could define a character in a game including features such as: the appearance of a character, how fast the character can run, how high the character can jump and how strong the character is. If weapons are involved, more rules are included defining the range of weapons to be used, the range of fire of each weapon and the kinds of terrain the game is set on.

Sometimes these game simulations are realistic, such as Formula One car racing games using real racing circuits. The game works by responding to inputs from the user devices including the throttle, the gears and the steering wheel. The user is given the impression of driving a real car including the visuals, sound effects and the sensation of acceleration.

More games involving virtual reality are appearing in amusement arcades, such as using skis on a ski game to give the user a more realistic experience. Advancements in technology have made gaming more realistic, such as surround sound systems and the development of 3D high-definition televisions. Using internet technology users can now play a game against each other from the comfort of their own homes, which may not even be in the same countries.

Mobile phones are also used to play games which have been downloaded from the provider network or the internet.

Basically anywhere that there is a processor and a screen a game can be played. ICT is used in the games industry to create highly specialised games which have 3D graphic effects and realistic sound and video. Games are now created which demand highly specified hardware to support them.

Advances in graphics, processing power, game design and complexity mean that the most up-to-date games make games designed a few years ago look simplistic in comparison. Technology has facilitated the growth in user expectations with regard to games. Young people are now accustomed to using highly interactive, 3D, action-packed games. As our expectations grow, the games industry is under pressure to meet them with more impressive gaming environments.

Computer gaming is a top leisure activity and many say that the skills gained from playing games can be transferred to others areas of education and training. Games motivate many people to succeed in attaining performance levels, for this reason gaming technologies and techniques are being used to create more effective learning materials for schools and colleges.

■ Computer control and data logging

Sensors and data logging

GLOSSARY TERMS
Sensor
Data logging

A **sensor** is an input device, which can be used to measure almost any physical quantity. Different types of sensors are used to measure different physical quantities. Light sensors can measure light intensity, temperature sensors can measure temperature changes, and sound sensors can measure the level of noise. In other words, sensors measure changes in environmental conditions. Sensors are used in **data logging** to collect data at regular time intervals automatically.

Data logging involves the automatic capture and storage of data, without human intervention. A computer normally collects data at regular time intervals depending on the requirements of the application, without the need for human supervision. This can happen twenty-four hours a day, seven days a week continuously. The use of computers to log data is more accurate, and in some cases safer than a human collecting data. Data can be stored over a period of time and then analysed by special/dedicated software. Since physical quantities such as temperature and light are continuously varying quantities, they are described as **analogue** signals, whereas computers can only process digital signals. Therefore there needs to be some form of analogue to digital conversion. The diagram below illustrates why light is an analogue signal.

GLOSSARY TERM
Analogue

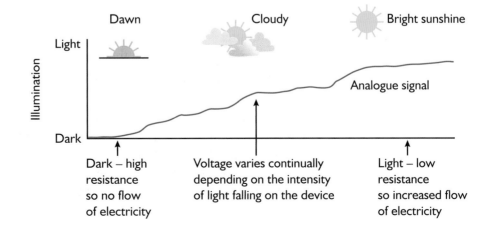

Analogue to digital conversion

An interface, or electrical device, called an analogue to digital converter (ADC) is used to change analogue data into digital data. The analogue data is best described as a varying voltage, whereas the digital signal is best described as a digital/binary pulse. To allow computers to be used in data-logging applications, the ADC is connected between the sensor and the computer. The ADC is built into the device and connected via a port using a cable.

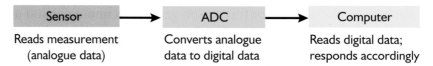

Sensor	ADC	Computer
Reads measurement (analogue data)	Converts analogue data to digital data	Reads digital data; responds accordingly

The table below illustrates the difference between an analogue and digital signal.

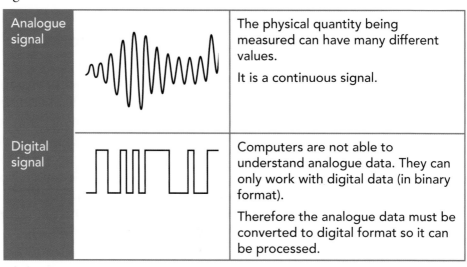

Analogue signal		The physical quantity being measured can have many different values. It is a continuous signal.
Digital signal		Computers are not able to understand analogue data. They can only work with digital data (in binary format). Therefore the analogue data must be converted to digital format so it can be processed.

The principle of feedback

Computer systems that can monitor their own activity through controlling the outputs according to the inputs, are said to have feedback.

Feedback is an important concept in **computer control**. To illustrate feedback we will consider a home heating system, which uses a temperature sensor to measure room temperature at regular intervals and this data is fed into the computer. When the computer processes the data, one of two possible outputs will occur, either to turn the heating on or turn the heating off.

To summarise the diagram on the next page we can say if the temperature sensor says it is cold the heating is turned on. This will lead to a rise in temperature. When the temperature reaches a certain limit the sensor will communicate this data to the computer and the output will result in turning the heat off.

GLOSSARY TERM
Computer control

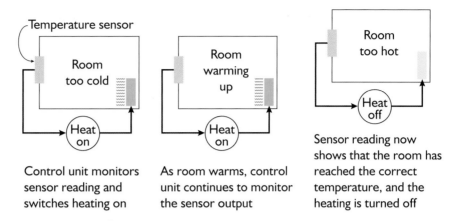

Control unit monitors sensor reading and switches heating on

As room warms, control unit continues to monitor the sensor output

Sensor reading now shows that the room has reached the correct temperature, and the heating is turned off

We will now examine how computer control is used in the following ICT applications:

- home control systems
- traffic control systems.

Home control systems

When a computer is used to control a device in your home by using a microprocessor which is inside the device, it is described as an 'embedded computer'. These devices include washing machines, burglar alarms, televisions, DVD players and microwave ovens to mention only some modern house appliances.

The embedded computer in each device will control the input and output devices attached to the device. Consider a typical automatic washing machine. When the user selects a washing program, the microprocessor carries out a pre-stored sequence of instructions. The microprocessor will carry out activities such as turning on and off switches for water intake and water outlet, the water heater to heat the water to a certain temperature, controlling the water pump and controlling the drum. To do all of these activities a number of sensors are used including water flow sensors, temperature sensors and door open/close sensors. During the washing cycle computer-controlled motors and pumps will also be used. Feedback is an important aspect to help monitor temperature settings and levels of water. The diagram below indicates some of the inputs, processes and outputs in a typical washing machine.

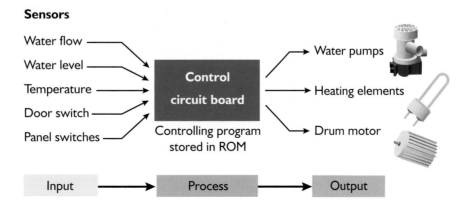

Computer systems in traffic control

These computer-controlled systems are mainly employed in large cities where traffic is a problem. The main aim of these systems is to keep traffic moving, particularly during rush hours (early morning/evening), to discourage speeding and to manage car parking. Computers are used in different aspects of traffic control such as traffic lights, car park management and vehicle speeding.

In cities, traffic lights are normally controlled at a central location. Each set of traffic lights can be programmed to vary in operation throughout the day. For example, a lot of traffic may arrive into the city in the morning, therefore the lights can be programmed to remain green on roads into a city for longer periods in the morning. Again in the evening, traffic lights out of the city can remain green for longer. The sequence during the rest of the day can also vary if the need arises. These systems are often called vehicle actuation systems. Feedback will help the computers to make decisions based on traffic flow.

Sensors can be placed on roads to detect and count the cars over a period of time.

This data is then sent back to the main computer, which in turn can send signals back to the lights that amend the timings of the light sequence. In the case of emergency vehicles such as fire engines, it would even be possible to ensure that the traffic lights are all green along its path.

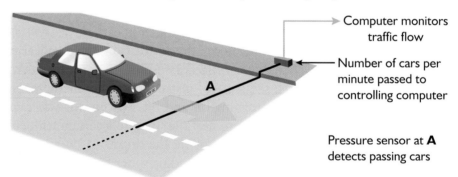

Computer monitors traffic flow

Number of cars per minute passed to controlling computer

Pressure sensor at **A** detects passing cars

Although most control of traffic lights in cities is centralised, each set of lights can also react automatically to local events such as people wishing to cross roads. By pressing a button, the local control box will allow the lights to be changed to red for a short period of time.

To assist in maintenance, traffic lights can be monitored, allowing faults to be detected automatically leading to prompt repairs.

In the area of car park management, computer-controlled systems can direct cars around a city to those car parks with available space. The system can calculate the number of vehicles entering and leaving a car park at regular time intervals, and then display on large electronic signposts, the number of empty spaces in a named car park. Sensors are used to automatically log each car on entry and exit.

As speed becomes more of an issue on our roads, police forces are making greater use of computer technology to sense and record the speeds of individual cars.

Camera   Sensor

This computer-controlled system consists of sensors, which are capable of detecting car speeds, and, if the speed is excessive, a camera that can automatically take a photograph of the car including registration number, speed, location and the time and date of incident. All these details can be superimposed onto the photograph. Using the registration plate the owner can easily be detected and a copy of the photo sent, with a fine and police follow up. The data logged by each camera can also be analysed to produce data about those roads where speeding is a problem. Special sensors built into traffic lights can also detect cars jumping or driving through red traffic lights.

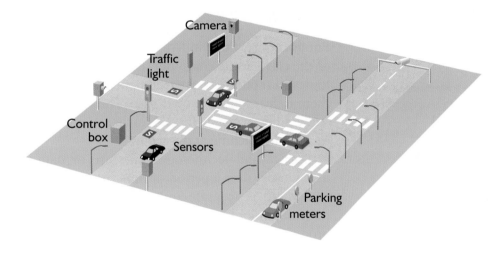

The application of ICT in education

The twenty-first century classroom makes use of many aspects of technology to enhance and assist with teaching and learning. Computers in classrooms can provide pupils with a wide variety of experiences and give the class teacher a sophisticated teaching tool.

Pupils can use these tools to create high-quality and well-presented homework, projects and coursework. Teachers can use them to develop better-quality teaching materials.

Interactive subject-specific learning materials are available using **multimedia** software to include on-screen moving pictures and sounds. Pupils can watch and learn within a stimulating environment. Special subject-specific packages such as Geometry Inventor for mathematics and online website links all contribute to enriching the classroom experience.

GLOSSARY TERM
Multimedia

A screen from the CAL package 'Everyone's a winner' which teaches students about the technicalities of soccer in preparation for a graded examination in PE

GLOSSARY TERM
Podcast

Pupils can use these individually while the teacher is working with the rest of the class. Some computer-assisted learning (CAL) packages can teach a topic in a multimedia environment. They can then assess students and allow them to learn at their own pace. These packages can automatically record student performance for the teacher to monitor. **Podcast**s can also be used to assist in teaching and learning.

Science and technology make use of data-logging equipment which uses sensors over a period of time to collect data. Data recorded using this equipment is accurate and can be processed by a computer to produce information or to draw graphs. CD writers and MIDI assist in learning and producing music, and DVD technology provides students with interactive films and real-life learning situations.

A data projector can project the computer screen on to a large whiteboard. It makes a single computer into a whole-class teaching tool. This lets all of the students see a particular demonstration at once.

Using a data projector and an interactive whiteboard, pupils can interact with the computer by pressing or clicking on the board. This allows students to collaborate on projects in a single group. The main advantages of using interactive whiteboards in the classroom include:

● allowing pupils to absorb information more easily.

● allowing pupils to participate in group discussions by freeing them from note taking.

● allowing pupils to work collaboratively around a shared task/work area.

● rapid learner feedback when used for whole-class interactive testing of understanding.

Technology can assist students with special educational needs or learning difficulties. There are accessibility tools built into many school networks. Examples of these are:

● Magnifier – magnifies text so that sight-impaired students can read it.

● On-screen keyboard – gives students with low mobility a keyboard on screen. Letters can be typed by simply placing the cursor over the letter.

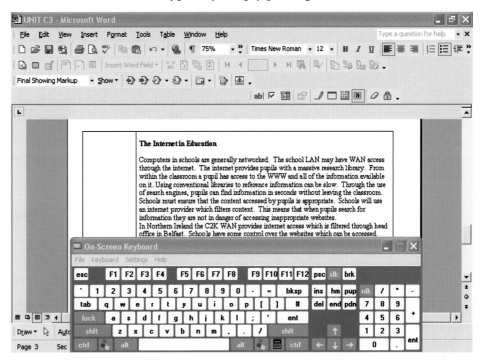

The on-screen keyboard which can be used with Windows applications.

● Voice recognition software – can be trained to understand the spoken word. These sounds are spoken into a microphone and the computer can be operated by speaking instead of using the mouse or keyboard.

● Braille keyboards and printers can also be incorporated to assist blind students in the use of technology.

● Talking word processors can help students with learning difficulties to produce error-free documents.

- Concept keyboards and trackerball mouse devices can help those with limited mobility to manipulate the hardware and software.

- Highly sophisticated movement sensors, which can sense eye or muscle movement, can allow people with little or no mobility to make use of a computer.

The internet in education

Computers in schools are generally networked. The school LAN may have WAN access through the internet. The internet provides pupils with a massive research library. From within the classroom a pupil has access to the WWW and all of the information available on it. Using conventional libraries to reference information can be slow. Through the use of search engines, pupils can find information in seconds without leaving the classroom. Schools must ensure that the content accessed by pupils is appropriate. Schools will use an internet provider which filters content. This means that when pupils search for information they are not in danger of accessing inappropriate websites.

In Northern Ireland the C2K WAN provides internet access which is filtered through head office in Belfast. Schools have some control over the websites which can be accessed. For example, students and staff can be prevented from accessing internet shopping or web email such as Yahoo! mail or Hotmail. This is done within the school by the C2K administrator or the C2K manager. Filtering is a means of controlling what a pupil can access on the web and it works by using word-recognition techniques and by pixel analysis on graphics or simply by disallowing a known web address.

■ Communication technologies in education

The use of communications technologies provides new opportunities for distance learning. Students and teachers can use email as a means of communicating. **Video conferencing** allows students to take part in two-way visual communication. The possibilities for this type of technology are endless.

GLOSSARY TERM
Video conferencing

Schools could video conference with companies or other schools on opposite sides on the world. On a smaller scale, schools which are remotely situated could video conference with larger schools who might share their teachers and resources. Students can exchange ideas interactively and produce joint projects regardless of where their schools are located. Bulletin boards and controlled interactive text-based discussion (similar to chat rooms) are also successfully used to allow the school community to extend beyond the school itself.

E-portfolios are a new technology which will allow students to create and maintain an electronic collection of projects and personal data. This would free them from gathering paper-based evidence of coursework and personal achievements. An e-portfolio can be web based. A student can access it from school and home. A teacher can access it and assess the student's work online. Parents can become more informed about their child's progress by browsing the e-portfolio.

A Virtual Learning Environment (VLE) is a tool which is used in many schools and universities to deliver courses using some of the technologies outlined. The VLE also allows lecturers to assess student work and even tracks their 'attendance' record within the course itself.

One word which could encompass the use of all of these technologies in education is the term 'e-learning' (electronic learning). This is the use of these technologies to enhance the learning experience of every student. The use of communications technology in education means that students have access to resources and teachers on a more flexible basis. The boundaries between home and school or university are blurred. Collaboration and collegiality between students and teachers from different schools becomes possible. The main advantages of e-learning and VLEs are:

- there is organised central storage of an increasing number of digital resources

- staff and pupils can share resources for collaborative teaching and learning

- the incorporation of multimedia into lessons, providing different learning styles

- they allow for learning beyond the classroom with 24/7 individual access to the VLE, both in and out of school

- absent or ill students can access lessons

- personalised learning is offered with lessons tailored to individual pupil requirements

- they support the embedding of ICT in subject teaching.

ICT and employment

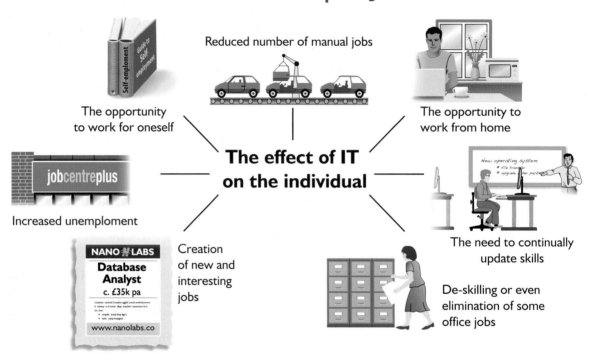

The opportunity to work for oneself

Reduced number of manual jobs

The opportunity to work from home

The effect of IT on the individual

Increased unemploment

Creation of new and interesting jobs

The need to continually update skills

De-skilling or even elimination of some office jobs

Information and communication technologies have been introduced in many aspects of working life. This has meant changes in the way we do our jobs. In manufacturing, for example, the introduction of robots means that the work of a number of workers is being done by a computer-controlled machine. In general, jobs which are highly repetitive and tedious for humans can now be carried out by a computer-controlled robot. Examples of ICT in the workplace include:

- Car manufacture – where paint spraying in car factories is now carried out by computer-controlled robots.

- Warehouse work – where stock is moved from one place to another using computer-controlled fork-lift trucks.

- Office workers make use of applications software packages to carry out administration tasks and use communications technologies to interact with fellow employees and customers.

Changes in work patterns

The change in technology used has led to changing work patterns for employees and their employers. Portable technology such as laptops and other mobile devices allow more people to carry out their work at home rather than at their employer's location. Employees can be contacted at any time using mobile telephones or PDAs. The working day is therefore extended and the boundaries between home and work become less defined. Employees can find it difficult to adjust to this environment.

Businesses who want to operate in the global marketplace must be available 24 hours a day because of the time difference between countries. This and the upsurge in 24-hour call centres has meant that employers are now using a 'global' workbase and employees from other countries. Local employees are also having to work in shifts which cover daytime and night-time hours.

The increased use of electronic mail has led to a greater proportion of the employee's day being set aside to read and answer emails.

Job displacement, retraining and opportunities

Many office jobs have been taken over by modern ICT systems. For example, there has been a reduction in clerical work, such as filing clerks, as organisations now use databases and spreadsheets to store and manage their data. Modern multimedia software allows users to produce professional documents with very little training. Because of this, workers feel that they are becoming de-skilled because their role in the workplace has changed.

In a changing technological work environment people require continuous training to enable them to carry out their job. In an office, for example, workers have to be trained as software is upgraded and new hardware is continuously replacing outdated hardware, such as a more modern digital telephone switchboard or a photocopying machine with more functionality. They have to learn the new skills necessary to operate the new equipment.

People need to be re-trained to take account of changing technology. In all areas of a person's working life there is a continual need to update skills. The nature and the type of jobs people are doing is always changing. This has led to lifelong learning courses resulting in employees having to attend training courses on a regular basis throughout their working lives.

New technologies have led to the creation of new jobs. In order to design and maintain ICT systems there is a need for programmers, software engineers, database administrators, network managers and ICT consultants. The World Wide Web and the growing number of websites has led to more web designers being required. The widespread use of electronic communication including mobile phone networks, digital television and wireless technology has led to a growth in employment opportunities, not least the need for ICT security experts. Most modern countries have encouraged ICT-related employment to help generate economic growth.

Teleworking

> **GLOSSARY TERMS**
> Teleworking
> Intranet

Teleworking is using ICT to work from home. The use of communications technology has made working from home much easier. Employees can stay in touch with the office through the use of the internet, email, video conferencing and hand-held devices such as PDAs. Employees can also log on to a company's **intranet** from home. People who work from home using ICT are called teleworkers or telecommuters.

As cities become more congested, both employers and employees are demanding an alternative way of working. This has been made possible with advances in communications technology and networks including wireless networks. It is common for telecommuters to spend a large part of their working time at home.

Advantages of teleworking

Cost	● Saves on travel cost and travel time to and from work for the employee. ● The employer is not liable for travel expenses.
Location	● The employee can live anywhere, there is no necessity to live within travelling distance of work. ● The employer can employ a more global workforce with the right skills regardless of where they live.
Flexibility	● The employee has flexible working hours and can carry out other activities such as child care. ● The employer is not restricted to 9–5pm working hours.
Overheads	● Organisations do not need to rent expensive city centre offices and pay heating and lighting costs.
Society	● The environment will benefit because there are fewer cars on the road, which will help with pollution and traffic congestion. ● Wealth is spread across a given country rather than concentrated in commuter belts near large cities.
Equality of opportunity	● Working from home will allow people with disabilities to carry out their jobs in an environment designed for them.

Disadvantages of teleworking

Social interaction	● Employees may feel isolated because of loss of social interaction and teamwork. ● Employees may not have a good understanding of the company's aims and vision.
Discipline	● Employees need an office or workroom at home, which may be difficult to find in a family home. ● Employees need to be disciplined to ensure that they distinguish between home and work activities. ● They need to work the required amount of time and complete tasks to deadlines. This could be made difficult by interruptions at home.
Monitoring	● Managers will find it more difficult to monitor employee activity and productivity since they are not in the office. ● Employees may be difficult to contact in an emergency.

GLOSSARY TERM
Hacker

■ The impact of ICT on leisure

Social networking

Social networking is using websites such as MySpace, Facebook and Twitter, which people can use to connect with others to share information such as photos, videos and personal messages. As the popularity of these social sites grows, so do the risks of using them. **Hacker**s and other criminals can follow the traffic with ease. To help with safety and security users should act responsibly by doing some of the following:

- Use care when you click hyperlinks that you receive in messages from your friends on your social website.

- Know exactly what you have uploaded about yourself. A common way that hackers break accounts is by clicking the 'Forgot your password?' link on the account login page. To break into your account, they search for the answers to your security questions which you may have on your profile.

- Don't always trust that a message is really from who it says it is from.

- Be selective about who you accept as a friend on a social network. Identity thieves might create fake profiles in order to get information from you.

- Choose your social network carefully as there are many of them available.

- Be careful about downloading extras on your site. Many social networking sites allow you to download free software, music and videos.

ICT in music and video

What is an MP3 player and how does it work?

Digital recordings of music are distributed on CD. Music files produced in this format are generally very large. The internet is fast becoming a major medium for the download of music both commercially and illegally. If music is to be downloaded in the same format as on CD it would take a long time and very fast internet connections would be required. MP3 is another audio file format for storing music files. It is a compressed format which makes the size of a music file up to 12 times smaller that a conventional music file on CD. This is achieved by eliminating frequencies and sounds on the soundtrack which the human ear cannot normally hear. Music files in MP3 format can be downloaded from the internet much quicker than music files in .wav or .aif format.

The development of MP3 technology means that more people are using the web to download music. Manufacturers have flooded the market with MP3 players, which are tiny in size and can hold thousands of songs. Users can download their favourite songs and store them on this tiny device. The songs can be overwritten again and again.

MP4 compression standards are now being introduced by the MPEG (Moving Pictures Expert Group). This is the compression standard relating not only to sound but to moving images and multimedia as well. MP4 players can play sound and pictures or movies.

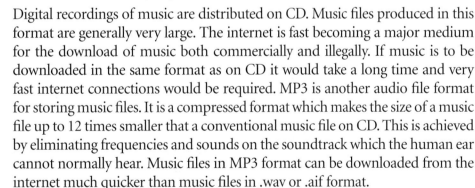

What is digital recording?

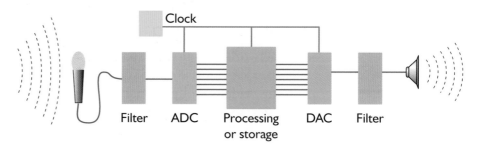

The components of a digital recording/playback system

Since the invention of CDs music has been recorded and stored digitally. Digital recording involves taking the analogue sounds produced when playing music and converting them into digital signals. This is done using an analogue to digital converter (ADC). It is the digital signals that are recorded onto the CD. When the music is played back, a digital to analogue converter (DAC) changes the digital signals to analogue and these signals are amplified and sent to speakers.

The two main aims of digital recording are:

● to produce a recording which is very similar to the original sound as it was played

● to ensure that the music sounds the same each time it is played.

Digital music can be recorded from many sources, it does not always have to be done using a microphone. MIDI keyboards can be plugged into a PC and music can be recorded directly from them. This music can be mixed with digital music from any source therefore making it a very versatile way of producing music. Music which has been digitally encoded onto a CD is highly durable and minor damage to the CD will have no impact on the sound produced.

Digital recording can be carried out successfully on a PC given the correct peripherals.

MIDI and sound effects

Musical Instrument Digital Interface or MIDI is a technology which allows musical instruments to be connected together or to a computer. Most MIDI keyboards can create sound from several instruments, for example flute, drums, violin and trumpet to name but a few. The notes or melodies composed are recorded as digital signals. These can be saved onto a computer or any digital storage medium. When they are loaded back onto the MIDI device it will play back the music which has been saved.

Digital music can be created by using the computer keyboard and mouse. Tracks made using different MIDI devices and the computer can be mixed together using computer software. This makes the creation of digital music using several different instruments easy for one person. The musician can record several different tracks using different instruments on the MIDI keyboard. These tracks can then be mixed to form a single track with several instruments being played at one time.

MIDI devices allow users to distort sound to produce sound effects. Notes played can be echoed, reverberated, lengthened or shortened. Most electronic instruments have their own sound effects built in. On a MIDI keyboard there are many sound effects such as bells, beeps, chimes, whistles and synthesizer functions allowing users to create their own sounds.

Because of the versatile nature of digital music, sound effects can be added to the music at a later stage to enhance or change the mood of the piece.

The advantages of using MIDI to produce music are:

- The sheet music can be generated automatically.
- The tempo, key and duration of the music can be changed easily.
- The instrument playing a particular section can be changed easily.
- Sound effects can be added after the music has been composed.
- Voice tracks can be integrated with the music.
- The music can be edited easily without having to re-write the whole piece again.
- Once produced the music can be played on any device which has digital audio facilities.
- Music can be produced by people who are not experts.

The use of digital technology has revolutionised the music industry. Production techniques have changed, the way in which music is sold has changed and the technology used to listen to music has become personalised and portable ensuring every person can listen to their own selection of music from wherever they wish.

The impact of ICT on the video industry

The first analogue video recorders captured pictures using video tape. Digital video (DV) cameras are now used to record moving pictures. DV is a method of recording movies in digital format onto a digital video tape. The movie can then be transferred directly onto a PC or Mac for editing and enhancing. This is done using either a USB cable connected to the DV-out port of the camera and the computer or by using firewire. Firewire is a special cable which permits the immediate transferral of digital video onto a computer.

A digital video camera can:

- take digital photographs directly onto DV tape or onto a memory stick for later download onto a computer
- be connected to a VHS recorder to download movie footage

- allow users to edit video footage and apply video effects using facilities on the camera
- be used as a video camera for video-conferencing.

Most DV cameras record onto a mini DV tape holding about one hour of video footage, around 11 GB of data. Some record onto small CD-R/RW or DVDs.

Analogue video recordings can be converted to digital recordings using a video digitiser. Digital videos produced in this way are not of the same high quality as those shot using a DV camera.

The falling cost of this technology means that more people are able to buy DV cameras. But it is the development of the DVD and video compression which has made the storage of digital movies much easier. Digital videos take up a large amount of storage space; a few minutes of video will take up 1 GB of storage space. In order to be edited the video must be transferred to the computer. Once edited it must be compressed before it is transferred onto a DVD which has a storage capacity of about 17 GB. A DVD player has a decoder which can uncompress data as we watch it. These advances in technology have resulted in the widespread use of DVDs and DVD players.

DVD technology has been used by the film industry in the distribution of films. All new movies are distributed on DVD. Movies on DVD have been compressed using MPEG 2 format and provide significant advantages for users.

The advantages of using DVD:

- The picture and sound is of a much higher quality. It is more like going to the cinema.
- DVDs have an on-screen menu allowing the user to select which frame or scene they wish to view. The scenes don't have to be viewed in order.
- DVDs provide subtitles in different languages.
- DVDs usually have additional features such as games associated with the movie or extra information about how the movie was made.
- DVD players can be used to play audio CDs.

DVD players are used in many homes and cost less than £100. Video games are also being distributed on DVD for use on home DVD players.

Digital TV

HD (High Definition) TV offers viewers high-quality sound and pictures in digital format. This type of transmission also includes many features not available in analogue television.

Feature	Explanation
More channels available	Because of the bandwidth used by digital television more channels can be transmitted and viewed.
EPG	Electronic program guide, which allows viewers to see what programs are being transmitted. The EPG usually gives some additional information about the program.
Reduced interference	Digital TV signals are not as prone to distortion through interference. This makes the pictures clearer and more pleasant to view.
Pay per view	Viewers can select programs they wish to watch and pay for if they are not part of the subscription package. Charges are usually made for key sporting events or new movies.
Digital recorders	Viewers can record one channel while watching another one.
Interactive TV	Interactive TV allows the user to make purchases or interact online. Information can flow in both directions, from the user to the TV or from the TV to the user. Some facilities available on interactive TV include games, home shopping and email.

GLOSSARY TERM
Interactive TV

Digital TV is no longer just a viewing service, it is a fully integrated home communication service. Advances in technology, such as the development of broadband, have moved digital TV in this direction. Viewers' expectations are higher in terms of quality of sound and picture and interactivity.

The impact of ICT on shopping

ICT has had a number of effects on how we do our shopping. Most people buying products now make use of credit or debit cards and fewer cash transaction takes place. Money is transferred using EFT (Electronic Funds Transfer). Credit and debit cards make use of the new 'chip and PIN' technology. Signatures will no longer be required at the POS (Point of Sale), the customer enters a PIN (Personal Identification Number) and funds are transferred from their account to the shop's account in seconds via the communications links. This technology has been introduced to cut down on credit card fraud. Special new computer systems have been installed in large supermarkets to enable the chip and pin system to be used.

E-commerce is the buying and selling of goods on the World Wide Web. It has had a major effect on shopping. Consumers using the internet for shopping have access to all the major stores 24 hours a day. Tesco have one

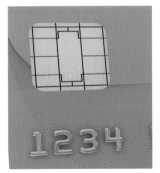

A section of the new credit cards showing the chip

GLOSSARY TERM
E-commerce

of the most successful online shopping stores. On this website it is possible to shop for groceries and book a delivery slot. Shoppers can access products bought on previous shopping trips through 'My Favourites'. The products are paid for by credit or debit card and the shopping is delivered to the door.

What are the advantages of shopping like this?

Advantages for the consumer:

- ✔ Shopping can be done from the comfort of your own home 24 hours a day, 7 days a week. This is helpful for busy people and those with young children who may find it difficult to visit the supermarket or shop.

- ✔ Elderly and disabled people can shop for heavy items and have them delivered without the inconvenience of visiting the store.

- ✔ Shoppers can use a wider variety of stores giving them a greater choice of items.

- ✔ The stores can be anywhere in the world.

- ✔ Customers are looking at a larger range of shops. Shops therefore have to be more competitive in their pricing to attract customers.

Advantages for the company:

- ✔ The website is open 24/7 and requires few personnel.

- ✔ Checkout operators are not required.

- ✔ The website can be accessed from anywhere in the world, so the company has the chance of getting more customers.

- ✔ If a small company sets up an e-commerce site, it can trade without the need to rent large city centre premises.

What are the concerns of shopping like this?

Concerns for the consumer:

✗ Not all consumers may have access to a computer or the internet.

✗ Not all consumers have the necessary skills to navigate the internet.

✗ There is the possibility of being defrauded if the website is not secure.

✗ Not all websites are authentic. Bogus websites could con customers into giving personal information or card details.

✗ Orders made on websites can be harder to rectify if an error is made.

✗ On authentic websites credit card details could be intercepted.

✗ Once personal data is submitted to a website it may be intercepted and used for different purposes.

What is a secure website?

The biggest concern most people have about buying online is security. Secure websites use an internet protocol called Secure Socket Layers (SSL) to protect card data. This performs several important things in the background. Data is encrypted or scrambled before being sent from your computer to the server. This means that hackers won't be able to get at your details. The data is then reconstructed when it reaches the company's server. Customers are at significantly more risk of fraud if they give their credit card to a retailer to swipe outside their view, for example at a restaurant.

Encryption is a mathematical process which uses formulae to scramble data before it is transmitted. In most cases encryption involves a key. The sender uses a secret key to encrypt the data and the receiver uses a private key to unscramble or decrypt the data.

Secure Electronic Transaction (SET) is a protocol used by Visa and Mastercard designed to make online purchases much more secure for card users. SET makes use of a two-stage authentication process using **digital signature**s and **digital certificate**s. The company sends the consumer a digital signature which confirms the company's identity. When sent the account details to pay for goods, customers send a digital signature which allows the bank to confirm the customer's identity. A digital certificate sent by the bank will confirm the customer's identity and ability to pay.

Definition of terms associated with SET:

> **GLOSSARY TERMS**
> Digital signature
> Digital certificate

Term	Definition
Digital certificate	An electronic identification that confirms that the user is an authentic person. A bank will issue this certificate which contains information about the user.
Digital signature	A code that guarantees a sender's identity. If an unauthorised person decrypts it, the digital signature will be altered, this means that the recipient will recognise that the code has been decrypted.

An easy way to see if the page you are on is secure is the closed padlock displayed at the bottom of most browsers, and URLs will usually start 'https' instead of 'http'.

■ Health and safety issues

As computers become fully integrated into the workplace, this has led to more people working at computers for longer periods every day, resulting in an increase in health and safety issues. Like all machinery and equipment in the workplace, computers have to be used correctly and safely. The Health and Safety legislation gives guidance regarding health and safety standards for the use of computers in the workplace.

There are a number of health problems and injuries which can arise because of the use of computers. It is the responsibility of an employer to provide a working environment which minimises the possibility of employees developing these problems. There are standards expected in areas such as:

- lighting
- furniture
- noise
- hardware
- software
- temperature control.

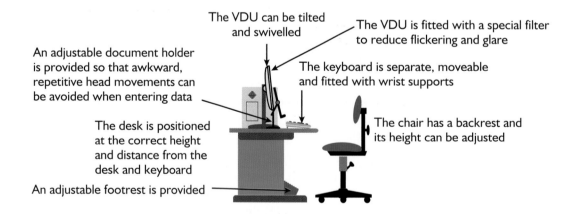

The VDU can be tilted and swivelled

The VDU is fitted with a special filter to reduce flickering and glare

An adjustable document holder is provided so that awkward, repetitive head movements can be avoided when entering data

The keyboard is separate, moveable and fitted with wrist supports

The chair has a backrest and its height can be adjusted

The desk is positioned at the correct height and distance from the desk and keyboard

An adjustable footrest is provided

The table opposite describes health problems and indicates how the organisation of furniture, lighting and choice of equipment can help reduce health and safety concerns.

Health problem	Description	How can it be reduced?
RSI – repetitive strain injury	Refers to a range of conditions affecting the neck, shoulders, arms, wrists and hands. The employee uses the same muscle groups to perform the same actions over and over again such as working at a keyboard all day. This can result in a condition of the wrists known as Carpal Tunnel Syndrome.	• Take regular breaks. • Use ergonomically designed keyboard and mouse. • Use appropriate furniture such as adjustable swivel chairs. • Use a wrist rest underneath the keyboard to avoid Carpal Tunnel Syndrome. • Use a foot rest. • Change the sitting position from time to time.
Eyestrain	A very common problem caused by over exposure to computer screens. It can also lead to headaches, blurred vision and a deterioration in eyesight. This condition can cause discomfort leading to less work being done.	• Use anti-glare screens. • Use swivel bases on screens to deflect light. • Use screens which have adjustable brightness and contrast. • Have good lighting in the office. • Use blinds to control sunlight. • Employer to provide regular free eye tests.
Back pain	Usually minor problems which can be debilitating periodically. The person may suffer back pain or immobility. The problem can be related to the sitting position at the computer.	• Use adjustable chairs which allow height adjustment and backrest tilting. • Take regular breaks and walk around to exercise muscles.
Radiation	Computer VDUs can give out extremely low frequency (ELF) radiation. The strength is similar to mild sunlight exposure. Illness may occur if the user is working for long periods in front of a computer screen. There are some concerns about pregnant women and the unborn child being exposed to computer radiation.	• Take regular breaks. • Use swivel screens to deflect the glare. • Anti-glare filters. • Use low-emission screens.

Safety in the workplace

The workplace must also be safe. A safe workplace means that employees will not meet with accidents because of the way in which the equipment is organised. Here are some measures employers can take to ensure the safety of their employees:

● Electricity switches, plugs, sockets and computer equipment should be in good repair and regularly checked.

- Computer cables and network leads should be safely organised using cable management. This will prevent accidents such as tripping over cables and electrocution.

- Extension leads should not be used in the office as overloading of electrical sockets could result in a fire.

- The temperature in the room should be controllable. High temperatures could make computers overheat or employees uncomfortable causing stress or illness.

- Anti-static carpet should be used in the room to avoid the build-up of electrostatic charge.

- Fire extinguishers, which can put out electrical fires, should be installed.

- Employees should not eat or drink near computers.

- Employees should be fully trained in the causes of accidents in the office and be made aware of the company policy on health and safety.

■ Computers and the law

The widespread use of computers has prompted the government to design laws to encourage the appropriate use of computers, digital information and software. The laws are:

- Computer Misuse Act 1990
- The Copyright, Designs and Patents Act 1988
- The Data Protection Act 1998.

Computer Misuse Act 1990

As general computer usage grew during the last century, so did the incidence of people using computers for criminal purposes, for example accessing and amending data in bank accounts. New digital crimes emerged and the people involved are known as hackers. These people were defined as intentionally accessing a computer system without consent or authorisation. Hacking is usually done remotely using telecommunication links through the internet. Most people involved in this process are motivated to 'beat the system'.

Some hackers are involved in the 'planting of viruses'. A **virus** can be defined as a program or a piece of software that has been designed to damage the normal operation of a computer. There are many types of viruses around but generally they tend to destroy user files, display annoying messages or graphics or store themselves as 'hidden' files on your hard drive. They can also be transmitted as 'unknown' attachments in your email account. Some viruses are set to trigger on certain dates, so you may not know you have one until the day it does the damage.

> GLOSSARY TERM
> Virus

Spyware is a program installed on a computer which automatically collects user information over a period of time without their knowledge or consent. Since the spyware program is hidden, it can be difficult for the user to detect its presence. It is secretly installed on the user's hard drive. Spyware programs can collect various types of personal information relating to the user, such as internet sites that have been visited, usernames and passwords and financial information such as bank account numbers. Spyware can also change your computer settings such as slowing down your internet connection speeds, changing your home page or causing loss of your internet connection. To eliminate the problem with spyware programs users can now obtain anti-spyware software that can be installed on your computer to prevent unauthorised access to your personal information.

To deal with these unhelpful situations the government introduced the **Computer Misuse Act 1990**. The main aim of the Act is to deal with problems involving hacking, viruses and other nuisances by making the following illegal:

GLOSSARY TERM
Computer Misuse Act

- unauthorised access to computer programs and data, such as hacking into a computer system

- unauthorised access to a computer system with intent to commit a serious crime, such as planting a virus

- unauthorised modification of computer material.

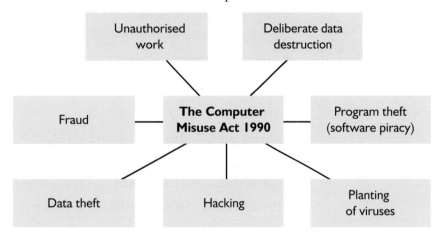

The Copyright, Designs and Patents Act 1988

This law was designed to protect the property rights of people and organisations that create and produce material based on original ideas. Material of this kind, sometimes referred to as 'intellectual property', includes books, articles, music, films, software, paintings and other individual creations. The law gives the owner of the material or idea the right to prevent it being circulated or copied freely. Consider the cost involved in making and distributing a music CD. Artists depend on the money made from the sales of the CD to pay their costs and also pay their wages. If the CD is copied by everyone rather than bought, the artists will receive no money and will be unable to pay the costs incurred during production or their living expenses. This is now illegal and is referred to as piracy. Piracy usually involves the illegal copying or distribution of other people's work. There are other areas where copyright can be breached, for example:

- photocopying pages from a text book and distributing them without the author's permission
- using photographs from a website or text book without permission
- copying films on DVD and distributing them
- using music in advertisements or presentations without the composer's permission
- presenting someone else's material or ideas as your own (plagiarism).

From a digital and ICT viewpoint, there are four main areas covered by legislation:

> **GLOSSARY TERM**
> **Software piracy**

- **software piracy**, which includes the illegal copying or downloading of software
- the 'theft' by one company of the ideas and methods of other ICT companies
- the use of ICT (including the internet) to copy or download material such as music/video/text-based files, thus avoiding the price of purchase
- using unlicensed software.

Software piracy

Software piracy takes two main forms:

- individual users borrowing CDs or DVDs or using the internet to copy a piece of software to install on their computers
- professional criminals making copies in bulk and selling them through illegal outlets.

The software industry believes that there are three negative effects of this piracy:

- Software piracy results in higher prices for those customers who are buying software legally.
- Software piracy discourages software houses and programming experts from being innovative.
- Software piracy means that artists and creators are not getting the correct and rightful income from the sale of their products.

Software licensing

Most organisations have installed a computer network to carry out their activities. When they buy a piece of software, they must also purchase a licence to cover the number of users. They are then legally permitted to distribute the software to the number of users specified in the licence. If the organisation wants more users to access the program, they have to pay for more licences. Some organisations distribute the software over their network without a proper licence and hence they break the Copyright, Designs and Patents Act 1988. Many of the major software producers such as Microsoft have helped fund an organisation known as FAST (Federation Against Software Theft) to protect against illegal use of their software.

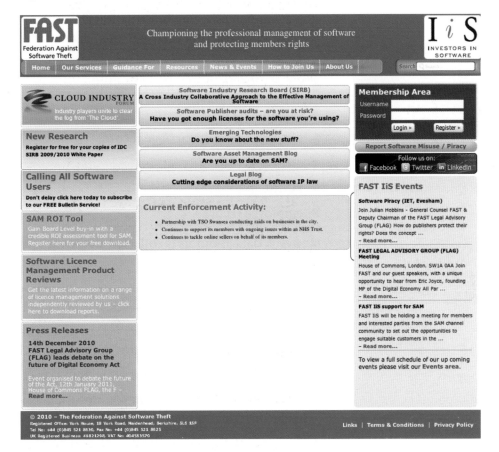

Data Protection Act 1998

As more personal information is stored on computers there are implications for us as individuals and for organisations that use our personal information. This means that there is a need to control what is stored in the interests of protecting individuals and their privacy. The digital nature of the information allows it to be easily distributed. Internet technology allows data to be sent anywhere in the world in seconds.

People are concerned that data about them is being shared between companies without their permission. Another major concern for individuals is that their personal data is being accessed by people who could misuse it. Personal data is a very sensitive area for most people.

What is personal data?

Personal data is data about an individual which they consider to be private. If someone answers a questionnaire or fills out a form for a company, they may not want the information to be shared with other companies. Before the Data Protection Act 1998, companies were allowed to share this information. Most forms now have a box included which can be ticked to stop a company sharing information about the person filling out the form.

Most people accept their personal data is stored in areas including:

- medical records
- school or college records
- criminal records
- birth, death and marriage records
- census records
- HMRC records
- employee records.

However, data about us is collected all the time, sometimes we may not even be aware of it.

- Loyalty cards at supermarkets collect data about our shopping habits and this is used to inform their stock, marketing and advertising departments.
- Speed cameras on sections of road record our speed and vehicle registration number as we travel.
- CCTV cameras monitor our activity in city centres and shopping malls.
- Mobile phones can transmit your location at any point in time when you make or receive a phone call.
- Each use of a credit or debit card gives banks and credit card companies information about our shopping patterns.
- When using the internet our personal computers can transmit an IP (Internet Protocol) address which can give details about our location. Cookies and spyware software can also be downloaded which record our activity on the internet.

If a company collects data about people, the expectation is that the information will be collected in an accurate way, used correctly and stored securely. This is now a legal requirement demanded by the Data Protection Act.

When mobile phones are switched on, their whereabouts can be located fairly accurately

Loyalty cards and credit cards link you to the purchases you make

ATMs (cash dispensers) record transaction details (date, time, location, amount withdrawn, etc.). Some will secretly take your photograph

Cameras at ports record the registration numbers of vehicles entering or leaving the country

Internet 'cookies' record details of the websites you have visited without you knowing

The Data Protection Act demands that those collecting and using data about others take responsibility for it. There are eight principles which companies must agree to.

The Data Protection Act Principles

The eight principles of the Data Protection Act are:

GLOSSARY TERM
Data subject

1 Personal data should be processed fairly and lawfully with the consent of the **data subject**.

2 Personal data should be used for the specified purpose only.

3 Personal data should be adequate and relevant for its intended purpose.

4 Personal data should be accurate and up to date.

5 Personal data should not be kept for longer than necessary.

6 Personal data should be processed in accordance with the rights of the data subject.

7 Personal data should be held securely, with no unauthorised access.

8 Personal data should not be transferred outside the EU.

Key terms used within the Data Protection Act:

Term	Definition
Personal data	Concerns a living person who can be identified from the data
Data subject	The individual who is the subject of the personal data
Information Commissioner	● Responsible for enforcing the Act ● Promoting good practice from those people responsible for processing personal data ● Making the general public aware of their rights under the Act
Data Controller	The person in a company who is responsible for controlling the way in which personal data is processed

GLOSSARY TERM
Information
  Commissioner

■ Environmental implications of ICT

The actions of ICT users, organisations and businesses that use ICT to carry out everyday activities are all generating carbon emissions and thus causing concerns for the environment. Scientists are telling us that by generating carbon emissions we are causing a climate change crisis across the world.

ICT users are being encouraged to reduce their carbon footprint. Organisations and businesses that use sophisticated ICT systems are not in a position to become 'totally carbon neutral', but they are keen to look at ways of reducing their carbon footprint in line with government policy.

In the global marketplace ICT solutions such as video conferencing allow firms to reduce their reliance on road transport and the demands for air travel. This can help reduce carbon emissions. Sophisticated ICT systems installed in vehicles can also cut carbon emissions by informing users of their petrol or diesel usage at different speeds.

Many users of ICT are now only purchasing energy-efficient equipment, which is a positive step forward. Educating ICT users to change their behaviour can make significant energy savings and financial savings on bills. Some of the following aspects of ICT can reduce our carbon footprints:

● **Power management** – this refers to settings on your computer to allow the computer to go into hibernation/sleep mode if it is not being used for a period of time. Screensavers are designed to help reduce power consumption but some use more energy than others; therefore it would be helpful to use only the ones that demand less energy.

- **Provide technical support** – this refers to giving advice to users on the energy usage on their digital devices and labelling each device with specific power-saving instructions. This involves giving advice on how to reduce the power when using the computer.

- **Peripheral usage** – this refers to encouraging users to purchase energy-saving devices, such as liquid crystal display (LCD) monitors which can draw less than 45 per cent of the power of cathode ray tube (CRT) monitors. Users should ensure monitors, projectors, peripherals and their mains adaptors are turned off and chargers are switched off when they are not charging. Users should look at the possibility of purchasing a multi-functional device such as a printer/scanner/fax commonly called an 'all-in-one' device.

- **Printer usage** – this refers to using printers and faxes and encouraging users to 'think before you print'. ICT users should be encouraged to optimise controls such as sleep-mode, duplex (double-sided printing) and greyscale. There is no need to print everything in colour. Some organisations, including schools, have purchased print management software packages to control the number of copies a user can print and a restriction on the choice of printers. This will help reduce the need for printing consumables such as ink and paper.

When equipment becomes obsolete we are now encouraged to break down the components for the purpose of recycling, which helps organisations become more responsible for the environment.

New legislation came into force in 2007 to cover waste electrical and electronic equipment (WEEE). The regulations have significant implications for those who manage recycling and for those organisations who are disposing of computer components. The law states that users must store, collect, treat, recycle and dispose of WEEE separately from other waste. It is now a requirement that all users who are disposing of WEEE, obtain and keep proof that equipment was given to a waste management company, and was treated and disposed of in an environmentally sound way.

Questions on Unit 3 Understanding ICT systems in everyday life

9 ICT components

1 Complete the following table.

Classify the following as Input (I), Output (O) or Storage (S)

Name	Classification – I, O or S
Hard disk	
VDU (monitor)	
Ink-jet printer	
Keyboard	
Mouse	
Laser printer	
Dot matrix printer	
Tracker pad	
Joystick	
Touch screen	
ROM	
Flat-bed scanner	
Hand-held scanner	
Graphics digitiser	
DVD drive	
Digital camera	
Microphone	
Concept keyboard	
CD-RW drive	

2 Copy and complete the table below, expanding the acronyms:

Acronym	Expand
RAM	
ROM	
LCD	
CD-RW	
PDA	
VDU	
USB	
DVD	
CPU	
GUI	

3 Name **three** components of a CPU.

4 a Explain the difference between ROM and RAM.
   b For each, suggest a suitable use.

5 Define the term 'concept keyboard'.

6 Name **two** different types of 'keying in' devices, and for each suggest a suitable use.

7 Name and describe the main features of **two** different input devices that could be used as an alternative to a mouse.

8 State **three** advantages of using a digital camera over a traditional camera for input.

9 Explain the following terms:
   a 2 GB of RAM
   b USB port
   c Icon
   d Menu
   e Cache memory.

10 Copy the table below. Tick the box which best fits the storage capacity of each device:

Device	50 GB	500 MB	500 GB	16 GB
Hard disk				
CD-R				
Blu-ray				
USB pen drive				

11 Distinguish between 'hard copy' output and 'soft copy' output.

12 State **two** advantages of using LCD screens over ordinary desktop monitors.

13 Define the terms 'pixel' and 'resolution' when describing output from a VDU.

14 Your neighbour asks you for advice before purchasing a printer. State **four** criteria that could be used when you are purchasing a printer.

15 Complete the following table for storage devices:

Device	Storage capacity
Hard disk	
CD-R	
DVD	
Blu-ray	
USB memory stick	

16 Suggest **two** uses for a hard disk on a typical PC.

17 Describe the main features of Blu-ray disks.

18 Define the term 'operating system'.

19 State **four** features of a typical operating system.

20 Name and describe **three** features available in a typical GUI.

10 Data and information

1 Copy and complete the table below, expanding the acronyms:

Acronym	Expand
ASCII	
CSV	
GIF	
JPEG	
MPEG	
MP3	
MP4	
OMR	
OCR	
PICT	
RTF	
TIFF	

2 a Explain the difference between data and information. Give an example of each.

b You are asked to design a paper-based or on-screen form which will allow the following details to be entered about members of a music club:

Member ID, Firstname, Surname, Date of Birth (must be over 14 years), Gender, Area of interest (can be Rock, Pop, Classical, Jazz), Contact telephone number, Email address.

Suggest data types for each field specified.

c List the information which could be created using the data in this database. An example would be 'A list of all female members registered.'

Higher-tier extension task

d Evaluate a form designed by another student and make three suggestions for improvement.

3 a Copy and complete the following table by entering a description of how the Input, Processing and Output associated with OCR and OMR occurs.

Method of data capture	Input	Processing	Output
OMR			
OCR			

b List the hardware associated with OMR and OCR systems.

4 Data capture is used to input data into computer systems. OMR and OCR are two types of data capture.

a Research and find **four** different applications of OMR.

b List **two** ways in which OCR is used.

c What are the advantages of using data capture instead of entering data using a keyboard?

5 Explain how each of the following validation checks works:

a Length

b Presence

c Type

d Range

e Format.

6 a Give an example of how each of the validation checks above could be used on the form you have designed in Question 2b?

b Suggest possible validation rules for each field in the database.

Higher-tier extension task

c What is the difference between validation and verification?

d Explain **two** methods of verification.

7 a What is a check digit?

b How is a check digit used in shops?

8 a What is data compression?

  b Which of the following file types are compressed file types?

    i CSV

    ii JPEG

    iii MPEG

    iv PICT

    v TXT.

9 a Why is file compression used?

  b Create a picture using Paint or a simple graphics editor. Save the file as a bitmap. Then save the same file as a jpeg. What differences do you see in the appearance and size of the files?

Higher-tier extension task

  c Research and find **three** file compression tools. List **four** features that they each provide.

  d Explain how file compression works when used to send files in an email.

  e Prepare a folder of information and use a compression tool to zip it. What differences do you see in the original folder and the zipped folder?

10 a What is data portability?

   b Why can 'data portability' be described as helpful to users?

11 Digital communication systems

1 Copy and complete the table below, expanding the acronyms:

Acronym	Expand
LAN	
WAN	
WWW	
ISP	
HTML	
URL	
ISDN	
PSTN	
ADSL	
PC	

2 a What is a LAN?

  b What are the differences between a LAN and a WAN?

  c What are the advantages of having a LAN?

  d List **four** devices you have seen connected to a LAN.

3   Copy and complete the table overleaf. Use the internet to find a picture of the named device and give its purpose. You can do this using a word processor, presentation software or web development software.

Device	Picture	Purpose
File server		
Network interface card		
Switch		
Router		

4   Create a poster for your classroom or a brochure which is designed to explain security on the network to Year 8 students. You should:

   a   List and explain **three** ways in which the data on a LAN can be protected.

   b   Explain the features of a good password.

   c   Explain why data should be backed up on the network.

   d   Explain the importance of virus protection software on the computer system.

   e   Remember to consider your target audience when completing this task.

5   a   In order for networks to communicate there are communications protocols. Explain the term communications protocols.

Higher-tier extension task

   b   Why are protocols required?

6   Wireless technology is used everyday.

   a   Make a list of the ways in which you have used wireless technology.

   b   Wi-Fi, 3G and Bluetooth are wireless technologies. Which technology would you recommend for each of the following? In each case state the feature that makes the technology suitable for this.

      i   Using laptops on a wireless network.

      ii   Transferring photographs between mobile phones.

      iii Accessing the internet using a mobile phone.

      iv   Connecting a mobile phone to the sound system in a car.

Higher-tier extension task

   c   List **five** other applications for each of the technologies named above.

7   a   Using the internet, select your favourite website. Take a screenshot of the webpage including the URL. Paste it into a Word document. Type the URL and explain the meaning of each part of the URL.

   b   Take a screenshot of the toolbar of a search engine you use. Paste it into a document. Annotate the different features available on the toolbar.

Higher-tier extension task

c What features of search engines are designed to improve the user's experience when browsing?

8 a There are many services available across the internet. Copy and complete the following table (you could produce a word-processed revision sheet).

Service	Explanation	Advantages	Disadvantages
Email			
Video conferencing			
VoIP			
Bulletin boards			

Higher-tier extension task

b Explain how bandwidth affects internet performance. Use the technologies mentioned above to help in your descriptions.

9 Investigate your school network. Copy and complete the table below:

User	What tasks can they perform on the network?
A pupil	
A teacher	
A technician/ network manager	

10 Eoin has discovered a worm and a Trojan horse on his computer. His friend describes them both as viruses.

a What is a virus?

b Explain to Eoin, the differences between a worm and a Trojan horse.

c Eoin also discovers that spyware is a problem. What is spyware and how can Eoin protect his computer system against it?

12 Applications of ICT

1 Copy and complete the table below, expanding the acronyms:

Acronym	Expand
EFTPOS	
HMD	
EAN	
PIN	
ICC	
VLE	
SET	
RSI	
MIDI	
ELF	

2 Suggest **three** reasons why a supermarket uses a barcoding system.
3 List **four** different hardware devices that are included in a typical EFTPOS.
4 State **four** different contents of a barcode on a supermarket product.
5 Apart from supermarkets, state **two** other applications that use barcodes.
6 State **three** activities available to a customer at an ATM.
7 State **two** benefits for the customer in using online banking.
8 What is meant by the term 'chip and PIN'?
9 Describe what happens during 'batch processing' in an electricity billing application.
10 Describe how computer simulation is used for training airline pilots.
11 Name and describe **one** other application that uses computer simulation.
12 Distinguish between a sensor and data logging.
13 Explain the principle of feedback as used in computer control applications.
14 Describe **three** different uses of ICT in education.
15 What is meant by teleworking?
16 Describe **three** advantages of teleworking to the employee.
17 Describe **two** different uses of computer systems in traffic control.
18 Discuss the implications to the consumer of using computers for:
   a Leisure
   b Digital TV.
19 State **three** health problems associated with ICT and explain how they can be minimised.
20 State **four** principles of the Data Protection Act 1998.
21 Name **two** other laws associated with ICT.
22 Describe **three** ways in which we can use ICT to reduce our carbon footprint.

Glossary/index

Broadband	118, 217	A telecommunications link that provides a wide bandwidth communication for high speed internet access.
Browser	207, 235	Software used to view webpages.
Cache memory	172	The type of memory used by the CPU. Cache memory is similar to RAM in that instructions can be read or written. It is small in capacity compared to RAM but has faster access speeds. Its purpose is to store frequently accessed program instructions.
Casual gaming	119	Games with simple rules and methods of interaction that require little practice for success. Casual games are often available as free downloads.
Character	163	A character is a letter, a digit, a punctuation mark, a symbol or a control code that can be stored by a computer. Each character is stored in digital format referred to as a byte.
Cheats	120	Shortcuts that allow users to skip elements of games they are having difficulty with.
Check digit	186, 227	A digit added to the beginning or end of a number to verify that the number entered is an authentic code. For example, ISBNs on books have a check digit added to the end. The reading computer calculates the check digit; if it matches the check digit at the end of the ISBN then it is a valid ISBN.
Chip and PIN	225	Chip and PIN has replaced the magnetic stripe on credit and debit cards. The silicon 'chip' can read and write data to/from a card. Whereas the PIN is the personal identification number used to validate the transaction.
Code view	134	Allows a website designer to view the HTML code comprising the website they are creating. Some website designers prefer to produce websites by writing all of the HTML code themselves.
Compressed	99	A file is said to be compressed when its overall size is reduced through the application of an algorithm to remove unnecessary data.
Compression	107	The use of an algorithm to reduce file size through the removal of unnecessary data.
Computer control	240	A computer control environment can process variables which are fed in; the output of the computer is used to control the process. Computer control is based on the principle of feedback.
Computer Misuse Act	261	This Act deals with problems involving hacking, viruses and other nuisances by making it illegal to hack into a computer system, plant a virus and modify computer material without authorisation.
Concept keyboard	160	A keyboard that can use a variety of programmed overlays. The overlays allow the keys to be defined as words and/or pictures.
Controls	120	The methods used by the user to interact with a computer game. Methods vary from cursor keys on keyboards to specialised input devices such as steering wheels, guitars, etc.
Crop	98	A tool in a graphics package that will allow you to select part of an image and discard everything else outside the selected area.
Data	175	Unprocessed facts and figures which on their own have no meaning. Data is entered into a computer and processed, it then becomes information.
Data collection	234	Using forms and devices to collect data from a variety of sources.
Data compression	191	Reducing the size of a file by using special software such as WinZip. Compressed data has to be decompressed before it can be used.

Data logging	239	Capturing data at regular intervals by a device such as a sensor. It is then stored by a computer for analysing at a later point.
Data subject	265	The individual whose personal data is being stored and used. The Data Protection Act will guide organisations on the legal use of personal data.
Decompression	107	The restoration of a compressed file to its original format for presentation using an appropriate output device.
Design view	134	Allows a website designer to view the multimedia elements comprising the website they are creating.
Digital	97, 106	Data in a format known as binary which consists of two digits: 0 and 1. These digits are known as BITs (Binary digITs).
Digital certificate	257	An attachment to an electronic message such as an email, used for security purposes. The most common use of a digital certificate is to verify the user sending a message and also to provide the receiver with the means to encode a reply.
Digital signature	257	A digital code attached to an electronic message which uniquely identifies and authenticates the sender.
E-commerce	255	This is a means of conducting business transactions over electronic networks, for example online banking.
Electronic mail (email)	209	A tool for sending and receiving messages electronically across a network of computers. It allows users to send messages and file attachments to other users on a network by using a system of electronic mailboxes. Mail that is sent is normally received immediately. To send and receive emails each user needs an email address.
Encryption	200	A way of encoding data before transmitting it on a network. Data is encoded by the sending computer using a software encoding key and sent along the communications line. The data can only be decoded by the receiving computer if it has the decoding key. This keeps data secure whilst it is being transmitted between computers. It is used on the internet for credit card transactions to ensure that the user's credit card number is not detected.
External memory	168	This refers to memory devices that are connected to the computer system and includes hard drives, DVD drives, USB memory pens and Blu-ray disks. They allow programs and data to be stored permanently.
Facsimile (Fax)	220	A device which is used to transfer paper-based information along telecommunications lines. Fax capability is commonly integrated into computer systems provided a scanner is used.
Feedback	117, 120, 237	This is a situation where the output can influence further inputs. It is used in real time processing situations.
Fibre optic	195	A data cable which has a glass or perspex core. It allows data to travel in pulses of light at high speeds and is less susceptible to interference.
File	180	A resource for storing data or information on a computer system. The file usually has a name and an extension which is related to the software which created it. For example Microsoft Word files have a .doc extension.
File server	195	The main computer on a network which holds applications and user data, and manages the security of the network.
Fill (flood fill)	99	A tool in a graphics package that allows a selected image component to be filled with the selected background colour.

Firewall	197	A device which contains software to protect a LAN or computer when using the internet. It prevents hackers and viruses from entering the network and can also prevent users from sending data out of the network.
Flash media	98	A multimedia application used to develop video and animation for publication on web pages. Can also be used to develop interactive multimedia applications.
Flash technologies	107	A non-volatile memory chip that stores data electronically.
Flip	99	A tool in a graphics package that will allow a selected graphic element to be rotated 180 degrees either vertically or horizontally.
Form design	176	The process of creating a layout for entering or capturing data on paper or electronically.
Frameset	134	A method of creating web pages where each element of a page is created separately and then combined onscreen when displayed through the user's browser.
Function key	160	Keys labelled with F followed by a number found along the top of a qwerty keyboard. They are programmed to carry out a user task.
Game genre	120	A grouping of games of similar characteristics and game play under one name or phrase for ease of identification, e.g. action games, adventure games, etc.
Game play	118	The rules that define how a user should interact with a computer game and the controls used to allow interaction with a computer game.
Games console	118	An interactive electronic device that uses video signals to display a video game.
Hacker	251	A person who gains unauthorised access to a computer system.
Haptic peripherals	117	Peripheral devices that use small motors to provide additional sensory feedback to users. For example, in gaming, steering wheels that shudder when you go over rough terrain in the computer game scenario.
Horizontal navigation	135	Displaying the main navigation elements of a web page as a series of options that are displayed down one side of a web page. Normally down the left hand side of the web page.
Hot key	161	This is known as a shortcut. It allows the user to use two or more keys to carry out a task as an alternative to using a mouse and menu. For example ctrl+p to print.
Hotspot	134	An area of a large image on a web page that has a hyperlink added to it.
Hub	197	A device which connects several devices on a network together. Data is made available to all devices through the hub.
Hyperlinks	134	A graphic/button/text on a website that when clicked on takes the user to another page/website/document.
Information	175	Data that has been processed and is presented in a way which is meaningful to users.
Information Commissioner	266	The organisation who is responsible for regulating compliance with the Data Protection legislation. This can differ from country to country.
Infrared	98, 161	Used to send data between computers and other devices, such as Personal Digital Assistants, over short distances. Also used with remote control devices where signals are generated using Light Emitting Diodes.

Motherboard	171	The main printed circuit board in the computer, which contains the CPU, memory boards and the other circuit boards required by a computer system.
Multimedia	165, 243	The combination of text, graphics, voice, video and sound to produce a presentation or a website.
Network	194	A number of computers or devices connected together using data cables or wireless technologies.
Network Interface Card (NIC)	197	A device fitted to a computer which enables it to connect to a network.
Online gaming	119	Playing computer games via the internet or another network.
Operating system	168	A software package that manages the computer system functions including allocating software and hardware to jobs, managing memory allocation for tasks requiring processing and managing overall system security.
Optical disk	168	Disks that are written and read by laser light. CD and DVD are examples of optical disks. Some disks are classified as R (recordable) and RW (rewriteable).
Optical storage media	107	Any storage medium that allows for the storage and reading of data using laser technology.
Optimise	107	The reduction of the file size of an image/document for internet transmission through the removal of unnecessary data.
Optimised	135	When files are compressed to facilitate storage or electronic tranmission across a communication link they are said to be optimised.
Password	196	A word, phrase or sequence of characters known only to the user or a group of users. The word must be known in order to provide access to a system or file. Passwords are sometimes used along with usernames to prevent unauthorised access to a computer system.
Pen drive	170	A flash memory card that plugs into the computer's USB port. It works similarly to a hard disk and allows data to be easily transferred from one computer to another.
Peripheral device	159	A hardware component connected to a computer. These can be categorised as input devices, output devices and storage devices.
Pixel	99, 164, 192	The smallest area on a VDU that can be edited, for example changing the colour. A picture is made up of pixels. The greater the number of pixels, the higher the resolution, hence a better quality image.
Podcast	244	A podcast is a series of digital media files (either audio or video) that are released episodically and often downloaded as multimedia files over the internet for playback on a mobile device or a personal computer.
Portability	187	The way in which users can transfer or reuse data across a range of applications.
Presence check	181	A validation check which ensures that data has been entered into a data field.
Preview mode	134	Allows a website designer to test their website to see how it will be displayed using a browser.
Processing	176	Taking input data and manipulating it to produce information.
Program	167	A set of instructions written in a computer based language to instruct the computer to carry out a given task.

Software piracy	262	The copying of software for distribution and resale without legal permission.
Sound card	168	A plug-in circuit board built into the motherboard that records and plays back sound. It acts as an input port for a microphone and output ports to speakers and amplifiers.
Spam	202	Unwanted emails selling or advertising products which are usually sent to large volumes of users.
Spyware	202	A program installed on a computer which automatically collects user information over a period of time without their knowledge or consent.
Storyboard	120	The production of diagramatic representation of scenes/pages in an application in the design stages of development.
Stretch	98	A tool in a graphics package that will allow a selected graphic element to be stretched in a given direction by clicking on the edge of the image and dragging in the required direction.
Stylus	164	Resembles a pencil in appearance and is used to allow the user to input data in 'freehand mode' using a graphics digitiser.
Switch	197	A single connection point for a group of computers or devices.
Tabs	135	Categorising user options as tabs on a web page. When a user clicks on a tab more options are provided.
Target audience	118	A description of the audience the game is aimed at. Used to help determine appropriate level of language, graphics, etc. at the game design stage.
Telepresence	237	This is used in medicine to describe a situation of creating a 'virtual patient' which can then be used by surgeons to practice for a forthcoming operation.
Teleworking	249	Use of ICT resources to work from home.
Thumbnail	135	A reduced version of a larger image displayed on a web page which provides the user with a preview of the image. When the user clicks on the reduced image a full size version of the image will be displayed.
Tool palette	99	A group of icons on a graphics package that provides shortcuts to the most commonly used editing tools.
Touch screen	162	An Input/Output device that is sensitive to human touch. The screen processes the position touched by using co-ordinates.
Tracker pad	161	A touch sensitive pad found on a laptop which functions similarly to a mouse. The pad can sense touch from human fingertips.
Transaction file	235	This involves storing data that will be used to update the master file at a later stage.
Transcription error	160	An error created when transferring data from one source to another source. Typically keying in data from a source document to a word processor package.
Type check	183	A validation check which ensures that data entered is of the correct data type, e.g numeric or character.
Uniform Resource Locator (URL)	212	A web address which when typed into the address bar of a browser will take the user to a website. An example of a URL is www.ccea.org.uk.